Frommer's®

Japanese PhraseFinder & Dictionary

2nd Edition

WILEY

John Wiley & Sons, Inc.

Published by:

John Wiley & Sons, Inc.

111 River St.
Hoboken, NJ 07030-5774

ISBN-13: 978-1-118-14363-6

Editor: Andrea Kahn
Photo Editor: Richard H. Fox
Illustrations by Maciek Albrecht

With special thanks to Yoshie Susan Higaki.

Translation, Copyediting, Proofreading, Production, and Layout by:
Language Line Translation Solutions, 15115 SW Sequoia Pkwy, Ste 200, Portland,
OR 97224

Front cover photo: Assorted bottles of sake in Japan. © ImageDJ / AGE Fotostock,
Inc.

Contents

HOW TO CONTACT US

In putting together this book, we've chosen the sayings and terms we believe travelers in Japanese-speaking countries will find most useful. We're sure you'll find others. Please tell us about them, so we can share the information with your fellow travelers in upcoming editions. If you were disappointed with any aspect of this book, we'd love to know that, too. Please write to:

Frommer's Japanese PhraseFinder & Dictionary, 2nd Edition
John Wiley & Sons, Inc.
111 River St.
Hoboken, NJ 07030-5774

ADVISORY & DISCLAIMER

Travel information can change quickly and unexpectedly, and we strongly advise you to confirm important details before traveling, including information on visas, health and safety, traffic and transport, accommodations, shopping, and eating out. We also encourage you to stay alert while traveling and to remain aware of your surroundings. Avoid civil disturbances, and keep a close eye on cameras, purses, wallets, and other valuables.

While we have endeavored to ensure that the information contained within this guide is accurate and up-to-date at the time of publication, we make no representations or warranties with respect to the accuracy or completeness of the contents of this work and specifically disclaim all warranties, including without limitation warranties of fitness for a particular purpose. We accept no responsibility or liability for any inaccuracy or errors or omissions, or for any inconvenience, loss, damage, costs, or expenses of any nature whatsoever incurred or suffered by anyone as a result of any advice or information contained in this guide.

TRAVEL RESOURCES AT FROMMERS.COM

Now that you have the language resources for your trip, visit our website, **www.frommers.com**, for travel information on more than 4,000 destinations. We update features regularly, giving you access to the most current trip-planning information and the best airfare, lodging, and car-rental bargains. You can also listen to podcasts, connect with other Frommers.com members through our active-reader forums, share your travel photos, read blogs from guidebook editors and fellow travelers, and much more.

INTRODUCTION: HOW TO USE THIS BOOK

More than 120 million people are native speakers of Japanese. Many more speak it as a second language. Japanese is a cosmopolitan tongue, heavily influenced by Chinese and receptive to foreign "loan" words (see page 20). Conversely, many Japanese words have entered the English language lexicon, in the worlds of technology, art, food, and more.

Although more and more Japanese—especially younger people and people in larger cities—can speak at least some English, most locals will appreciate your attempt, no matter how limited, to speak their language. Being able to communicate in this rich and historic tongue will prove both challenging and rewarding, and it will also help you to make new friends.

Our intention is not to teach you Japanese; a class or audio program is better for that. Our aim is to provide a portable travel tool that's easy to use. The problem with most phrasebooks is that you practically have to memorize the contents before you know where to look for a term you need on the spot. This phrasebook is designed for fingertip referencing, so you can whip it out and find the words you need fast.

Part of this book organizes terms by chapters, like the sections in a Frommer's guide—getting a room, getting a good meal, etc. Within those divisions, we tried to organize phrases intuitively, according to how frequently most readers would be likely to use them. The most unique feature, however, is the two-way PhraseFinder dictionary in the back, which lists words as well as phrases organized by keyword. Say a taxi driver hands you ¥500 instead of ¥1,000. Look up "change" in the dictionary and discover how to say: "Sorry, but this isn't the correct change."

To make best use of the content, we recommend that you spend some time flipping through it before you depart for your trip. Familiarize yourself with the order of the chapters. Read through the pronunciations section in chapter one and practice pronouncing random phrases throughout the book. Try looking up a few phrases in the phrasebook section as well as in the dictionary. This way, you'll be able to locate phrases faster and speak them more clearly when you need them.

What will make this book most practical? What will make it easiest to use? These are the questions we asked ourselves repeatedly as we assembled these travel terms. Our immediate goal was to create a phrasebook as indispensable as your passport. Our far-ranging goal, of course, is to enrich your experience of travel. And with that, we wish you *Ganbatte kudasai!* (Good luck!)

CHAPTER ONE

SURVIVAL JAPANESE

If you tire of toting around this phrasebook, tear out this chapter. You should be able to navigate your destination with only the terms found in the next 36 pages. *For an explanation of pronunciations, please see "Japanese Grammar & Pronunciation Basics," later in this chapter.*

BASIC GREETINGS

For a full list of greetings, see p97.

Hello.	こんにちは。
	kon nichi wa.
How are you?	お元気ですか?
	ogenki desu ka.
I'm fine, thanks.	元気です、どうもありがとう。
	genki desu, dōmo arigatō.
And you?	あなたもお元気ですか?
	anata mo ogenki desu ka.
My name is ____.	____と申します。
	____ *to mōshimasu.*
And yours?	あなたのお名前は?
	anata no onamae wa.
It's a pleasure to meet you.	あなたにお会いできて嬉しいです。
	anata ni oai dekite ureshii desu.
Please.	どうぞ。
	dōzo.
Thank you.	どうもありがとう。
	dōmo arigatō.
Yes.	はい。
	hai.
No.	いいえ。
	iie.
Okay.	オッケイ。
	okkei.

No problem.	いいですよ。 *ii desu yo.*
I'm sorry, I don't understand.	すみませんが、わかりません。 *sumi masen ga, wakari masen.*
Would you speak slower please?	もう少しゆっくり話していただけませんか? *mō sukoshi yukkuri hanashite itadake masen ka.*
Would you speak louder please?	もう少し大きな声で話していただけませんか? *mō sukoshi ōkina koe de hanashite itadake masen ka.*
Do you speak English?	英語を話しますか? *eigo o hanashi masu ka.*
Do you speak any other languages?	他の国の言葉も話しますか? *hoka no kuni no kotoba mo hanashi masu ka.*
I speak ____ better than Japanese.	日本語よりも____の方が うまく話せます。 *nihongo yori mo ____ no hō ga umaku hanase masu.*
Would you please repeat that?	もう一度繰り返していただけますか? *mō ichido kuri kaeshite itadake masu ka.*
Would you please point that out in this dictionary?	この辞書でそれを指していただけませんか? *kono jisho de sore o sashite itadake masen ka.*

THE KEY QUESTIONS

With the right hand gestures, you can get a lot of mileage from the following list of single-word questions and answers.

Who?	誰? *dare.*
What?	何? *nani.*

When?

いつ?

itsu.

Where?

どこ?

doko.

To where?

どこへ?

doko e.

Why?

なぜ?

naze.

How?

どう?

dō.

Which?

どれ?

dore.

How many? / How much?

いくつ / いくら、どれくらい?

ikutsu / ikura, dorekurai

THE ANSWERS: WHO

For full coverage of pronouns, see p25.

I	私
	watashi
you	あなた
	anata
he	彼
	kare
she	彼女
	kanojo
we	私たち
	watashi tachi
they	彼ら/彼女ら
	karera/kanojyora

THE ANSWERS: WHEN

For full coverage of time-related terms, see p16

now	今
	ima
later	後で
	atode

afterwards	後で *ato de*
earlier	前に *mae ni*
in a minute	すぐ *sugu*
today	今日 *kyō*
tomorrow	明日 *ashita*
yesterday	昨日 *kinō*
the day after tomorrow	あさって *asatte*
the day before yesterday	おととい *ototoi*
in a week	1週間後に *isshū kango ni*
next week	来週 *raishū*
last week	先週 *senshū*
next month	来月 *raigetsu*
last month	先月 *sengetsu*
At ____.	____に。 ____ *ni.*
ten o'clock this morning	今朝の10時 *kesa no jū ji*
two o'clock this afternoon	今日の午後2時 *kyō no gogo ni ji*
seven o'clock this evening	今晩7時 *konban shichi ji*

For full coverage of numbers, see p7.

THE ANSWERS: WHERE

here	ここ
	koko
there	そこ
	soko
near	近い
	chikai
closer	もっと近い
	motto chikai
closest	一番近い
	ichiban chikai
far	遠い
	tōi
farther	もっと遠い
	motto tōi
farthest	一番遠い
	ichiban tōi
across from	の向かい
	no mukai
next to	の隣
	no tonari
behind	の後ろ
	no ushiro
straight ahead	ここをまっすぐ
	koko o massugu
left	左
	hidari
right	右
	migi
up	上
	ue
down	下
	shita
lower	もっと低い
	motto hikui

higher	もっと高い
	motto takai
above	上に
	ue ni
below	下に
	shita ni
forward	前に
	maeni
backward	後ろに
	ushiro ni
around	周り
	mawari
across the street	この道の向こう側
	kono michi no mukō gawa
down the street	この道（の先）
	kono michi (no saki)
on the corner	角に
	kado ni
kitty-corner	斜め向かい
	naname mukai
＿＿＿ blocks from here	ここから＿＿＿目の角
	koko kara ＿＿＿ me no kado

For a full list of numbers used for blocks, see the section "Generic Inanimate Objects" on p. 12.

THE ANSWERS: WHICH

this (this one)	これ
	kore
that (that one, close by)	それ
	sore
(that one, in the distance)	あれ
	are
these (these here)	これら
	korera
those (those there, close by)	それら
	sorera

HELP & EMERGENCIES

Can you help me?	助けてください。
	tasukete kudasai.
I'm lost.	道に迷いました。
	michi ni mayoi mashita.
Help!	助けて!
	tasukete!
Call the police!	警察を呼んでください!
	keisatsu o yonde kudasai!
I need a doctor.	医者をお願いします。
	isha o onegai shimasu.
Thief!	泥棒!
	dorobō!
My child is missing.	私の子供が迷子になりました。
	watashi no kodomo ga maigo ni nari mashita.
Call an ambulance.	救急車を呼んでください。
	kyūkyūsha o yonde kudasai.

NUMBERS & COUNTING

one	一	eight	八
	ichi		*hachi*
two	二	nine	九
	ni		*kyū*
three	三	ten	十
	san		*jū*
four	四	eleven	十一
	shi / yo / yon		*jū ichi*
five	五	twelve	十二
	go		*jū ni*
six	六	thirteen	十三
	roku		*jū san*
seven	七	fourteen	十四
	shichi / nana		*jū shi*

fifteen	十五	forty	四十
	jū go		*yon jū*
sixteen	十六	fifty	五十
	jū roku		*go jū*
seventeen	十七	sixty	六十
	jū shichi /		*roku jū*
	jū nana	seventy	七十
eighteen	十八		*nana jū*
	jū hachi	eighty	八十
nineteen	十九		*hachi jū*
	jū kyū	ninety	九十
twenty	二十		*kyū jū*
	ni jū	one hundred	百
twenty-one	二十一		*hyaku*
	ni jū ichi	two hundred	二百
thirty	三十		*ni hyaku*
	san jū	one thousand	千
			sen

COUNTERS

When counting objects, you need to use a counter. In English you simply put a number before the item you wish to count and pluralize it; for example, one car, two cars, etc. In Japanese, which has no plural form, you instead use a separate counter word that varies depending on the type of thing you wish to count. The item being counted comes first, followed by the number, which is in turn followed by the counter word. The counters vary according to the type, shape, or size of each item. The pronunciation of either the number or the counter will vary in some instances. Note that the numbers four (*shi*), seven (*shichi*) and nine (*kyu*) can also be *yon*, *nana*, and *ku* when counting objects.

People

one person   一人

hitori

two people	二人
	futari
three people	三人
	sannin
four people	四人
	yonin
five people	五人
	gonin
six people	六人
	rokunin
seven people	七人
	shichinin / nananin
eight people	八人
	hachinin
nine people	九人
	kyūnin / kunin
ten people	十人
	jūnin

Mechanical Objects

one mechanical object	一台
	ichidai
two mechanical objects	二台
	nidai
three mechanical objects	三台
	sandai
four mechanical objects	四台
	yondai
five mechanical objects	五台
	godai
six mechanical objects	六台
	rokudai
seven mechanical objects	七台
	nanadai
eight mechanical objects	八台
	hachidai

| nine mechanical objects | 九台
kyūdai |
| ten mechanical objects | 十台
jūdai |

Flat Objects

one flat object	一枚 *ichimai*
two flat objects	二枚 *nimai*
three flat objects	三枚 *sanmai*
four flat objects	四枚 *yonmai*
five flat objects	五枚 *gomai*
six flat objects	六枚 *rokumai*
seven flat objects	七枚 *nanamai*
eight flat objects	八枚 *hachimai*
nine flat objects	九枚 *kyūmai*
ten flat objects	十枚 *jūmai*

Small Animals

one small animal	一匹 *ippiki*
two small animals	二匹 *nihiki*
three small animals	三匹 *sanbiki*
four small animals	四匹 *yonhiki*

five small animals	五匹	*gohiki*
six small animals	六匹	*roppiki*
seven small animals	七匹	*nanahiki*
eight small animals	八匹	*happiki*
nine small animals	九匹	*kyūhiki*
ten small animals	十匹	*juppiki*

Cylindrical Objects

one cylindrical object	一本	*ippon*
two cylindrical objects	二本	*nihon*
three cylindrical objects	三本	*sanbon*
four cylindrical objects	四本	*yonhon*
five cylindrical objects	五本	*gohon*
six cylindrical objects	六本	*roppon*
seven cylindrical objects	七本	*nanahon*
eight cylindrical objects	八本	*hachihon / happon*
nine cylindrical objects	九本	*kyūhon*
ten cylindrical objects	十本	*juppon*

A Little Tip

Double consonants in Japanese are *kk*, *ss*, *tt* and *pp*. They are pronounced as a single consonant preceded by a short pause. For example:

bikkuri *(bee-(k)-koo-ree)*
zasshi *(zah-(s)-shee)*
matte! *(mah-(t)-teh!)*
ippai *(ee-(p)-pah-ee)*

Generic Inanimate Objects

one object	一つ
	hitotsu
two objects	二つ
	futatsu
three objects	三つ
	mittsu
four objects	四つ
	yottsu
five objects	五つ
	itsutsu
six objects	六つ
	muttsu
seven objects	七つ
	nanatsu
eight objects	八つ
	yattsu
nine objects	九つ
	kokonotsu
ten objects	十
	tō

FRACTIONS & DECIMALS

one eighth	8分の1
	hachi bun no ichi

one quarter	4 分の 1
	yon bun no ichi
one third	3 分の 1
	san bun no ichi
one half	2 分の 1
	ni bun no ichi
two thirds	3 分の 2
	san bun no ni
three quarters	4 分の 3
	yon bun no san
double	2 倍
	ni bai
triple	3 倍
	san bai
one tenth	10 分の 1
	jū bun no ichi
one hundredth	100 分の 1
	hyaku bun no ichi
one thousandth	1000 分の 1
	sen bun no ichi

ORDINAL NUMBERS

first	1 番目
	ichi ban me
second	2 番目
	ni ban me
third	3 番目
	san ban me
fourth	4 番目
	yon ban me
fifth	5 番目
	go ban me
sixth	6 番目
	roku ban me
seventh	7 番目
	nana ban me

eighth	8番目
	hachi ban me
ninth	9番目
	kyū ban me
tenth	10番目
	jū ban me
last	最後
	saigo

MEASUREMENTS

Measurements will usually be metric, though you may need a few American measurement terms.

inch	インチ
	inchi
foot	フット
	futto
mile	マイル
	mairu
millimeter	ミリメートル
	miri mētoru
centimeter	センチメートル
	senchi mētoru
meter	メートル
	mētoru
kilometer	キロメートル
	kiro mētoru
hectare	ヘクタール
	hekutāru
squared	平方形の
	hēhōkei no
milliliters	ミリリットル
	miri rittoru
liter	リットル
	rittoru
kilo	キロ
	kiro

ounce	オンス
	onsu
cup	カップ
	kappu
pint	パイント
	painto
quart	クォート
	kuōto
gallon	ガロン
	garon

QUANTITY

some	いくつか（の）/ いくらか（の）
	ikutsuka (no) / ikuraka (no)
none	少しもない、全くない
	sukoshi mo nai, mattaku nai
all	すべて / すべての
	subete / subete no
many / much	沢山の
	takusan no
a little bit (can be used for quantity or for time)	少し
	sukoshi
a dozen	ダース
	dāsu
too much	多すぎ
	ōsugi
not enough	十分でない
	jūbun de nai

SIZE

short	短い
	mijikai
long	長い
	nagai
small	小さい
	chiisai
the smallest (literally "the most small")	もっとも小さい
	mottomo chiisai

medium	中位の
	chū kurai no
big	大きい
	ōkii
the biggest	一番大きい
	ichi ban ōkii
fat	太った
	futotta
wide	広い
	hiroi
narrow	狭い
	semai

TIME

Time in Japanese is referred to, literally, by the hour. "What time is it?" translates literally as "What hour is it?"
For full coverage of number terms, see p7.

HOURS OF THE DAY

What time is it?	今何時ですか?
	ima nan ji desu ka?
At what time?	何時に?
	nan ji ni?
For how long?	どのくらい?
	dono kurai?
It's one o'clock.	1 時です。
	ichi ji desu.
It's two o'clock.	2 時です。
	ni ji desu.
It's two thirty.	2 時半 (2 時 30 分) です。
	ni ji han (ni ji san juppun) desu.
It's two fifteen.	2 時 15 分です。
	ni ji jū go fun desu.
It's a quarter to three.	2 時 45 分です。
	ni ji yon jū go fun desu.
It's noon.	正午です。
	shōgo desu.

It's midnight.	真夜中です。
	mayonaka desu.
It's early.	早いです。
	hayai desu.
It's late.	遅いです。
	osoi desu.
in the morning	午前 / 朝
	gozen / asa
in the afternoon	午後 / 昼間
	gogo / hiruma
at night	夜に
	yoru ni
at dawn	夜明けに
	yo ake ni
A.M.	午前
	gozen
P.M.	午後
	gogo

DAYS OF THE WEEK

Sunday	日曜日
	nichi yō bi
Monday	月曜日
	getsu yō bi
Tuesday	火曜日
	ka yō bi
Wednesday	水曜日
	sui yō bi
Thursday	木曜日
	moku yō bi
Friday	金曜日
	kin yō bi
Saturday	土曜日
	do yō bi

DAYS OF THE MONTH

When saying or writing the date in Japanese, the month always precedes the day.

1	1日 *tsuitachi*	17	17日 *jūshichi nichi*
2	2日 *futsuka*	18	18日 *jūhachi nichi*
3	3日 *mikka*	19	19日 *jūku nichi*
4	4日 *yokka*	20	20日 *hatsuka*
5	5日 *itsuka*	21	21日 *nijūichi nichi*
6	6日 *muika*	22	22日 *nijūni nichi*
7	7日 *nanoka*	23	23日 *nijūsan nichi*
8	8日 *yōka*	24	24日 *nijūyokka*
9	9日 *kokonoka*	25	25日 *nijūgo nichi*
10	10日 *tōka*	26	26日 *nijūroku nichi*
11	11日 *jūichi nichi*	27	27日 *nijūshichi nichi*
12	12日 *jūni nichi*	28	28日 *nijūhachi nichi*
13	13日 *jūsan nichi*	29	29日 *nijūku nichi*
14	14日 *jūyokka*	30	30日 *sanjū nichi*
15	15日 *jūgonichi*	31	31日 *sanjūichi nichi*
16	16日 *jūroku nichi*		

MONTHS OF THE YEAR

January	一月	*ichi gatsu*
February	二月	*ni gatsu*
March	三月	*san gatsu*
April	四月	*shi gatsu*
May	五月	*go gatsu*
June	六月	*roku gatsu*
July	七月	*shichi gatsu*
August	八月	*hachi gatsu*
September	九月	*ku gatsu*
October	十月	*jū gatsu*
November	十一月	*jū ichi gatsu*
December	十二月	*jū ni gatsu*

SEASONS OF THE YEAR

in spring	春に	*haru ni*
in summer	夏に	*natsu ni*
in autumn	秋に	*aki ni*
in winter	冬に	*fuyu ni*

"JAPLISH"

Gairaigo is not to be confused with what is often known as 'Japlish,' or badly misused English that is sometimes incomprehensible and often amusing. While the prevalence of Japlish is decreasing as English is more widely used in Japan, it is still not unusual to encounter signs warning you to "Take care of your feet" (i.e., watch your step) or department store specials on "flying pans."

Another form of Japlish is English words that are used strictly for their sound or even visual appearance as text, without regard for their literal meanings. This is a common practice among packagers and manufacturers. A popular soft drink bears the name Poccari Sweat; presumably, it does not reveal anything about the ingredients.

Gairaigo (Japanese Loan Words)

Gairaigo refers to Japanese terms that originated from words in foreign languages, mostly English. Though similar in pronunciation to the words of origin, their relationships to the original meanings are sometimes obscure. Here are some examples.

aisu (アイス) : i.e., 'ice'; ice cream, ice pop
baikingu (バイキング): i.e., 'Viking'; buffet, smorgasbord
bebiikaa (ベビーカー): i.e., 'baby car'; stroller, carriage
depāto (デパート): i.e., 'department'; department store
eakon (エアコン): i.e., 'air con'; air conditioning
furiidaiyaru (フリーダイヤル): i.e., 'free dial'; toll-free call
igirisu (イギリス): i.e., Inglez in Portuguese; Englishperson;
 the UK
kasutera (カステラ): i.e., castela in Dutch; sponge cake
saabisu (サービス): i.e., 'service'; gratis, free-of-charge
sumaato (スマート): i.e., 'smart' (British); slender, svelte
tabako (タバコ): i.e., 'tobacco'; cigarette

JAPANESE GRAMMAR & PRONUNCIATION BASICS

Compared to Western languages, little is known about the origins of Japanese or its connections to other tongues. The most popular theory places it in the family that includes Turkish, Mongolian, and Korean. Another theory links it to Polynesian and other languages in the South Pacific. In its present form, Japanese consists of native words as well as loan words from Chinese and Western languages such as English, Portuguese, and German (see page 20).

PRONUNCIATION

Most Japanese syllables consist of either a single vowel, or a consonant + a vowel.

Vowels are either short or long. The sound does not change, only the length of the syllable. However, a short or long vowel can change the meaning of a word entirely. For instance, *shujin* (husband) vs. *shūjin* (prisoner).

PRONUNCIATION GUIDE

Vowels

a:	ah like the a in father; hana *(hah-nah)*
ā:	elongated a (aah); okāsan *(oh-kaah-sahn)*
i:	ee like the ee in feed; migi *(mee-ghee)*
ī:	elongated i (eee); kīroi *(keee-ro-ee)*
u:	oo like the u in blue; sugu *(soo-ghoo)*
ū:	elongated u (ooo); kūkan *(kooo-kah-n)*
e:	eh like the e in bed; te *(teh)*
ē:	elongated e (eeh); dēta *(deeh-tah)*
o:	oh like the o in rose; omoi *(oh-moh-ee)*
ō:	elongated o (ooh); ōkii *(ooh-kee-ee)*

Vowel Combinations

ai:	kaidan *(kah-ee-dah-n)*
ae:	mae *(mah-eh)*
ao:	aoba *(ah-oh-bah)*
au:	kau *(kah-oo)*
ue:	tsukue *(tsoo-koo-eh)*

oi: oi *(oh-ee)*

oe: koe *(koh-eh)*

Consonants

k: as in English, like the k in kick; kekkon *(keh-k-koh-n)*

g: as in English, like the g in gum; genkan *(geh-n-kah-n)*

s: as in English, like the s in see; sara *(sah-rah)*

j: as in English, like the j in jump; jikan *(jee-kah-n)*

z: as in English, like the z in zoo; zubon *(zoo-boh-n)*

t: as in English, like the t in time; takai *(tah-kah-ee)*

d: as in English, like the d in dog; daikon *(dah-ee-koh-n)*

n: as in English, like the n in name, or at the end of a word, run;
      naka *(nah-kah)*, hon *(hoh-n)*

h: as in English, like the h in home; hashi *(hah-shee)*

b: as in English, like the b in baby; ban *(bah-n)*

p: as in English, like the p in pepper; pan *(pah-n)*

f: softer than English f and closer to h, like hf; fūsen
      (hfoo-seh-n)

m: as in English, like the m in man; manzoku
      (mah-n-zoh-koo)

y: as in English, like the consonant y in yes; yama *(yah-mah)*

r: closer to English l than r; tap the roof of your palate with
      your tongue; raku *(rah-koo)*

w: as in English, like the w in woman; wakai
      (wah-kah-ee)

Consonant Combinations

ky: ki *(kee)* + ya *(yah)*, yu *(yoo)* or yo *(yoh)*, pronounced almost
       simultaneously; kyaku *(kee-yah-koo)*, Kyōto *(kee-yooh-toh)*,
       kyūkei *(kee-yooo-keh-ee)*

sh: as in English, like sh in she; shabu-shabu *(shah-boo s
       hah-boo)*

ch: as in English, like the ch in cherry; chōcho *(chooh choh)*

tsu: like ts at the end of hats in English, followed by u, although
       the u is nearly silent when it is followed by a consonant;
       tsukuru *(ts(oo)-koo-roo)*

ry: this is possibly the most difficult sound for non-native
        speakers to pronounce; ri *(ree)* + ya *(yah)*, yu *(yoo)* or yo
        (yoh), pronounced almost simultaneously, remembering
        the r is closer to the English l; ryaku *(ree-yah-koo)*, ryūkō
        (ree-yooo-kooh); ryōri *(ree-yooh-ree)*

WORD PRONUNCIATION

Japanese has no accented syllables, unlike English, which has
accented and unaccented syllables (e.g., Is THIS the FACE
that LAUNCHED a THOUsand SHIPS?). In spoken Japanese,
all syllables receive the same level of stress. Some commonly
mispronounced Japanese words or names:

	Incorrect	Correct
karate	*kah-RAH-tee*	*kah-rah-teh*
sashimi	*sah-SHEE-mee*	*sah-shee-mee*
sayōnara	*SAH-yoh-NAH-rah*	*sah-yooh-nah-rah*
sukiyaki	*SOO-kee-YAH-kee*	*soo-kee-yah-kee*
Toyota	*toh-YOH-tah*	*toh-yoh-tah*

SENTENCE CONSTRUCTION

The basic sentence construction in English is:
    subject – verb – object
    i.e. I read a book.

In Japanese, the basic sentence structure is:
    subject – object – verb
    i.e. Watashi wa hon o yomimashita.

The position of subject and object can alternate (Hon o watashi
wa yomimashita), but the verb always goes at the end of the
sentence.

Subjects and objects are distinguished in the sentence by
particles, or case markers, which follow them.

Particles

wa / ga (no English equivalent) subject **wah / gah**
    Watashi wa ringo o tabemashita.

I ate an apple.
Watashi ga ringo o tabemashita.
It is I who ate the apple.

o (no English equivalent) direct object **oh**
Jane wa hon o kaimashita.
Jane bought a book.

Particles also specify such things as to, from, when and where an event is taking place.

de (in, by, with, at) how, where, in what **deh** circumstance
Te de sētā o araimashita.
I washed the sweater by hand.
Mary wa doitsu de kenkyū shite imasu.
Mary is doing research in Germany.
Watashi wa mainichi basu de kayotteimasu.
I commute by bus everyday.

e (to, toward) direction toward **eh**
Otōsan wa nyū yōku e ikimasu ka?
Is your father going to New York?

ka (or) or **kah**
Kurīmu ka satō wa ikaga desu ka?
Would you like cream or sugar?

kara (from) starting point **kah-rah**
Kare wa bosuton kara unten shitekimashita.
He drove from Boston.

made (up to, until) destination, end point **mah-deh**
Kuji kara goji made shigoto o shimasu.
I work from nine until five.

ni (to, on, at) target; direction; when **nee**
Okāsan ni hana o agemashita.
I gave my mother flowers.

Watashitachi wa furansu ni ryokō ni ikimasu.
We are traveling to France.
Asa rokuji ni okiru yotei desu.
I plan to get up at six o'clock.

to (and) and **toh**
Onīsan to Onēsan wa hawai ni sunde imasu.
My older brother and older sister live in Hawaii.

PERSONAL PRONOUNS

I, me	watashi	wah-tah-shee
I, me	boku (male, informal)	boh-koo
I, me	atashi (female, informal)	ah-tah-shee
we, us	watashitachi	wah-tah-shee-tah-chee
you (sing.)	anata	ah-nah-tah
you (pl.)	anatatachi	ah-nah-tah-tah-chee
he, him	kare	kah-reh
she, her	kanojo	kah-noh-joh
they, them	karera/kanojyora	kah-reh-rah/ kah-noh-joh-rah

Anata (you) is rarely used and can sound presumptuous and unnatural in the wrong context. For second-person direct address (you familiar), the safest bet is to use a proper name (either given or surname, depending on your relationship to that person) + *san*. With small children, *san* becomes *chan* or *kun* (see page 27). Or, if you are asking a question, you can drop the pronoun altogether and use just the interrogative verb form: For example, instead of saying

Anata ga kimasu ka? (Are you coming?),

you would say

Kimasu ka?

POSSESSIVE PRONOUNS

I becomes **my**, **he** becomes **his**, and **she** becomes **hers**, etc., when the particle no (noh) is added after the pronoun.

I (watashi)	my (watashi no)	watashi no kaban (my bag)
he (kare)	his (kare no)	kare no tokei (his watch)
she (kanojo)	her (kanojo no)	kanojo no kuruma (her car)
we (watashitachi)	our (watashitachi no)	watashitachi no resutoran (our restaurant)
they (karera)	their (karera no)	karera no ie (their home)

A Little Tip

Japanese people introduce themselves with the surname first, followed by the given name (e.g., Watanabe Ken, instead of Ken Watanabe). However, it isn't necessary for non-Japanese to follow suit (e.g., "I'm Smith John"), as most people understand the difference in Japanese and Western conventions.

FORMS OF ADDRESS

As in English, the way you address another person in Japanese depends on your relationship, the context, and your relative social status. But for the most part, the question in English is whether to use a person's first name or last, in Japanese it is a bit more intricate. The honorific title is a suffix that is attached to a person's name (either given or surname).

Title	Appropriate for
-chan *(chah-n)*	young children; used with given name
-kun *(koo-n)*	boys' given name, 'subordinate' males
-sama *(sah-mah)*	after superior's, VIP's or customer's surname; also used in letters
-san *(sah-n)*	the most common and safest option, especially when meeting someone for the first time; can be used with either the given name or surname

As mentioned on page 23, the use of *anata* is not advisable in most situations. To politely address people whose names you do not know, you can use titles based on age and gender. See introductions on page 99.

AGE- & GENDER-BASED FORMS OF ADDRESS
bōya *(booh-yah)* young boy
o-bocchan *(oh-boh-t-chah-n)* young boy
ojō-san *(oh-jooh-sah-n)* young girl
onī-san *(oh-neee-sah-n)* young man; lit. 'big brother'
onē-san *(oh-neeh-sah-n)* young woman; lit. 'big sister'
oji-san *(oh-jee-sah-n)* middle-aged man; lit. 'uncle'
oba-san *(oh-bah-sah-n)* middle-aged woman; lit. 'aunt'
ojī-san *(oh-jeee-sah-n)* elderly man; lit. 'grandfather'
obā-san *(oh-baah-sah-n)* elderly woman; lit. 'grandmother'

PROFESSIONAL TITLES
buchō *(boo-chooh)* department manager
kachō *(kah-chooh)* section chief; manager
kōchō *(kooh-chooh)* school principal
sensei *(seh-n-seh-ee)* teacher, professor; also, doctor
shachō *(shah-chooh)* company president
tenchō *(teh-n-chooh)* store manager

VERBS

Unlike verbs in other languages, Japanese verbs are not conjugated according to person, gender, or number. Whether the subject is I, he, she, or they, the verb to walk is always *aruku*. Verbs are conjugated to show tense, negation, and level of completion or duration, as well as the status of the speaker or subject. In informal situations with family or friends, the plain, or dictionary, form of a verb is appropriate. In more formal settings, the polite, or –*masu*, form is called for.

Verbs consist of what is called a stem form, plus an ending. They are categorized according to the endings of their plain forms. The stem form does not change, except in the case of irregular verbs. They are conjugated by changing the endings, or adding a suffix.

'U' Verbs

These are verbs that end with 'u,' or [stem form] + u. They are conjugated by dropping the u and changing the syllable that immediately precedes it.

HANASU: 'to speak'

Plain present	hanasu	hah-nah-soo
Plain past	hanashita	hah-nah-shee-tah
Plain present negative	hanasanai	hah-nah-sah-nah-ee
Plain past negative	hanasanakatta	hah-nah-sah-nah-kah-t-tah
Polite present affirmative	hanashimasu	hah-nah-shee-mah-soo
Polite past affirmative	hanashimashita	hah-nah-shee-mah-shee-tah
Polite present negative	hanashimasen	hah-nah-shee-mah-seh-n
Polite past negative	hanashimasen deshita	hah-nah-shee-mah-seh-n deh-shee-tah

KIKU: to hear, listen

Plain present	kiku	kee-koo
Plain past	kiita	kee-ee-tah
Plain present negative	kikanai	kee-kah-nah-ee
Plain past negative	kikanakatta	kee-kah-nah-kah-t-tah
Polite present affirmative	kikimasu	kee-kee-mah-soo
Polite past affirmative	kikimashita	kee-kee-mah-shee-tah
Polite present negative	kikimasen	kee-kee-mah-seh-n
Polite past negative	kikimasen deshita	kee-kee-mah-seh-n deh-shee-tah

'Ru' Verbs

These are verbs that end with '*ru*', or [stem form] + *ru*. They are conjugated by dropping the *ru*.

TABERU: 'to eat'

Plain present	taberu	tah-beh-roo
Plain past	tabeta	tah-beh-tah
Plain present negative	tabenai	tah-beh-nah-ee
Plain past negative	tabenakatta	tah-beh-nah-kah-t-tah
Polite present affirmative	tabemasu	tah-beh-mah-soo
Polite past affirmative	tabemashita	tah-beh-mah-shee-tah
Polite present negative	tabemasen	tah-beh-mah-seh-n
Polite past negative	tabemasen deshita	tah-beh-mah-seh-n deh-shee-tah

MIRU: 'to see'

Plain present	miru	mee-roo
Plain past	mita	mee-tah
Plain present negative	minai	mee-nah-ee
Plain past negative	minakatta	mee-nah-kah-t-tah
Polite present affirmative	mimasu	mee-mah-soo
Polite past affirmative	mimashita	mee-mah-shee-tah
Polite present negative	mimasen	mee-mah-seh-n
Polite past negative	mimasen deshita	mee-mah-seh-n deh-shee-tah

Irregular Verbs
These are verbs whose stem and ending change in conjugation.

SURU: 'to do'

Plain present	suru	soo-roo
Plain past	shita	shee-tah
Plain present negative	shinai	shee-nah-ee
Plain past negative	shinakatta	shee-nah-kah-t-tah
Polite present affirmative	shimasu	shee-mah-soo
Polite past affirmative	shimashita	shee-mah-shee-tah
Polite present negative	shimasen	shee-mah-seh-n
Polite past negative	shimasen deshita	shee-mah-seh-n deh-shee-tah

KURU: 'to come'

Plain present	kuru	koo-roo
Plain past	kita	kee-tah
Plain present negative	konai	koh-nah-ee
Plain past negative	konakatta	koh-nah-kah-t-tah
Polite present affirmative	kimasu	kee-mah-soo
Polite past affirmative	kimashita	kee-mah-shee-tah
Polite present negative	kimasen	kee-mah-seh-n
Polite past negative	kimasen deshita	kee-mah-seh-n deh-shee-tah

Te (or de) Form

By itself, this verb form is used as an informal request. It is commonly combined with other verbs or suffixes. To denote either past or present, the second, or auxiliary, verb is conjugated.

U Verbs

| OYOGU | oyoide *(oh-yoh-ee-deh)* | Swim. |
| KAKU | kaite *(kah-ee-teh)* | Write it. |

Ru Verbs

| OKIRU | okite *(oh-kee-teh)* | Wake up. |
| NERU | nete *(neh-teh)* | Go to sleep. |

Irregular Verbs

| SURU | shite *(shee-teh)* | Do. |
| KURU | kite *(kee-teh)* | Come. |

Te + IMASU: present progression; "to be doing"
Densha o matte imasu.	I am waiting for a train.
Terebi o mite imasu.	He is watching TV.
Kaban o sagashite imasu.	She is looking for her bag.

Te + KUDASAI: Please (do something); polite request
Namae o kaite kudasai	Please write your name.
Hayaku okite kudasai.	Please wake up early.
Yoku benkyō shite kudasai.	Please study well.

Te + AGEMASU: to do something for someone else; a favor to someone else.

Musume ni purezento o katte agemasu.
I will buy my daughter a present.

Gohan o tsukutte agemashita.
I made dinner (for them).

Akachan no furo o junbi shite agemasu.
I will draw the baby's bath.

Note: The *te agemasu* can sound patronizing unless it's used in a proper way. For instance, to say "I bought my daughter a present", *katte agemasu* is OK, but if it is your mother, you would not use the te-agemasu form. Instead, you would simply say *Haha ni purezento o kaimashita.* (I bought my mother a present.) It should be used very carefully when speaking to someone senior or superior to you, or even among equals. It is best to avoid using it whenever in doubt.

Te + MORAU: someone doing something for you; a favor received

Kare ni kuruma o aratte moraimasu.
He is going to wash my car.

Kanojo ni doa o akete moraimashita.
She opened the door for me.

Haha ni shukudai o mite moratte imasu.
My mother is checking my homework.

DESU: to be

The word *desu* is a combination of the particle *de*, the verb *aru* (to exist) and the polite ending *masu*. It is used to express condition or identity, and like all verbs, appears at the end of a sentence.

Plain present	da	dah
Plain past	datta	dah-t-tah
Plain present negative	ja nai	jah-nah-ee
Plain past negative	ja nakatta	jah-nah-kah-t-tah
Polite present affirmative	desu	deh-soo
Polite past affirmative	deshita	deh-shee-tah
Polite present negative	de wa arimasen	deh-wah-ah-ree-mah-seh-n
Polite past negative	de wa arimasen deshita	deh-wah-ah-ree-mah-seh-n deh-shee-tah

ADJECTIVES

In Japanese the adjective appears either before the noun it is modifying, or at the end of the sentence preceding the word desu in conjugated form. For instance,

> **Sore wa takai tokei desu.**
> That's an expensive watch.
> **Sono tokei wa takai desu.**
> The watch is expensive.

There are two types of adjectives—the *I* adjectives, which are adjectives that end in i, and the *na* adjectives, which are combined with the suffix *–na* when modifying a noun (e.g., *jōzu na hito*, a skilled person). One exception is the word *kirei*, which means pretty or neat. Although it ends with the letter *i*, it is conjugated as a *na* adjective.

I-Adjective
warui: 'bad'

Plain present	warui	wah-roo-ee
Plain past	warukatta	wah-roo-kah-t-tah
Plain present negative	warukunai	wah-roo-koo-nah-ee
Plain past negative	warukunakatta	wah-roo-koo-nah-kah-t-tah
Polite present affirmative	warui desu	wah-roo-ee deh-soo
Polite past affirmative	warukatta desu	wah-roo-kah-t-tah deh-soo
Polite present negative	waruku arimasen	wah-roo-koo ah-ree-mah-seh-n
Polite past negative	waruku arimasen deshita	wah-roo-koo ah-ree-mah-seh-n deh-shee-tah

Na-Adjective
damena: 'failed'

Plain present	dame na	dah-meh nah
Plain past	dame datta	dah-meh dah-t-tah
Plain present negative	dame janai	dah-meh jah nah-ee
Plain past negative	dame janakatta	dah-meh jah nah-kah-t-tah
Polite present affirmative	dame desu	dah-meh deh-soo
Polite past affirmative	dame deshita	dah-meh deh-shee-tah
Polite present negative	dame de wa arimasen	dah-meh deh-wah ah-ree-mah-seh-n
Polite past negative	dame de wa arimasen deshita	dah-meh deh-wah ah-ree-mah-seh-n deh-shee-tah

CHAPTER TWO

GETTING THERE & GETTING AROUND

This section deals with every form of transportation. Whether you've just reached your destination by plane or you're renting a car to tour the countryside, you'll find the phrases you need in the next 28 pages.

BY PLANE

ARRIVING AT THE AIRPORT

I am looking for ____.	____はどこですか。
	____ wa doko desu ka.
a porter	ポーター
	pōtā
the check-in counter	チェックイン カウンター
	chekku in kauntā
the ticket counter	チケット カウンター
	chiketto kauntā
arrivals	到着ロビー
	tōchaku robī
departures	出発ロビー
	shuppatsu robī
security	荷物検査
	nimotsu kensa
immigration	入国審査
	nyūkoku shinsa
customs	税関
	zeikan
gate number ____	____番ゲート
	____ ban gēto

For full coverage of numbers, see p7.

the waiting area	待合室
	machiai shitsu

the men's restroom	男性用トイレ *dansei yō toire*
the women's restroom	女性用トイレ *josei yō toire*
the police station	警察の派出所 *keisatsu no hashutsusho*
a security guard	警備員 *keibi in*
the smoking area	喫煙所 *kitsu en jo*
the information booth	案内窓口 *annai madoguchi*
a public telephone	公衆電話 *kōshū denwa*
an ATM	ATM 機 *ATM ki*
baggage claim	手荷物引き渡し所 *tenimotsu hikiwatashi jo*
a luggage cart	荷物運搬カート *nimotsu unpan kāto*
a currency exchange	両替所 *ryōgae jo*
a café	喫茶店 *kissaten*
a restaurant	レストラン *resutoran*
a bar	バー *bā*
a bookstore or newsstand	本屋か新聞雑誌売り場 *hon ya ka shinbun zasshi uriba*
a duty-free shop	免税店 *menzei ten*
Is there Wi-Fi here?	ここには Wi-Fi アクセスはありますか? *koko niwa Wi-Fi akusesu wa arimasu ka.*

| I'd like to page someone. | 呼び出し放送をしていただけますか。
*yobidashi hōsō o shite itadake
masu ka.* |
| Do you accept credit cards? | クレジットカードは使えますか?
kurejitto kādo wa tsukae masu ka |

CHECKING IN

I would like a one-way ticket to ____.	____行きの片道航空券を買いたい のですが。 *____ yuki no katamichi kōkūken o kaitai no desuga.*
I would like a round-trip ticket to ____.	____行きの往復航空券を買いたい のですが。 *____ yuki no ōfuku kōkūken o kaitai no desuga.*
How much are the tickets?	その航空券の値段はいくらですか? *sono kōkūken no nedan wa ikura desu ka.*
Do you have anything less expensive?	もう少し安いのはありませんか? *mō sukoshi yasui nowa arimasen ka.*
How long is the flight?	飛行時間はどのくらいですか? *hikō jikan wa dono kurai desu ka.*

For full coverage of number terms, see p7.
For full coverage of time, see p16.

What time does flight ____ leave?	____便は何時に出発しますか? *____ bin wa nanji ni shuppatsu shimasu ka.*
What time does flight ____ arrive?	____便は何時に到着しますか? *____ bin wa nanji ni tōchaku shimasu ka.*
Do I have a connecting flight?	接続便はありますか? *setsuzoku bin wa arimasu ka.*
Do I need to change planes?	飛行機を乗り換える必要がありますか? *hikōki o norikaeru hitsuyō ga arimasu ka.*

Common Airport Signs

到着	Arrivals
出発	Departures
ターミナル	Terminal
ゲート	Gate
チケット取扱い	Ticketing
税関	Customs
手荷物引き渡し所	Baggage Claim
押す	Push
引く	Pull
禁煙	No Smoking
入口	Entrance
出口	Exit
男性用	Men's
女性用	Women's
シャトルバス	Shuttle Buses
タクシー	Taxis

My flight leaves at ____.	私のフライトは ____ に出発します。 *watashi no furaito wa ____ ni* *shuppatsu shimasu.*

For full coverage of numbers, see p7.
For full coverage of time, see p16.

What time will the flight arrive?	その便は何時に到着しますか？ *sono bin wa nanji ni tōchaku* *shimasu ka.*
Is the flight on time?	その便は定刻通りに出発しますか？ *sono bin wa teikoku dōri ni shuppatsu* *shimasu ka.*
Is the flight delayed?	その便は予定より遅れていますか？ *sono bin wa yotei yori okurete* *imasu ka.*

From which terminal is flight ____ leaving?

_____便の出発ターミナルはどれですか?

_____ bin no shuppatsu tāminaru wa dore desu ka._

From which gate is flight ____ leaving?

_____便の出発ゲートは何番ですか?

_____ bin no shuppatsu gēto wa nan ban desu ka._

How much time do I need for check-in?

チェックインの手続きにどのくらい時間がかかりますか?

chekku in no tetsuzuki ni dono kurai jikan ga kakarimasu ka.

Is there an express check-in line?

特別優先チェックインカウンターはありますか?

tokubetsu yūsen chekku in kauntā wa arimasu ka.

Is online check-in available?

オンラインチェックインはできますか?

onrain chekku in wa deki masu ka.

I would like ____ ticket(s) in ____.

_____の航空券を_____枚ください。

_____ no kōkūken o _____ mai kudasai._

first class

ファースト クラス

fāsuto kurasu

business class

ビジネス クラス

bijinesu kurasu

economy class

エコノミー クラス

ekonomī kurasu

I would like ____.

_____がいいのですが。

_____ ga ii no desuga._

Please don't give me ____.

_____以外のものをください。

_____ igai no mono o kudasai._

a window seat

窓側の座席

mado gawa no zaseki

an aisle seat

通路側の座席

tsūro gawa no zaseki

an emergency exit row seat	非常用出口に一番近い座席
	hijōyō deguchi ni ichiban chikai zaseki
a bulkhead seat	仕切り壁前の座席
	shikiri kabe mae no zaseki
a seat by the restroom	トイレ近くの座席
	toire chikaku no zaseki
a seat near the front	前方の座席
	zenpō no zaseki
a seat near the middle	中央部の座席
	chūōbu no zaseki
a seat near the back	後方の座席
	kōhō no zaseki
Is there a meal on the flight?	機内食は出ますか?
	kinaishoku wa demasu ka.
I'd like to order ____.	____をください。
	____ o kudasai.
a vegetarian meal	ベジタリアン料理
	bejitarian ryōri
a vegan meal	ベーガンの食事
	bēgan no shokuji
a kosher meal	コーシャの食事
	kōsha no shokuji
a gluten-free meal	グルテン抜きの食事
	guruten nuki no shokuji
a diabetic meal	糖尿病食
	tōnyōbyō shoku
I am traveling to ____.	____に旅行に行きます。
	____ ni ryokō ni ikimasu.
I am coming from ____.	____から来ます。
	____ kara kimasu.
I arrived from ____.	____から到着しました。
	____ kara tōchaku shimashita.

For full coverage of country terms, see English / Japanese dictionary.

I'd like to change / cancel / confirm my reservation.	予約の変更 / 取り消し / 確認をしたいのですが。 yoyaku no henkō / torikeshi / kakunin o shitai no desuga.
I have ____ bags to check.	預ける荷物は____個あります。 azukeru nimotsu wa ____ ko arimasu.

For full coverage of numbers, see p7.

Questions You May Be Asked

パスポートをお願いします。 pasupóto o onegai shimasu.	Your passport, please.
訪問の目的は何ですか? hōmon no mokuteki wa nani desu ka?	What is the purpose of your visit?
滞在は何日間ですか? taizai wa nan nichi kan desu ka?	How long will you be staying?
どこに滞在しますか? doko ni taizai shimasu ka?	Where are you staying?
申告する持ち物はありますか? shinkoku suru mochimono wa arimasu ka?	Do you have anything to declare?
かばんを開けてください。 kaban o akete kudasai.	Open this bag, please.

Passengers with Special Needs

Is it wheelchair accessible?	車椅子で入れますか? kurumaisu de haire masu ka.
May I have a wheelchair / walker please?	車椅子か歩行器をお借りできますか? kurumaisu ka hokō ki o okari dekimasu ka.
I need some assistance boarding.	搭乗するのを手伝っていただきたいのですが。 tōjō suru no o tetsudatte itadakitai no desuga.

I need to bring my service dog.	介護犬を連れて行く必要があります。
	kaigo ken o tsurete iku hitsuyō ga arimasu.
Do you have services for the hearing impaired?	聴覚障害者のためのサービスはありますか？
	chōkaku shōgaisha no tame no sābisu wa arimasu ka.
Do you have services for the visually impaired?	視覚障害者のためのサービスはありますか？
	shikaku shōgaisha no tame no sābisu wa arimasu ka.

Trouble at Check-In

How long is the delay?	どのくらい遅れていますか？
	donokurai okurete imasu ka.
My flight was late.	飛行機の出発が遅れました。
	hikōki no shuppatsu ga okure mashita.
I missed my flight.	飛行機に乗り遅れました。
	hikōki ni nori okure mashita.
When is the next flight?	次の便はいつ出発しますか？
	tsugi no bin wa itsu shuppatsu shimasu ka?
May I have a meal voucher?	食事利用券をいただけますか。
	shokuji riyō ken o itadake masu ka?
May I have a room voucher?	客室利用券をいただけますか。
	kyakushitsu riyō ken o itadake masu ka?

AT CUSTOMS / SECURITY CHECKPOINTS

I'm traveling with a group.	団体で旅行しています。
	dantai de ryokō shite imasu.
I'm on my own.	個人で旅行しています。
	kojin de ryokō shite imasu.
I'm traveling on business.	仕事で来ています。
	shigoto de kite imasu.

I'm on vacation.	休暇中です。 *kyūka chū desu.*
I have nothing to declare.	申告するものはありません。 *shinkoku suru mono wa arimasen.*
I would like to declare ____.	____を申告します。 ____ *o shinkoku shimasu.*
I have some liquor.	お酒を買いました。 *osake o kai mashita.*
I have some cigars.	タバコを買いました。 *tabako o kai mashita.*
They are gifts.	これらはもらい物です。 *kore wa morai mono desu.*
They are for personal use.	個人用です。 *kojin yō desu.*

GETTING THERE & AROUND

Listen Up: Security Lingo

靴を脱いでください。 *kutsu o nuide kudasai.*	Please remove your shoes.
上着 / セーターを脱いでください。 *uwagi / sētā o nuide kudasai.*	Remove your jacket / sweater.
身に付けている貴金属をはずしてください。 *mi ni tsukete iru kikinzoku o hazushite kudasai.*	Remove your jewelry.
カバンをベルトコンベヤーに載せてください。 *kaban o beruto konbeyā ni nosete kudasai.*	Place your bags on the conveyor belt.
横に移動してください。 *yoko ni idō shite kudasai.*	Step to the side.
手で身体検査を行います。 *te de shintai kensa o okonai masu.*	We have to do a hand search.

That is my medicine.	それは私の薬です。 *sore wa watashi no kusuri desu.*
I have my prescription.	処方薬を持っています。 *shohōyaku o motte imasu.*
I'd like a male / female officer to conduct the search.	検査するのは男性 / 女性の係員にしていただきたいです。 *kensa suru nowa dansei / josei no kakari in ni shite itadaki tai desu.*

Trouble at Security

Help me. I've lost _____.	_____を失くしてしまったのですが、探すのを手伝っていただけませんか。 *_____ o nakushite shimatta no desuga, sagasu no o tetsudatte itadake masen ka.*
my passport	私のパスポート *watashi no pasupōto*
my boarding pass	私の搭乗券 *watashi no tōjōken*
my identification	私の身分証明書 *watashi no mibun shōmei sho*
my wallet	私の財布 *watashi no saifu*
my purse	私のハンドバッグ *watashi no hando baggu*
Someone stole my purse / wallet!	誰かに財布を盗まれました! *dareka ni saifu o nusumare mashita.*

IN FLIGHT

It's unlikely you'll need much Japanese on the plane, but these phrases will help if a bilingual flight attendant is unavailable or if you need to talk to a Japanese-speaking neighbor.

I think that's my seat.	それは私の席だと思いますが。 *sore wa watashi no seki dato omoi masuga.*

May I have _____ ?	_____をいただけますか？
	_____ o itadake masu ka.
water	水
	mizu
sparkling water	炭酸水
	tansan sui
orange juice	オレンジ ジュース
	orenji jūsu
soda	ソーダ
	sōda
diet soda	ダイエット ソーダ
	daietto sōda
a beer	ビール
	bīru
wine	ワイン
	wain

For a complete list of drinks, see p81.

a pillow	枕
	makura
a blanket	毛布
	mōfu
a hand wipe	お絞り
	oshibori
headphones	ヘッドホーン
	heddo hōn
a magazine or	雑誌か新聞
newspaper	zasshi ka shinbun
When will the meal be served?	食事はいつ出ますか？
	shokuji wa itsu demasu ka.
How long until we land?	あとどれくらいで着きますか？
	ato dore kurai de tsuki masu ka.
May I move to another seat?	別の席に移ってもいいですか？
	betsu no seki ni utsuttemo iidesu ka.
How do I turn the light on / off?	どうやって点灯 / 消灯しますか？
	dōyatte tentō / shōtō shimasu ka.

Trouble in Flight

These headphones are broken.	このヘッドホーンは壊れています。
	kono heddo hōn wa kowarete imasu.
I spilled something.	何かをこぼしました。
	nanika o koboshi mashita.
My child spilled something.	子供が何かをこぼしました。
	kodomo ga nanika o koboshi mashita.
My child is sick.	子供の具合が悪いのですが。
	kodomo no guai ga waruino desuga.
I need an airsickness bag.	飛行機酔いの袋をいただけますか。
	hikōki yoi no fukuro o itadeke masuka.
I smell something strange.	変なにおいがします。
	henna nioi ga shimasu.
That passenger is behaving suspiciously.	あの乗客の様子が変です。
	ano jōkyaku no yōsu ga hen desu.

AT BAGGAGE CLAIM

Where is baggage claim for flight ____?	____便の手荷物引き渡し所はどこですか?
	____ bin no tenimotsu hikiwatashi jo wa doko desu ka.
Would you please help with my bags?	荷物を手伝っていただけませんか?
	nimotsu o tetsudatte itadake masen ka.
I am missing ____ bags.	荷物が ____ つ見つかりません。
	nimotsu ga ____ tsu mitsukari masen.

For a full list of numbers used for bags, see the section "Generic Inanimate Objects" on p12.

My bag is ____	私の荷物____
	watashi no nimotsu ____

lost.	が失くなりました。 *ga nakunari mashita.*
damaged.	が損傷しました。 *ga sonshō shi mashita.*
stolen.	が盗まれました。 *ga nusumare mashita.*
a suitcase.	はスーツケースです。 *wa sūtsukēsu desu.*
a briefcase.	はブリーフケースです。 *wa burīfukēsu desu.*
a carry-on.	は機内持込み用です。 *wa kinai mochikomi yō desu.*
a suit bag.	はスーツバッグです。 *wa sūtsubaggu desu.*
a trunk.	は旅行カバンです。 *wa ryokō kaban desu.*
golf clubs.	はゴルフクラブです。 *wa gorufu kurabu desu.*

For full coverage of color terms, see English / Japanese Dictionary.

hard.	は硬いです。 *wa katai desu.*
made out of ____.	____製です。 *____ sei desu.*
canvas	キャンバス地 *kyanbasu ji*
vinyl	ビニール *binīru*
leather	皮 *kawa*
hard plastic	硬いプラスチック *katai purasuchikku*
aluminum	アルミニウム *aruminiumu*

BY CAR

RENTING A VEHICLE

Is there a car rental agency in the airport?

空港内にレンタカー会社はありますか?

kūkō nai ni rentakā gaisha wa arimasu ka.

I have a reservation.

予約してあります。

yoyaku shite arimasu.

Vehicle Preferences

I would like to rent _____.

_____を借りたいのですが。

_____ *o karitai no desuga.*

an economy car

エコノミー車

ekonomī sha

a midsize car

中型車

chūgata sha

a convertible

オープンカー

ōpun kā

a van

バン

ban

a sports car

スポーツカー

supōtsu kā

a 4-wheel-drive vehicle

4輪駆動車

yon rin kudō sha

a motorcycle

バイク

baiku

a scooter

スクーター

sukūtā

Do you have one with _____?

_____が付いているのはありますか?

_____ *ga tsuite iru nowa arimasu ka.*

air conditioning

エアコン

eakon

a sunroof

サンルーフ

san rūfu

a CD player	**CD プレーヤー**
	CD purēyā
an iPod connection	**iPod 接続**
	iPod setsuzoku
a GPS system	**GPS システム**
	GPS shisutemu
a DVD player	**DVD プレーヤー**
	DVD purēyā
a child seat	**チャイルドシート**
	chairudo shīto
Do you have a ____?	**____はありますか?**
	____ wa arimasu ka.
smaller car	**もっと小さい車**
	motto chiisai kuruma
bigger car	**もっと大きい車**
	motto ōkii kuruma
cheaper car	**もっと安い車**
	motto yasui kuruma
Do you have a non-smoking car?	**禁煙車はありますか?**
	kinen sha wa arimasu ka.
I need an automatic transmission.	**オートマチック車が欲しいのですが。**
	ōtomachikku sha ga hoshii no desuga.
A standard transmission is okay.	**マニュアル車でもいいです。**
	manyuaru sha demo ii desu.
May I have an upgrade?	**アップグレードできますか?**
	appu gurēdo dekimasu ka.

Money Matters

What's the daily rate?	**1日の料金はいくらですか?**
	ichi nichi no ryōkin wa ikura desu ka.
What's the weekly rate?	**週料金はいくらですか?**
	shū ryōkin wa ikura desu ka.
What's the monthly rate?	**月額料金はいくらですか?**
	getsugaku ryōkin wa ikura desu ka.

What is the mileage rate?	走行距離料金はいくらですか？
	sōkōkyori ryōkin wa ikura desu ka.
How much is insurance?	保険はいくらかかりますか？
	hoken wa ikura kakari masu ka.
Are there other fees?	その他にもかかる料金はありますか？
	sono hoka nimo kakaru ryōkin wa arimasu ka.
Is there a weekend rate?	週末料金はありますか？
	shūmatsu ryōkin wa arimasu ka.

Technical Questions

What kind of fuel does it take?	使用燃料の種類は何ですか？
	shiyō nenryō no shurui wa nan desu ka.
Do you have the manual in English?	英語のマニュアルはありますか？
	eigo no manyuaru wa arimasu ka.
Do you have a booklet in English with the local traffic laws?	この地方の交通規則の英語版はありますか？
	kono chihō no kōtsū kisoku no eigoban wa arimasu ka.

AT THE GAS STATION

Fill it up with ____.	____で満タンにしてください。
	de mantan ni shite kudasai.
Regular	レギュラー・ガソリン
	regyurā gasorin
Diesel	ディーゼル
	dīzeru
Unleaded	無鉛ガソリン
	muen gasorin

CAR TROUBLE

See diagram on p51 for car parts.

It is already dented.	すでに凹みがあります。
	sudeni hekomi ga arimasu.
It is scratched.	傷があります。
	kizu ga arimasu.

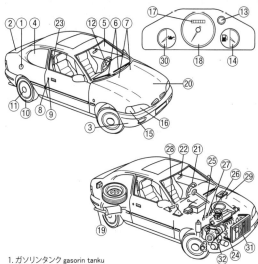

1. ガソリンタンク gasorin tanku
2. トランク toranku
3. バンパー banpā
4. 窓 mado
5. フロントガラス furonto garasu
6. ワイパー waipā
7. フロントガラス ウォッシャー
　furonto garasu wosshā
8. ドア doa
9. ロック rokku
10. タイヤ taiya
11. ホイールキャップ hoīru kyappu
12. ハンドル handoru
13. 非常灯 hijō tō
14. 燃料メーター nenryō mētā
15. ウィンカー winkā
16. ヘッドライト heddo raito
17. 走行距離計 sōkō kyori kei

18. 速度計 sokudo kei
19. マフラー mafurā
20. ボンネット bon netto
21. ハンドル handoru
22. バックミラー bakku mirā
23. シートベルト shīto beruto
24. エンジン enjin
25. アクセル akuseru
26. クラッチ kuracchi
27. ブレーキ burēki
28. サイドブレーキ saido burēki
29. バッテリー batterī
30. オイルゲージ oiru gēji
31. ラジエーター rajiētā
32. ファン ベルト fan beruto

The windshield is cracked.	フロントガラスにヒビが入っています。
	furonto garasu ni hibi ga haitte imasu.
The _____ doesn't work.	_____が機能しません。
	_____ *ga kinō shimasen.*

See diagram on p51 for car parts.

The tires look low.	タイヤの空気圧が低いようです。
	taiya no kūkiatsu ga hikui yō desu.
It has a flat tire.	タイヤがパンクしています。
	taiya ga panku shite imasu.
Whom do I call for service?	サービスを頼むには誰に電話をかければよいですか?
	sābisu o tanomu niwa dare ni denwa o kakereba yoi desuka.
It won't start.	エンジンがかかりません。
	enjin ga kakari masen.
It's out of gas.	ガソリンが入っていません。
	gasorin ga haitte imasen.
The Check Engine light is on.	エンジンのチェックランプが点灯しています。
	enjin no chekku ranpu ga tentō shite imasu.
The oil light is on.	オイル ランプが点灯しています。
	oiru ranpu ga tentō shite imasu.
The brake light is on.	ブレーキ ランプが点灯しています。
	burēki ranpu ga tentō shite imasu.
It runs rough.	走る時激しく振動します。
	hashiru toki hageshiku shindō shimasu.
The car is over-heating.	車がオーバーヒートしています。
	kuruma ga ōbāhīto shite imasu.

ASKING FOR DIRECTIONS

Excuse me, please.	ちょっとすみませんが。 *chotto sumimasen ga.*
How do I get to ___?	___への行き方を教えていただけますか? *___ eno ikikata o oshiete itadake masu ka.*
Go straight.	まっすぐ行きます。 *massugu iki masu.*
Turn left.	左に曲がります。 *hidari ni magari masu.*
Continue right.	そのまま右に進みます。 *sonomama migi ni susumi masu.*
It's on the right.	右側にあります。 *migi gawa ni arimasu.*
Can you show me on the map?	地図で示していただけませんか? *chizu de shimeshite itadake masen ka.*
What are the GPS coordinates?	GPS のコーディネートは何ですか? *GPS no kōdinēto wa nani desu ka.*
How far is it from here?	ここからどれくらいの距離がありますか? *kokokara dore kurai no kyori ga arimasu ka.*
Is this the right road for ___?	___へ行きたいのですがこの道で合っていますか? *___ e ikitai no desu ga kono michi de atte imasu ka.*
I've lost my way.	道に迷ってしまいました。 *michi ni mayotte shimai mashita.*
Would you repeat that?	もう一度言っていただけませんか? *mō ichido itte itadake masen ka.*
Thanks for your help.	どうもありがとうございました。 *dōmo arigatō gozai mashita.*

For full coverage of direction-related terms, see p5.

GETTING THERE & AROUND

SORRY, OFFICER

What is the speed limit?	制限速度は何キロですか？ *seigen sokudo wa nan kiro desu ka.*
I wasn't going that fast.	それほどスピードは出していません でした。 *sorehodo supīdo wa dashite imasen deshita.*
How much is the fine?	罰金はいくらですか？ *bakkin wa ikura desu ka.*
Where do I pay the fine?	罰金はどこで払えばよいですか？ *bakkin wa doko de haraeba yoi desu ka.*
Do I have to go to court?	裁判所に行かなければなりませんか？ *saibansho ni ikanakereba narimasen ka.*
I had an accident.	事故に遭いました。 *jiko ni ai mashita.*
The other driver hit me.	相手の運転手が私にぶつかりました。 *aite no untenshu ga watashi ni butsukari mashita.*

Road Signs

制限速度	Speed Limit
停止	Stop
道を譲る	Yield
危険	Danger
行き止まり	No Exit
一方通行	One Way
進入禁止	Do Not Enter
道路閉鎖中	Road Closed
有料	Toll
現金のみ	Cash Only
駐車禁止	No Parking
駐車料金	Parking Fee
車庫	Parking Garage

I'm at fault.	私に落ち度があります。 *watashi ni ochido ga arimasu.*

BY TAXI

Where is the taxi stand?	タクシー乗り場はどこにありますか? *takushī noriba wa doko ni arimasu ka.*
Is there a ____ for my hotel?	ホテル行きの____はありますか? *hoteru yuki no ____ wa arimasu ka.*
limo	リムジン *rimujin*
bus	バス *basu*
van	バン *ban*
I need to get to ____.	____に行きたいのですが。 *____ ni ikitai no desuga.*
How much will that cost?	料金はいくらくらいかかりますか? *ryōkin wa ikura kurai kakari masu ka.*
How long will it take?	どのくらい時間がかかりますか? *dono kurai jikan ga kakari masu ka.*
Can you take me to the train station?	駅までお願いします。 *eki made onegai shimasu.*

Listen Up: Taxi Lingo

乗ってく下さい! *notte kudasai.*	Get in!
荷物はそこに置いてください。 　私がやります。 *nimotsu wa soko ni oite kudasai.* 　*watashi ga yarimasu.*	Leave your luggage. I got it.
何人乗りますか? *nan nin norimasu ka.*	How many passengers?
お急ぎですか? *oisogi desu ka.*	Are you in a hurry?

I am in a hurry.	ちょっと急いでいるんです。
	chotto isoide iru n desu.
Slow down.	速度を落としてください。
	sokudo o otoshite kudasai.
Am I close enough to walk?	ここからだと歩いていけますか？
	kokokara dato aruite ikemasu ka.
Let me out here.	ここで降ろしてください。
	koko de oroshtie kudasai.
That's not the correct change.	おつりが間違っています。
	otsuri ga machigatte imasu.

BY TRAIN

How do I get to the train station?	駅へはどう行きますか？
	eki ewa dō iki masu ka.
Would you take me to the train station?	駅までお願いします。
	eki made onegai shimasu.
How long is the trip to ____?	____まではどのくらいかかりますか？
	____ made wa dono kurai kakari masu ka.
When is the next train?	次の電車はいつ来ますか？
	tsugi no densha wa itsu kimasu ka.
Do you have a schedule?	時刻表はありますか？
	jikoku hyo wa arimasu ka.
Do I have to change trains?	電車を乗り換える必要がありますか？
	densha o norikaeru hitsuyō ga arimasu ka.
I'd like a ____.	____を買いたいです。
	____ o kai tai desu.
one-way ticket	片道切符
	katamichi kippu
round-trip ticket	往復切符
	ōfuku kippu
Which platform does it leave from?	何番線から発車しますか？
	nan ban sen kara hassha shimasu ka.

Is there a bar car?	ビュッフェはありますか？ *byuffe wa arimasu ka.*
Is there a dining car?	食堂車はありますか？ *shokudō sha wa arimasu ka.*
Which car is my seat in?	私の座席は何号車にありますか？ *watashi no zaseki wa nangōsha ni arimasu ka.*
Is this seat taken?	この席は空いていますか？ *kono seki wa aite imasu ka.*
Where is the next stop?	次の停車駅はどこですか？ *tsugi no teisha eki wa doko desu ka.*
How many stops to ____?	____までは停車駅が何個ありますか？ *____ made wa teisha eki ga nan ko arimasu ka.*
What's the train number?	電車の番号と行き先は何ですか？ *densha no bangō to ikisaki wa nan desu ka?*

BY BUS

How do I get to the bus station?	バス停に行く道を教えていただけませんか？ *basutei ni iku michi o oshiete itadake masen ka.*
Would you take me to the bus station?	バス停まで連れて行っていただけませんか？ *basutei made tsurete itte itadake masen ka.*
May I have a bus schedule?	バスの時刻表をもらえますか？ *basu no jikokuhyō o moraemasu ka.*

Which bus goes to ____?	____行きのバスはどれですか？
	_____ yuki no basu wa dore desuka._
Where does it leave from?	それはどこから発車しますか？
	sore wa doko kara hassha shimasu ka.
How long does the bus take?	このバスでどのくらいかかりますか？
	kono basu de dono kurai kakari masu ka.
How much is it?	それはいくらですか？
	sore wa ikura desu ka.
Is there an express bus?	特急バスはありますか？
	tokkyū basu wa arimasu ka.
Does it make local stops?	各停留所に停車しますか？
	kaku teiryūjo ni teisha shimasu ka.
Does it run at night?	夜間も運行しますか？
	yakan mo unkō shimasu ka.
When does the next bus leave?	次のバスはいつ発車しますか？
	tsugi no basu wa itsu hassha shimasu ka.
I'd like a ____.	____を買いたいです。
	_____ o kai tai desu._
one way ticket	片道チケット
	katamichi chiketto
round trip ticket	往復チケット
	ōfuku chiketto
How long will the bus be stopped?	このバスはどのくらいの時間停車しますか？
	kono basu wa dono kurai no jikan teisha shimasu ka.
Is there an air-conditioned bus?	冷房のあるバスはありますか？
	reibō no aru basu wa arimasu ka.
Is this seat taken?	この席は空いていますか？
	kono seki wa aite imasu ka.
Where is the next stop?	次の停留所はどこですか？
	tsugi no teiryūjo wa doko desu ka.

Please tell me when we reach ____.

____に着いたら教えていただけますか。

____ ni itsuitara oshiete itadake masu ka.

Let me off here.

ここで降ろしてください。

koko de oroshite kudasai.

BY BOAT OR SHIP

Would you take me to the port?

港までお願いします。

minato made onegai shimasu.

When does the ship sail?

この船はいつ出航しますか?

kono fune wa itsu shukkō shimasu ka.

How long is the trip?

目的地まではどのくらいかかりますか?

mokutekichi made wa dono kurai kakari masu ka.

Where are the life preservers?

救命用具はどこにありますか?

kyūmei yōgu wa doko ni arimasu ka.

I would like a private cabin.

船室は個室にしてください。

senshitsu wa koshitsu ni shite kudasai.

Is the trip rough?

航行中揺れますか?

kōkōchū yuremasu ka.

I feel seasick.

船酔いしたみたいです。

funayoi shita mitai desu.

I need some seasickness pills.

船酔いに効く薬がほしいのですが。

funayoi ni kiku kusuri ga hoshii no desuga.

Where is the bathroom?

トイレはどこですか?

toire wa doko desu ka.

Does the ship have a casino?

船内にカジノはありますか?

sennai ni kajino wa arimasu ka.

Will the ship stop at ports along the way?

途中で停まる港はありますか?

tochū de tomaru minato wa arimasu ka.

BY SUBWAY

Where's the subway station?	**地下鉄の駅 はどこにありますか?** *chikatetsu no eki wa doko ni arimasu ka.*
Where can I buy a ticket?	**切符はどこで買えますか?** *kippu wa doko de kaemasu ka.*
Could I have a map of the subway?	**地下鉄の地図をいただけますか?** *chikatetsu no chizu o itadake masu ka.*
Which line should I take for ____?	**____へ行くにはどの線に乗ればいいですか?** *____ e iku niwa dono sen ni noreba ii desu ka.*

SUBWAY TICKETS

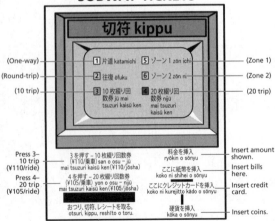

Is this the right line for ____?	____へ行きたいのですがこの線でいいですか？
	____ e ikitai no desuga kono sen de ii desu ka.
Which stop is it for ____?	____へ行くにはどの駅で降りればいいですか？
	____ e iku niwa dono eki de orireba ii desu ka.
How many stops is it to ____?	____まで停車駅は何個ありますか？
	____ made teisha eki wa nan ko arimasu ka.
Is the next stop ____?	次の駅は____ですか？
	tsugi no eki wa ____ desu ka.
Where are we?	ここはどこですか？
	koko wa doko desu ka.
Where do I change to ____?	____へ行くにはどこで乗り換えればよいですか？
	____ e iku niwa doko de norikaereba yoi desu ka.
What time is the last train to ____?	____ 行きの最終電車は何時ですか？
	____ yuki no saishū densha wa nanji desu ka.

CONSIDERATIONS FOR TRAVELERS WITH SPECIAL NEEDS

Do you have wheelchair access?	車椅子で移動できますか？
	kurumaisu de idō dekimasu ka.
Do you have elevators? Where?	エレベータはありますか？ どこですか。
	erebēta wa arimasu ka. doko desu ka.
Do you have ramps? Where?	スロープはありますか？ どこですか。
	surōpu wa arimasu ka. doko desu ka.
Are the restrooms wheelchair accessible?	トイレには車椅子で入れますか？
	toire niwa kurumaisu de hairemasu ka.

Do you have audio assistance for the hearing impaired?

聴覚障害者のための補聴アシスタンス がありますか？

chōkaku shōgaisha no tame no hochō ashisutansu ga arimasu ka.

I am deaf.

私は、耳が聞こえません。

watashi wa mimi ga kikoe masen.

I am hearing impaired.

私は、耳が不自由です。

watashi wa mimi ga fujiyū desu.

I am blind.

私は、目が見えません。

watashi wa me ga mie masen.

I am visually impaired.

私は、目が不自由です。

watashi wa me ga fujiyū desu.

May I bring my service dog?

介護犬を連れて行ってもいいですか？

kaigo ken o tsurete ittemo ii desu ka.

I need to charge my power chair.

電動車椅子を充電する必要があり ます。

dendō kurumaisu o jūden suru hitsuyō ga arimasu.

CHAPTER THREE

LODGING

This chapter will help you find the right accommodations, at the right price, and the amenities you might need during your stay.

FINDING A HOTEL

Please recommend ____.	____を選んでいただけますか。
	____ o erande itadake masu ka.
a clean hostel	清潔なホステル
	seiketsu na hosuteru
a moderately priced hotel	手頃な値段のホテル
	tegoro na nedan no hoteru
a moderately priced B&B	手頃な値段のB & B
	tegoro na nedan no B ando B
a good hotel / motel	良いホテル / モーテル
	yoi hoteru / mōteru
Does the hotel have ____?	そのホテルに____はありますか?
	sono hoteru ni ____ wa arimasu ka.
an indoor / outdoor pool	室内プール / 屋外プール
	shitsunai pūru / okugai pūru
a casino	カジノ
	kajino
suites	スイートルーム
	suīto rūmu
balconies	バルコニー
	barukonī
a fitness center	ジム
	jimu
a spa	スパ
	supa
a private beach	プライベート ビーチ
	puraibēto bīchi
a tennis court	テニスコート
	tenisu kōto

| air-conditioned rooms | エアコン付きの部屋
eakon tsuki no heya |
| free Wi-Fi | 無料 Wi-Fi
muryō Wi-Fi |

ROOM PREFERENCES

| I would like a room for ____. | ____の部屋をお願いします。
____ no heya o onegai shimasu. |

For full coverage of number terms, see p7.

I would like ____.	____がいいのですが。 *____ ga ii no desuga.*
a king-sized bed	キングサイズのベッド *kingu saizu no beddo*
a double bed	ダブル サイズのベッド *daburu saizu no beddo*
twin beds	ツイン サイズのベッド *tsuin saizu no beddo*
adjoining rooms	続き部屋 *tsuzuki beya*
a smoking room	喫煙できる部屋 *kitsu en dekiru heya*
a non-smoking room	禁煙の部屋 *kin en no heya*

Listen Up: Reservations Lingo

ただいま空き室がございません。 *tadaima aki shitsu ga gozaimasen.*	We have no vacancies.
何日ご滞在ですか? *nan nichi gotaizai desu ka.*	How long will you be staying?
喫煙または禁煙のどちらがよろしいですか? *kitsu en matawa kin en no dochira ga yoroshii desu ka.*	Smoking or non smoking?

a private bathroom	プライベート バスルーム
	puraibēto basurūmu
a shower	シャワー
	shawā
a bathtub	浴槽
	yokusō
air conditioning	エアコン
	eakon
television	テレビ
	terebi
cable	ケーブル
	kēburu
satellite TV	衛星テレビ
	eisei terebi
a telephone	電話
	denwa
Internet access	インターネット接続
	intānetto setsuzoku
Wi-Fi	Wi-Fi
	Wi-Fi
a refrigerator	冷蔵庫
	reizōko
a beach view	ビーチの見える
	bīchi no mieru
a city view	街の景色の見える
	machi no keshiki no mieru
a kitchenette	簡易キッチン
	kan i kicchin
a balcony	バルコニー
	barukonī
a suite	スイートルーム
	suīto rūmu
a penthouse	ペントハウス
	pento hausu
I would like a room ____.	____部屋をお願いしたいのですが。
	____ heya o onegai shitai no desuga.

LODGING

on the ground floor	1 階にある
	ikkai ni aru
near the elevator	エレベーターに近い
	erevētā ni chikai
near the stairs	階段に近い
	kaidan ni chikai
near the pool	プールに近い
	pūru ni chikai
away from the street	道路から離れた
	dōro kara hanareta
I would like a corner room.	角部屋をお願いしたいのですが。
	kado beya o onegai shitai no desuga.
Do you have ____?	____はありますか?
	____ *wa arimasu ka.*
a crib	ベビーベッド
	bebī beddo
a foldout bed	折りたたみ式ベッド
	oritatami shiki beddo

FOR GUESTS WITH SPECIAL NEEDS

I need a room with ____.	____部屋をお願いします。
	____ *heya o onegai shimasu.*
wheelchair access	車椅子で移動できる
	kurumaisu de idō dekiru
services for the visually impaired	視覚障害者のための設備のある
	shikaku shōgaisha no tame no setsubi no aru.
services for the hearing impaired	聴覚障害者のための設備のある
	chōkaku shōgaisha no tame no setsubi no aru
I am traveling with a service dog.	介護犬を連れているのですが。
	kaigo ken o tsurete iru no desuga.

MONEY MATTERS

| I would like to make a reservation. | 予約をしたいのですが。 |
| | *yoyaku o shitai no desuga.* |

How much per night?	一泊の料金はいくらですか？
	ippaku no ryōkin wa ikura desu ka.
Do you have a ____?	____はありますか？
	____ wa arimasu ka.
weekly rate	週料金
	shū ryōkin
monthly rate	月額料金
	getsugaku ryōkin
weekend rate	週末料金
	shūmatsu ryōkin
We will be staying for ____ days / weeks.	____日間 / 週間滞在する予定です。
	____ nichikan / shūkan taizai suru yotei desu.

For full coverage of number terms, see p7.

What is the checkout time?	チェックアウトは何時ですか？
	chekku auto wa nanji desu ka.

For full coverage of time-related terms, see p16.

Do you accept credit cards?	クレジットカードに対応していますか？
	kurejitto kādo ni taiō shite imasu ka.
May I see a room?	お部屋を見せていただけますか？
	oheya o misete itadake masu ka.
How much are taxes?	税金はいくらですか？
	zeikin wa ikura desu ka.
Is there a service charge, or is it included?	サービス料は取られますか？それとも含まれていますか？
	sābisu ryō wa torare masuka. soretomo fukumarete imasu ka.
Is breakfast included?	朝食込みですか？
	chōshoku komi desu ka.
I'd like to speak with the manager.	マネージャーとお話ししたいのですが。
	manējā to ohanashi shitai no desuga.

IN-ROOM AMENITIES

I'd like to place an international call.	国際電話をかけたいのですが。
	kokusai denwa o kaketai no desuga.

I'd like to place a long-distance call.	市外電話をかけたいのですが。 *shigai denwa o kaketai no desuga.*
I'd like directory assistance in English.	英語の番号案内にかけたいのですが。 *eigo no bangō annai ni kaketai no desuga.*
I'd like room service.	ルームサービスをお願いします。 *rūmu sābisu o onegai shimasu.*
I'd like maid service.	メードのサービスをお願いします。 *mēdo no sābisu o onegai shimasu.*
I'd like the front desk.	フロントデスクをお願いします。 *furonto desuku o onegai shimasu.*
Do you have room service?	ルームサービスはありますか？ *rūmu sābisu wa arimasu ka?*
When is the kitchen open?	食事は何時からできますか？ *shokuji wa nanji kara deki masu ka.*

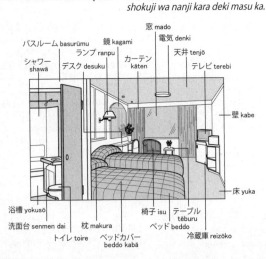

| When is breakfast served? | 朝食は何時ですか？ |
| | *chōshoku wa nan ji desu ka.* |

For full coverage of time-related terms, see p16.

Do you offer massages?	マッサージのサービスはありますか？
	massāji no sābisu wa arimasu ka.
Do you have a lounge?	ラウンジはありますか？
	raunji wa arimasu ka.
Do you have a business center?	ビジネス センターはありますか？
	bijinesu sentā wa arimasu ka.
Do you serve breakfast?	朝食は出ますか？
	chōshoku wa demasu ka.
Do you have Wi-Fi?	ワイヤーレスインターネット はありますか？
	waiyāresu intānetto wa arimasu ka.
Is there Wi-Fi in the rooms, or in the lobby only?	部屋には Wi-Fi はありますか？それともロビーのみですか？
	heya niwa Wi-Fi wa arimasu ka. soretomo robī nomi desu ka.

Listen Up: Dialing Instructions

他の部屋に電話をかけるには部屋番号をダイヤルします。 *hoka no heya ni denwa o kakeru niwa, heya bangō o daiyaru shimasu.*	To call another room, dial the room number.
市内電話をかけるには、最初に9をダイヤルします。 *shinai denwa o kakeru niwa, saisho ni kyū o daiyaru shimasu.*	To make a local call, first dial 9.
オペレーターを呼びだすには、0をダイヤルします。 *operētā o yobi dasu niwa, zero o daiyaru shimasu.*	To call the operator, dial 0.

LODGING

What is the Wi-Fi password?	**Wi-Fi のパスワードは何ですか?** *Wi-Fi no pasuwādo wa nani desu ka.*
May I have a newspaper in the morning?	**朝、新聞をもらえますか?** *asa, shinbun o morae masu ka.*
Do you offer a tailor service?	**仕立屋のサービスはありますか?** *shitateya no sābisu wa arimasu ka.*
Do you offer laundry service?	**ランドリー サービスはありますか?** *randorī sābisu wa arimasu ka.*
Do you offer dry cleaning?	**ドライ クリーニングのサービスはありますか?** *dorai kurīningu no sābisu wa arimasu ka.*
May we have ____?	**____いただけませんか?** *____ itadake masen ka.*
clean sheets today	**今日、きれいなシーツ** *kyō, kirei na shītsu*
more towels	**タオルをもっと** *taoru o motto*
more toilet paper	**トイレット ペーパーをもっと** *toiretto pēpā o motto*
extra pillows	**枕をもっと** *makura o motto*
shampoo	**シャンプー** *shanpū*
toothpaste	**歯磨き粉** *hamigakiko*
a toothbrush	**歯ブラシ** *haburashi*
an adapter	**アダプター** *adaputā*
a bottle opener	**栓抜き** *sennuki*
Do you have an ice machine?	**製氷機はありますか?** *seihyō ki wa arimasu ka.*
Did I receive any ____?	**私に____はありますか?** *watashi ni ____ wa arimasu ka.*

messages	伝言
	dengon
mail	手紙
	tegami

A spare key, please. スペアー キーをください。
supeā kī o kudasai.

More hangers, please. ハンガーをもっとください。
hangā o motto kudasai.

I am allergic to down pillows. 私は羽毛の枕にアレルギー反応が起きます。
watashi wa umō no makura ni arerugī hannō ga okimasu.

I'd like a wake-up call. モーニング コールをお願いします。
mōningu kōru o onegai shimasu.

For full coverage of time-related terms, see p16.

Do you have alarm clocks? 目覚まし時計はありますか？
mezamashi dokei wa arimasu ka.

Is there a safe in the room? 室内に金庫はありますか？
shitsu nai ni kinko wa arimasu ka.

Does the room have a hair dryer? 室内にヘアー ドライヤーはありますか？
shitsu nai ni heā doraiyā wa arimasu ka.

HOTEL ROOM TROUBLE

May I speak with the manager? マネージャーとお話したいのですが。
manējā to ohanashi shitai no desuga.

The television does not work. テレビが見れないんです。
terebi ga mirenai n desu.

The telephone does not work. 電話が使えないんです。
denwa ga tsukaenai n desu.

The air conditioning does not work. エアコンがきかないんです。
eakon ga kikanai n desu.

The Internet does not work. インターネットが使えません。
intānetto ga tsukae masen.

The cable TV does not work. ケーブルテレビが見れないんです。
kēburu terebi ga mirenai n desu.

There is no hot water.

お湯が出ないんです。
oyu ga denai n desu.

The toilet is over flowing!

トイレの水が溢れているんです!
toire no mizu ga afurete irun desu!

This room is _____.

この部屋は _____
kono heya wa _____

  too noisy

騒音がひど過ぎます。
sōon ga hido sugi masu.

  too cold

寒すぎます。
samu sugi masu.

  too warm

暖か過ぎます。
atataka sugi masu.

  dirty

汚いです。
kitanai desu.

This room has _____.

この部屋に_____がいます。
kono heya ni_____ ga imasu.

  bugs

虫
mushi

  mice

ねずみ
nezumi

I'd like a different room.

別の部屋に替えていただけませんか。
betsu no heya ni kaete itadake masen ka.

Do you have a bigger room?

これより大きい部屋はありますか?
kore yori ōkii heya wa arimasu ka.

I locked myself out of my room.

ドアに鍵がかかってしまい部屋に入ることができないんです。
doa ni kagi ga kakatte shimai heya ni hairu koto ga deki nai n desu.

I lost my key.	鍵をなくしました。
	kagi o nakushi mashita.
Do you have a fan?	扇風機はありますか?
	senpūki wa arimasu ka.
The sheets are not clean.	シーツが汚れています。
	shītsu ga yogorete imasu.
The towels are not clean.	タオルが汚れています。
	taoru ga yogorete imasu.
The room is not clean.	部屋が汚れています。
	heya ga yogorete imasu.
The guests next door are being very loud.	隣の客室がとてもうるさいです。
	tonari no kyaku shitsu ga totemo urusai desu.
The guests above are being very loud.	上の客室がとてもうるさいです。
	ue no kyaku shitsu ga totemo urusai desu.
The guests below are being very loud.	下の客室がとてもうるさいです。
	shita no kyaku shitsu ga totemo urusai desu.

CHECKING OUT

May I leave these bags?	このかばんを預けてもいいですか?
	kono kaban o azukete mo ii desu ka.
I'm missing ____.	____が見当たりません。
	____ ga miatari masen.
I've lost ____.	____をなくしました。
	____ o nakushi mashita.
I think this charge is a mistake.	この請求額は間違っていると思います。
	kono seikyū gaku wa machigatte iru to omoi masu.
Please explain this charge to me.	なぜこの請求額になるのか説明していただけますか。
	naze kono seikyūgaku ni naru noka setsumei shite itadake masu ka.

LODGING

Thank you, we enjoyed our stay.	楽しく滞在しました。ありがとうございました。 *tanoshiku taizai shimashita. arigatō gozaimashita.*
The service was excellent.	サービスがとてもよかったです。 *sābisu ga totemo yokatta desu.*
The staff is very professional and courteous.	スタッフはとてもプロフェッショナルで親切です。 *sutaffu wa totemo purofesshonaru de shinsetsu desu.*
Please call a cab for me.	タクシーを呼んでいただけますか。 *takushī o yonde itadake masu ka.*
Would someone please get my bags?	どなたか 私の荷物を取ってきていただけませんか？ *donata ka watashi no nimotsu o totte kite itadake masen ka.*

HAPPY CAMPING

I'd like a site for ____.	____場所が欲しいんですが。 *____ basho ga hoshii n desuga.*
a tent	テントを張る *tento o haru*
a camper	キャンパーのための *kyanpā no tame no*
Are there ____?	ここに____はありますか？ *koko ni ____ wa arimasu ka.*
bathrooms	トイレ *toire*
showers	シャワー *shawā*
Is there running water?	ここに水道水はありますか？ *koko ni suidōsui wa arimasu ka.*
Is the water drinkable?	この水は飲めますか？ *kono mizu wa nome masu ka.*
Where is the electrical hookup?	電気の接続部はどこにありますか？ *denki no setsuzoku bu wa doko ni arimasu ka.*

CHAPTER FOUR

DINING

This chapter includes a menu reader and the language you need to communicate in a range of dining establishments and food markets.

FINDING A RESTAURANT

Would you recommend a good ____?	お勧めの良い____はありますか? *osusume no yoi ____ wa arimasu ka.*
local restaurant	地元のレストラン *jimoto no resutoran.*
Japanese restaurant	和食の店 *washoku no mise*
Chinese restaurant	中華料理店 *chūka ryōri ten*
family restaurant	ファミリーレストラン *famirī resutoran*
French restaurant	フランス料理店 *furansu ryōri ten*
Indian restaurant	インド料理店 *indo ryōri ten*
Italian restaurant	イタリア料理店 *itaria ryōri ten*
gastropub / dining bar	居酒屋 *izakaya*
Korean restaurant	韓国料理店 *kankoku ryōri ten*
pizza restaurant	ピザ屋 *piza ya*
steakhouse	ステーキハウス *sutēki hausu*
Thai restaurant	タイ料理店 *tai ryōri ten*

Western restaurant	洋食レストラン *yōshoku resutoran*
vegetarian restaurant	ベジタリアンレストラン *bejitarian resutoran*
buffet	バイキング *baikingu*
inexpensive (budget) restaurant	あまり高くない（手ごろな）レストラン *amari takaku nai (tegoro na) resutoran*
Which is the best restaurant in town?	この街で最高のレストランはどれですか？ *kono machi de saikō no resutoran wa dore desu ka.*
Is there a late-night restaurant nearby?	この近くに深夜営業しているレストランはありますか？ *kono chikaku ni shinya eigyō shite iru resutoran wa arimasu ka.*
Is there a restaurant that serves breakfast nearby?	この近くに朝食を出すレストランはありますか？ *kono chikaku ni chōshoku o dasu resutoran wa arimasu ka.*
Is it very expensive?	値段はとても高いですか？ *nedan wa totemo takai desu ka.*
Do I need a reservation?	予約が必要ですか？ *yoyaku ga hitsuyō desu ka.*
Do I have to dress up?	正装しなければなりませんか？ *seisō shinakere ba nari masen ka.*
Do they serve lunch?	ランチはやってますか？ *ranchi wa yatte masu ka.*
What time do they open ____?	____は何時に始まりますか？ *____ wa nanji ni hajimari masu ka.*
for dinner	夕食 *yūshoku*
for lunch	昼食 *chūshoku.*

What time do they close?	何時に閉店しますか？ *nan ji ni heiten shimasu ka.*
Do you have a take out menu?	持帰り用のメニューはありますか？ *mochi kaeri yō no menyū wa arimasu ka.*
Do you have a bar?	バーはありますか？ *bā wa arimasu ka.*
Is there a café nearby?	この近くに喫茶店はありますか？ *kono chikaku ni kissa ten wa arimasu ka.*

GETTING SEATED

Are you still serving?	まだ開いていますか？ *mada aite imasu ka.*
How long is the wait?	どのくらい待ちますか？ *dono kurai machi masu ka.*
May I see a menu?	メニューを見せてください。 *menyū o misete kudasai.*
Do you have a no-smoking section?	禁煙席はありますか？ *kin en seki wa arimasu ka.*
A table for ____, please.	＿＿＿人座れるテーブルをお願いします。 *____ nin suwareru tēburu o onegai shimasu.*

For a full list of numbers, see p7.

Do you have a quiet table?	静かなテーブル席はありますか？ *shizukana tēburu seki wa arimasu ka.*
Do you have highchairs?	ハイチェアーはありますか？ *hai cheā wa arimasu ka.*
May we sit outside / inside please?	外 / 中に座ってもいいですか？ *soto / naka ni suwattemo ii desu ka.*
May we sit at the counter?	カウンターに座ってもいいですか？ *kauntā ni suwatte mo ii desu ka.*

Listen Up: Restaurant Lingo

喫煙席と禁煙席、どちらがよろしいですか？ *kitsu en seki to kin en seki, dochira ga yoroshii desu ka.*	Smoking or nonsmoking?
上着とネクタイが要ります。 *uwagi to nekutai ga iri masu.*	You'll need a tie and jacket.
申し訳ございませんが 半ズボンではお入りいただけません。 *mōshiwake gozai masen ga han zubon dewa o hairi itadake masen.*	I'm sorry, no shorts are allowed.
何かお飲み物をお持ちしましょうか？ *nani ka onomimono o omochi shima shō ka.*	May I bring you something to drink?
ワインリストをご覧になりますか？ *wain risuto o goran ni narimasu ka.*	Would you like to see a wine list?
当店のスペシャルをご説明しましょうか？ *tōten no supesharu o gosetsumei shima shō ka.*	Would you like to hear our specials?
ご注文はお決まりですか？ *gochūmon wa okimari desu ka*	Are you ready to order?
申し訳ございませんが、クレジットカードが拒否されました。 *mōshiwake gozai masen ga, kurejitto kādo ga kyohi sare mashita.*	I'm sorry, sir, your credit card was declined.

ORDERING

Do you have a special tonight?	今夜はスペシャルはありますか？ *konya wa supesharu wa arimasu ka.*
What do you recommend?	何がお勧めですか？ *nani ga osusume desu ka.*
May I see a wine list?	ワインリストを見せていただけますか？ *wain risuto o misete itadake masu ka.*
Do you serve wine by the glass?	グラスワインはありますか？ *gurasu wain wa arimasu ka.*
May I see a drink list?	飲み物のメニューを見せていただけますか？ *nomi mono no menyū o misete itadake masu ka.*
I would like it cooked ____.	____でお願いします。 *____ de onegai shimasu.*
rare	レア *rea*
medium rare	ミディアム レア *midiamu rea*
medium	ミディアム *midiamu*
medium well	ミディアム ウェル *midiamu weru*
well	ウェルダン *werudan*
charred	ベリーウェル *berī weru*
Do you have a ____ menu?	____向けメニューはありますか？ *____ muke menyū wa arimasu ka.*
vegetarian	ベジタリアン *bejitarian*

children's	子供
	kodomo
Do you have any ____ options?	____ のオプションはありますか?
	____ *no opushon wa arimasu ka.*
vegan	ベーガン料理
	bēgan ryōri
gluten-free	グルテン抜きの料理
	guruten nuki no ryōri
kosher	コーシャ料理
	kōsha ryōri
What is in this dish?	この料理には何が入っていますか?
	kono ryōri niwa nani ga haitte imasu ka.
How is it prepared?	どのように調理されていますか?
	donoyō ni chōri sarete imasu ka.
What kind of oil is that cooked in?	これにはどんな油が 使われていますか?
	kore niwa donna abura ga tsukawarete imasu ka.
I am allergic to ____.	____にアレルギーがあります。
	____ *ni arerugī ga arimasu.*
seafood	魚介類
	gyokairui
shellfish	貝類
	kai rui
nuts	ナッツ類
	nattsu rui
peanuts	ピーナッツ
	pīnattsu
I am lactose intolerant.	私は乳糖不耐症です。
	watashi wa nyuto futaisyo desu.
Would you recommend something without milk?	牛乳が入っていないものでは何がお勧めですか?
	gyūnyū ga haitte inai mono dewa nani ga osusume desu ka.

Do you have any low-salt dishes?	減塩の料理はありますか？
	gen en no ryōri wa arimasu ka.
On the side, please.	横に添えてください。
	yoko ni soete kudasai.
May I make a substitution?	ほかのものに替えていいですか？
	hoka no mono ni kaete ii desu ka.
I'd like to try that.	それを食べてみます。
	sore o tabete mimasu.
Is that fresh?	それは新鮮ですか？
	sore wa shinsen desu ka.
Extra butter, please.	バターをもう少しください。
	batā o mō sukoshi kudasai.
No butter, thanks.	バターは要りません。
	batā wa iri masen.
No cream, thanks.	クリームは要りません。
	kurīmu wa iri masen.
Dressing on the side, please.	ドレッシングを横に添えてください。
	doressingu o yokoni soete kudasai.
No salt, please.	塩を入れないでください。
	shio o ire naide kudasai.
Water _____, please.	_____で水をください。
	_____ de mizu o kudasai.
with ice	氷入り
	kōri iri
without ice	氷なし
	kōri nashi

DRINKS

cocktail	カクテル
	kakuteru
neat / straight	ストレートで
	sutorēto de
on the rocks	ロックで
	rokku de

with (seltzer or soda) water	(炭酸水またはソーダ) 水で *(tansansui / sōda) sui de*
draft beer	生ビール *nama bīru*
bottle beer	ビンビール *bin bīru*
wine	ワイン *wain*
sweet wine	甘口ワイン *amakuchi wain*
dry white wine	辛口白ワイン *karakuchi shiro wain*
red wine	赤ワイン *aka wain*
champagne	シャンパン *shanpan*
scotch	スコッチ *sukocchi*
whiskey	ウイスキー *uisukī*
brandy	ブランデー *burandē*
cognac	コニャック *konyakku*
gin	ジン *jin*
vodka	ウオッカ *uokka*
rum	ラム *ramu*
hot chocolate	ホット チョコレート *hotto chokorēto*
lemonade	レモネード *remonēdo*

milkshake	ミルクセーキ
	miruku sēki
milk	ミルク
	miruku
tea	紅茶
	kōcha
coffee	コーヒー
	kōhī
espresso	エスプレッソ
	esupuresso
iced coffee	アイス コーヒー
	aisu kōhī
fruit juice	フルーツ ジュース
	furūtsu jūsu

DURING THE MEAL

Excuse me!	すみません!
(to summon a waiter)	*sumi masen.*
More water, please.	もっと水をください。
	motto mizu o kudasai.
More bread, please.	もっとパンをください。
	motto pan o kudasai.
More butter, please.	もっとバターをください。
	motto batā o kudasai.
May I have some oil, please?	油をもらえますか?
	abura o morae masu ka.
Could I have another ____ please?	____をもう1つください。
	____ o mō hitotsu kudasai.
fork	フォーク
	fōku
knife	ナイフ
	naifu
spoon	スプーン
	supūn

napkin	ナプキン
	napukin
glass	コップ
	koppu
plate	お皿
	osara

I'm sorry, I don't think this is what I ordered.	すみませんが、これは私が注文したのと違うようです。
	sumi masen ga, kore wa watashi ga chūmon shita no to chigau yō desu.
My meat is a little over / under cooked.	肉が少し焼けすぎています / よく焼けていません。
	niku ga sukoshi yake sugite imasu / yoku yakete imasen.
My vegetables are a little over / under cooked.	野菜が少し煮えすぎています / よく煮えていません。
	yasai ga sukoshi nie sugite imasu / yoku niete imasen.
My food is cold.	私の料理は冷たいです。
	watashi no ryōri wa tsumetai desu.
There's a bug in my food!	食べ物の中に虫が入っています！
	tabemono no naka ni mushi ga haitte imasu.
May I have a refill?	お代わりをいただけますか？
	okawari o itadake masu ka.
A dessert menu, please.	デザートのメニューを見せてください。
	dezāto no menyū o misete kudasai.

For a full list of fruits, see p88.

SETTLING UP

I'm stuffed.	お腹が一杯です。
	onaka ga ippai desu.
Could I have the check, please?	お会計をお願いします。
	okaikei o onegai shimasu.

The meal was excellent.	とてもおいしかったです。
	totemo oishikatta desu
There's a problem with my bill.	お勘定が違うようなんですが。
	okanjō ga chigau yō nan desuga.
My compliments to the chef!	シェフにとてもおいしかったと伝えてください!
	shefu ni totemo oishikatta to tsutaete kudasai.
Check, please.	お勘定をお願いします。
	okanjō o onegai shimasu.

MENU READER

Japanese cuisine is far more varied than the offerings of most overseas Japanese restaurants, ranging from astronomically expensive haute cuisine to street food. While this is not a comprehensive guide, it will give you some idea of the diversity of the foods of Japan.

KAISEKI (懐石、会席)

These elaborate multi-course meals are becoming increasingly popular in the US. There are two types of *kaiseki*. One is based on the traditional *cha-kaiseki* (茶懐石), or food served during the traditional tea ceremony. Similar to the French menu *dégustation*, it involves multiple courses of small but elaborate dishes that vary according to season. The courses are predetermined; you do not order individual items. It is usually served at high-end Japanese restaurants known as *ryōtei* (料亭) and *kappō* (割烹), although nowadays, the word has become a catch-all name for any high-end tasting menu, so it is not unusual to find places offering French *kaiseki* menus.

The other form of *kaiseki* (会席) is served at banquets and is tailored toward drinking, featuring many dishes that go well with alcohol, which include *sashimi, tempura, aemono* and *sunomono*. The first part consists of an appetizer (*zensai*, 前菜), clear soup (*suimono*, 吸い物), and sashimi. The second part includes dishes that are grilled (*yakimono*, 焼物), steamed (*mushimono*, 蒸物), simmered (*nimono*, 煮物) and deep-fried (*agemono*, 揚物). An alternative to these would be a one-pot stew (*nabemono*, 鍋物). A salad, either vinegared (*sunomono*, 酢の物) or marinated (*aemono*, 和え物), also comes with this course. The final part is a course of boiled plain rice (*gohan*, 御飯), miso soup (*miso shiru*, 味噌汁), and pickles (*tsukemono*, 漬け物), served with green tea and some kind of fresh fruit.

BENTO (弁当)

Typically prepared for school and office lunchboxes, the bento is a boxed meal consisting of rice, pickles, and assorted finger foods. These can be found at any convenience store, supermarket or kiosk at a large train station. Bento sold at train stations are called *ekiben* (駅弁), and often contain some local flavor.

TEISHOKU (定食)

Teishoku are inexpensive set meals, usually consisting of meat or fish, some sides, soup and rice, which are all served at once. Restaurants that specialize in them, *teishoku-ya*, are comparable to luncheonettes or diners in the US.

SUSHI (江戸前)

The popular combo of raw fish and vinegar-seasoned rice comes from an ages-old means of preserving fish. Sushi comes in a variety of forms:

Nigirizushi (握りずし): a small handful of rice topped with fish or other seafood and a dab of wasabi paste; also sometimes known as *Edomae* (江戸前) *sushi*.

Makizushi (巻ずし): rice and fillings rolled inside a wrapping of dried seaweed (*nori*) with the use of a flexible bamboo mat. The best-known example is *tekkamaki* (てっか巻き), or raw tuna.

Chirashizushi (散らしずし): sometimes called *barazushi* (ばらずし), or literally 'scattered sushi.' It consists of various, usually colorful, toppings attractively arranged on top of a bed of seasoned rice. Unlike *nigirizushi* or *makizushi*, which can be eaten by hand, it must be eaten with utensils.

Inarizushi (いなりずし): sushi rice stuffed into pockets of sweetened thin, deep-fried tofu called *abura-age* (あぶらあげ). *Inari* is a Shinto deity who is associated with foxes. Foxes were believed to have a fondness for *abura-age*, hence the name.

Oshizushi (おしずし): A style of sushi that originated in Osaka, it consists of sushi rice and fish pressed into a rectangular box and then cut into slices. The best-known version is *battera*, which is rice topped with seasoned mackerel and a thin slice of *konbu* (昆布).

FOOD TERMS

CONDIMENTS / SAUCES / SPICES

bajiru バジル: basil
furikake ふりかけ: topping for hot rice, usually ground dried fish and nori, with salt
goma 胡麻: sesame
karashi からし: Japanese mustard
kinako 黄粉: soybean flour
kōshinryō 香辛料: spice
kuro koshō くろこしょう: black pepper
mirin みりん: sweet liquid flavoring
miso 味噌: fermented soybean paste
paseri パセリ: parsley
ponzu ぽん酢: condiment of citrus juice, vinegar and soy sauce
satō 砂糖: sugar
shio 塩: salt
shōyu 醤油: soy sauce

nin niku にんにく: garlic
tare たれ: sauce
tōgarashi 唐辛子: chili pepper
wasabi わさび: Japanese horseradish

FRUITS

anzu 杏: apricot
banana バナナ: banana
budō ぶどう: grapes
burūberī ブルーベリー: blueberry
gurēpufurūtsu グレープフルーツ: grapefruit
ichigo いちご: strawberry
kaki 柿: persimmon
kiui キウイ: kiwi
mango マンゴー: mango
meron メロン: melon
mikan みかん: tangerine
momo もも: peach
nashi 梨: pear
orenji オレンジ: orange
painappuru パイナップル: pineapple
puramu プラム: plum
raimu ライム: lime
razuberii ラズベリー: raspberry
remon レモン: lemon
ringo りんご: apple
sakuranbo さくらんぼ: cherry
suika スイカ: watermelon
yuzu 柚子: Japanese citron

GARNISHES / SIDES

fukujinzuke 福神漬け: pickled vegetables
gari がり: thinly sliced vinegared ginger
hijiki ひじき: seaweed
kinpira gobō きんぴらごぼう: burdock
konbu 昆布: kelp
nattō 納豆: fermented soybeans
nori のり: dried laver
shōga 生姜: ginger
takuan 沢庵: pickled daikon radish
tsukemono 漬け物: pickles
umeboshi 梅干し: pickled japanese plum
wakame わかめ: seaweed

GRAINS / RICE / RICE DISHES

chāhan チャーハン: fried rice
donburi 丼: bowl of rice with toppings
genmai 玄米: brown rice
gohan 御飯: cooked rice
gomoku meshi 五目飯: rice dish with chicken and assorted vegetables
kama meshi 釜飯: rice cooked in a large pot over a hearth
katsudon カツ丼: pork donburi
kayu 粥: rice porridge
kome 米: rice
meshi 飯: informal term for food or meal
mochi もち: rice cake
mugi 麦: grain; usually refers to barley
ojiya おじや: rice gruel; also called zōsui (雑炊)
oyako donburi 親子丼: chicken and egg donburi

MEATS / POULTRY

butaniku 豚肉: pork
gibie ジビエ: wild game in season
gyūniku 牛肉: beef
hitsuji 羊: lamb
horumon ホルモン: offal, variety meats
kamo 鴨: duck
katsu カツ: breaded and deep-fried meat, fish or chicken
motsu もつ: giblets, viscera
niku 肉: meat
nikujaga 肉じゃが: simmered dish of meat, potatoes and vegetables
shamo しゃも: gamecock, game fowl
tamago 卵 **or** 玉子: egg
toriniku 鳥肉: chicken meat

NOODLES

kitsune soba / udon きつねそば / うどん: noodles served with abura-age
rāmen ラーメン: Chinese-style noodles served in stock
soba そば: buckwheat noodles
sōmen 素麺: thin wheat noodles
udon うどん: soft, thick wheat noodles
udonsuki うどんすき: udon cooked in clear soup with vegetables and chicken or fish

SEAFOOD

aji あじ: horse mackerel
anago 穴子: saltwater conger eel
ankō あんこう: angler fish
awabi あわび: abalone
ayu 鮎: freshwater sweetfish
dojō どじょう: loach, a freshwater fish
ebi えび: prawn, shrimp, lobster
fugu ふぐ: puffer, blowfish
hamaguri はまぐり: clam

hamo はも: freshwater eel

hokke ほっけ: mackerel

hotategai 帆立て貝: scallop

ika いか: squid

ikura イクラ: salmon eggs

inada いなだ: young yellowtail tuna, also called hamachi (はまち)

iwashi いわし: sardine

kai 貝: mollusk

kaki かき: oyster

kamaboko 蒲鉾: processed fish paste

kani かに: crab

karasumi からすみ: dried mullet roe

katsuo かつお: bonito

katsuobushi カツオ節: dried bonito

kazunoko 数の子: herring roe

kegani 毛がに: hairy crab

koi 鯉: carp

maguro まぐろ: northern bluefin tuna

mentaiko 明太子: salted, spicy pollack roe

saba さば: chub mackerel

sakana 魚: fish

sanma さんま: Pacific saury

sake さけ: salmon

shirako 白子: soft roe; fish semen

suppon すっぽん: snapping turtle

surume するめ: dried squid

tai 鯛: sea bream; red snapper

tako たこ: octopus

takoyaki たこやき: grilled chopped octopus in batter

tara たら: cod

toro とろ: fatty tuna meat

unagi うなぎ: sea-born eel that migrates to freshwater

uni うに: sea urchin

SOUPS / STEWS / STOCK

chirinabe ちり鍋: *nabemono* of meat or fish, tofu and vegetables served with dipping sauce

dashi だし: soup stock made with fish and kelp

miso shiru 味噌汁: miso soup

mizutaki 水炊き: chicken *nabemono*

nabemono 鍋物: one-pot dish; stew

suimono 吸い物: clear soup

sumashijiru すまし汁: clear soup

zōni ぞうに: *mochi* in soup

SWEETS / SNACKS / DESSERTS

anko あんこ: sweet red bean paste

annindōfu 杏仁豆腐: almond jelly

kasutera カステラ: Castella cake

manjū まんじゅう: steamed bun with sweet or savory filling

senbei 煎餅: rice cracker

taiyaki たいやき: sweet cake shaped like a sea bream

wagashi 和菓子: Japanese confections, cakes, candy, cookies

yōkan 羊羹: sweet red bean jelly

TEA

bancha 番茶: common green tea

cha 茶: tea

genmaicha 玄米茶: green tea with roasted rice grains added for flavor

hōjicha 焙じ茶: roasted green tea

maccha 抹茶: powdered green tea

mugicha 麦茶: barley tea

sencha 煎茶: higher-quality green tea usually reserved for guests

VEGETABLES

abogado アボガド: avocado
ao mame 青豆: green beans
ātichōku アーティチョーク: artichoke
azuki 小豆: red bean
burokkorī ブロッコリー: broccoli
daikon 大根: Japanese radish
edamame 枝豆: soybean
enoki 榎: winter mushroom
gobo ごぼう: burdock
hōrensō ほうれん草: spinach
jagaimo じゃがいも: potato
kabocha かぼちゃ: pumpkin
karifurawā カリフラワー: cauliflower
kinoko きのこ: mushroom
kuri くり: chestnut
kuromame 黒豆: black bean
kyūri きゅうり: cucumber
mame 豆: beans
matsutake 松茸: Matsutake mushroom
moyashi もやし: bean sprouts
nasu なす: eggplant
negi ねぎ: leek
ninjin にんじん: carrot
okura おくら: okra
pīman ピーマン: Japanese green pepper
renkon れんこん: lotus root
retasu レタス: lettuce
satsumaimo さつまいも: sweet potato
serori セロリ: celery
shitake しいたけ: Shītake mushroom

takenoko 竹の子: bamboo shoot
tamanegi たまねぎ: onion
tomato トマト: tomato
tōmorokoshi とうもろこし: corn
uri うり: squash
yamaimo やまいも: yam

BUYING GROCERIES

In Japan, groceries can be bought at convenience stores, neighborhood stores, or large supermarkets.

AT THE SUPERMARKET

For a complete list of food terms, see p87.

Where can I find ____?	____はどこににありますか？
	____ wa doko ni arimasu ka.
spices	スパイス
	supaisu
toiletries	化粧品
	keshōhin
paper plates and napkins	紙皿とナプキン
	kamizara to napukin
canned goods	缶詰
	kanzume
frozen food	冷凍食品
	reitō shokuhin
snack food	軽食
	keishoku
baby food	ベビーフード
	bebī fūdo
water	水
	mizu
juice	ジュース
	jūsu
bread	パン
	pan

milk	牛乳
	gyūnyū
eggs	卵
	tamago
cheese	チーズ
	chīzu
fruit	果物
	kudamono
vegetables	野菜
	yasai
cookies	クッキー
	kukkī
Where is the checkout counter?	チェックアウトカウンターはどこですか?
	chekku auto kauntā wa doko desu ka.

AT THE BUTCHER SHOP

Is the ____ fresh?	この____は新鮮ですか?
	kono ____ wa shinsen desu ka.
meat	肉
	niku
fish	魚
	sakana
seafood	シーフード
	shīfūdo
Do you sell fresh ____?	新鮮な____はありますか?
	shinsen na ____ wa arimasu ka.

For a complete list of food terms, see p87.

May I smell it?	そのにおいをかいでもいいですか?
	sono nioi o kaide mo ii desu ka.
Would you please ____?	____いただけませんか?
	____ itadake masen ka.

filet it

おろして
oroshite

debone it

骨を取り除いて
hone o tori nozoite

remove the head and
tail

頭と尻尾を取り除いて
atama to shippo o tori nozoite

CHAPTER FIVE

SOCIALIZING

Whether you're meeting people in a bar or a park, you'll find the language you need, in this chapter, to make new friends.

GREETINGS

Hello.	こんにちは。 *kon nichi wa.*
How are you?	お元気ですか? *ogenki desu ka.*
Fine, thanks.	元気です。どうもありがとう。 *genki desu. dōmo arigatō.*
And you?	あなたもお元気ですか? *anata mo ogenki desu ka.*
I'm exhausted from the trip.	旅行で疲れました。 *ryokō de tsukare mashita.*
I have a headache.	頭痛がしています。 *zutsū ga shite imasu.*
I'm terrible.	体の調子が悪いです。 *karada no chōshi ga warui desu.*
I have a cold.	カゼを引きました。 *kaze o hiki mashita.*
Good morning.	おはようございます。 *ohayō gozai masu.*
Good evening.	こんばんは。 *kon ban wa.*
Good afternoon.	こんにちは。 *kon nichi wa.*
Good night.	おやすみなさい。 *oyasumi nasai.*

Listen Up: Common Greetings

お会いできて嬉しいです。	It's a pleasure.
oai dekite ureshii desu.	
とても嬉しいです。	Delighted.
totemo ureshii desu.	
ご用を承ります。／ご希望通りに。	At your service. / As you wish.
goyō o uke tamawari masu. / gokibō dōrini.	
嬉しいです。	Charmed.
ureshii desu.	
ごきげんよう。	Good day. (shortened)
gokigen yō.	
お元気ですか？	How's it going?
ogenki desu ka.	
最近どう？	What's up?
saikin dō?	
何をしているのですか？	What's going on?
nani o shite iru no desu ka	
さようなら。	Goodbye.
sayōnara	
それじゃ、また後で。	See you later.
soreja, mata ato de.	

OVERCOMING THE LANGUAGE BARRIER

I don't understand.	わかりません。
	wakari masen.
Please speak more slowly.	もっとゆっくり話してください。
	motto yukkuri hanashi te kudasai.
Please speak louder.	もっと大きな声で話してください。
	motto ōkina koe de hanashi te kudasai.

Do you speak English?	英語を話しますか？ *eigo o hanashi masu ka.*
I speak ＿＿ better than Japanese.	日本語より＿＿の方がうまく話せます。 *nihongo yori ＿＿ no hō ga umaku hanase masu.*
Please spell that.	つづりを言ってもらえますか。 *tsuzuri o itte morae masu ka.*
Please repeat that?	もう一度お願いします。 *mō ichido onegai shimasu.*
How do you say ＿＿?	＿＿は何と言いますか？ *＿＿ wa nan to iimasu ka.*
Would you show me that in this dictionary?	それをこの辞書で示してもらえますか。 *sore o kono jisho de shimeshite morae masu ka.*

GETTING PERSONAL

People in Japan are generally friendly, but more formal than Americans or Europeans.

INTRODUCTIONS

What is your name?	あなたの名前は何ですか？ *anata no namae wa nan desu ka.*
My name is ＿＿.	私は＿＿です。 *watashi wa ＿＿ desu.*
I'm very pleased to meet you.	お会いできて嬉しいです。 *oai dekite ureshii desu.*
May I introduce my ＿＿?	私の＿＿を紹介します。 *watashi no ＿＿ o shōkai shimasu.*
How is your ＿＿?	＿＿はお元気ですか？ *＿＿ wa ogenki desu ka.*
wife	奥さん 　*oku san*
husband	ご主人 　*go shujin*

child	お子さん
	oko san
boyfriend / girlfriend	ボーイフレンド / ガールフレンド
	bōi furendo / gāru furendo
family	ご家族
	go kazoku
mother / father	お父さん / お母さん
	otōsan / okāsan
brother / sister	ご兄弟 / ご姉妹
	go kyōdai / go shimai
friend	お友達
	o tomodachi
neighbor	ご近所の方
	go kinjo no kata
boss	上司
	jōshi
cousin	いとこ
	itoko
aunt / uncle	おばさん / おじさん
	oba san / oji san
fiancée / fiancé	婚約者
	kon yaku sha
partner	パートナー
	pātonā
niece / nephew	姪御さん / 甥御さん
	meigo san / oigo san
How are your ____?	____はお元気ですか。
	____ ha ogenki desu ka.
parents	ご両親
	goryōshin
grandparents	おじいさんとおばあさん
	ojīsan, obāsan

He / She is doing well, thanks.	ありがとうございます、彼 / 彼女は元気です。 *arigatō gozai masu, kare / kanojo wa genki desu.*
They are doing well, thanks.	ありがとうございます、彼らは元気です。 *arigatō gozai masu, karera wa genki desu.*
Are you married / single?	ご結婚していますか / 独身ですか？ *go kekkon shite imasu ka / dokushin desu ka.*
I'm married.	結婚しています。 *kekkon shite imasu.*
I'm single.	独身です。 *dokushin desu.*
I'm divorced.	離婚しました。 *rikon shima shita.*
I'm a widow / widower.	未亡人 / やもめです。 *mibōjin / yamome desu.*
We're separated.	別居しています。 *bekkyo shite imasu.*
I live with my boyfriend / girlfriend.	ボーイフレンド / ガールフレンドと一緒に暮らしています。 *bōi furendo / gāru furendo to issho ni kurashite imasu.*
I live with a roommate.	私はルームメートと住んでいます。 *watashi wa rūmu mēto to sunde imasu.*
How old are you?	何歳ですか？ *nan sai desu ka.*
How old is ____?	____ は何歳ですか？ *____ wa nansai desu ka.*

your son	あなたの息子さん
	anata no musuko san
your daughter	あなたの娘さん
	anata no musume san
your child	あなたのお子さん
	anata no oko san

How old are your children?
お子さんは何歳ですか?
oko san wa nan sai desu ka.

I am ____ years old.
私は____歳です。
watashi wa ____ sai desu.

He is / She is ____ years old.
彼 / 彼女は____歳です。
kare / kanojo wa ____ sai desu.

They are ____ years old.
彼らは____歳です。
karera wa ____ sai desu.

For a complete list of numbers, see p7.

Wow! That's very young.
まあ! とてもお若いですね。
ma! totemo owakai desu ne.

No you're not! You're much younger.
違いますよ! あなたの方がずっと若いです。
chigai masuyo. anata no hō ga zutto wakai desu.

Your wife / daughter is beautiful.
あなたの奥さん / お嬢さんは美人ですね。
anata no oku san / ojō san wa bijin desu ne.

Your husband / son is handsome.
あなたのご主人 / 息子さんはハンサムですね。
anata no goshujin / musuko san wa hansamu desu ne.

What a beautiful baby!
可愛い赤ちゃんですね!
kawaii aka chan desu ne.

Are you here on business?
ここへは商用で来られましたか?
koko ewa shōyō de korare mashita ka.

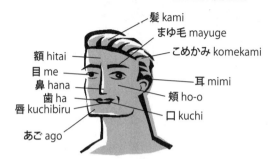

髪 kami
まゆ毛 mayuge
こめかみ komekami
額 hitai
目 me
鼻 hana
歯 ha
唇 kuchibiru
あご ago
耳 mimi
頬 ho-o
口 kuchi

I am vacationing.	私は休暇で来ました。
	watashi wa kyūka de kimashita.
I'm attending a conference.	会議に参加します。
	kaigi ni sanka shimasu.
How long are you staying?	どのくらい滞在しますか?
	dono kurai taizai shimasu ka.
What are you studying?	何を勉強していますか?
	nani o benkyō shite imasu ka.
I'm a student.	私は学生です。
	watashi wa gakusei desu.
Where are you from?	どこから来ましたか?
	doko kara kimashita ka.

For full coverage of nationalities, see p106.
See diagram, p150 for body parts.

DISPOSITIONS & MOODS

sad	悲しい
	kanashii
happy	嬉しい
	ureshii
angry	怒っている
	okotte iru

tired	疲れている
	tsukarete iru
depressed	落ち込んだ気分の
	ochikonda kibun no
anxious	心配している
	shinpai shite iru
stressed	ストレスを感じた
	sutoresu o kanjite iru
confused	混乱している
	konran shite iru
enthusiastic	熱心である
	nesshin de aru

PROFESSIONS

What do you do for a living?	仕事は何をされていますか?
	shigoto wa nani o sarete imasu ka.
Here is my business card.	私の名刺をお渡しします。
	watashi no meishi o owatashi shimasu.
I am ____.	私は____です。
	watashi wa ____ desu.
a doctor	医者
	isha
an engineer	エンジニア
	enjinia
a lawyer	弁護士
	bengoshi
a salesperson	販売員
	hanbai in
a writer	作家
	sakka
an editor	編集者
	henshū sha
a designer	デザイナー
	dezainā

an educator	教育者
	kyōiku sha
an artist	芸術家
	geijutsu ka
a craftsperson	職人
	shoku nin
a homemaker	主婦
	shufu
an accountant	会計士
	kaikei shi
a nurse	看護師
	kango shi
a web designer	ウェッブデザイナー
	webbu dezainā
a computer programmer	コンピューター プログラマー
	konpyūtā puroguramā
a musician	音楽家
	ongaku ka
a military professional	職業軍人
	shokugyō gunjin
a government employee	公務員
	kōmu in

TOPICS OF CONVERSATION

As in the United States or Europe, the weather and current affairs are common conversation topics.

THE WEATHER

It's so ____ .	とても____。
	totemo ____ 。
Is it always so ____ ?	いつもそんなに____か?
	itsumo sonna ni ____ ka.
sunny	晴れています
	harete imasu

Listen Up: Nationalities

私は台湾人です。 *watashi wa taiwan jin desu.*	I'm Taiwanese.
私はチベット人です。 *watashi wa chibetto jin desu.*	I'm Tibetan.
私は韓国人です。 *watashi wa kankoku jin desu.*	I'm Korean.
私はフィリピン人です。 *watashi wa firipin jin desu.*	I'm Filipino.
私は中国人です。 *watashi wa chūgoku jin desu.*	I'm Chinese.
私はマカオ人です。 *watashi wa makao jin desu.*	I'm Macanese.
私はタイ人です。 *watashi wa tai jin desu.*	I'm Thai.
私はマレーシア人です。 *watashi wa marēshiya jin desu.*	I'm Malaysian.
私はベトナム人です。 *watashi wa betonamu jin desu.*	I'm Vietnamese.
私はネパール人です。 *watashi wa nepāru jin desu.*	I'm Nepalese.
私はラオス人です。 *watashi wa raosu jin desu.*	I'm Laotian.
私はインド人です。 *watashi wa indo jin desu.*	I'm Indian.
私はビルマ人です。 *watashi wa biruma jin desu.*	I'm Burmese.
私はイタリア人です。 *iwatashi wa itaria jin desu.*	I'm Italian.
私は日本人です。 *watashi wa nihon jin desu.*	I'm Japanese.

For a full list of nationalities, see English / Japanese dictionary.

rainy	雨が降ります
	amega furi masu
cloudy	曇っています
	kumotte imasu
humid	湿気があります
	shikke ga arimasu
warm	暖かいです
	atatakai desu
cool	涼しいです
	suzushii desu
windy	風が強いです
	kaze ga tsuyoi desu

Do you know the weather forecast for tomorrow?
明日の天候予報を知っていますか？
ashita no tenki yohō o shitte imasu ka.

THE ISSUES

What do you think about ____?	____についてどう思いますか？
	____ ni tsuite dō omoi masu ka.
the government	政府
	seifu
democracy	民主主義
	minshu shugi
socialism	社会主義
	shakai shugi
the environment	環境
	kankyō
climate change	気候変動
	kikōhendō
the economy	経済
	keizai
the economic situation in ____	____での経済状況
	____ deno keizai jōkyō

the political situation
in _____

____での政治情勢
_____ *deno seijijōsei*

the upcoming election
in _____

____での次期選挙
_____ *deno jikisenkyo*

the war in _____

____での戦争
_____ *deno sensō*

What political party do
you belong to?

あなたはどの政党に属しています
か？
*anata wa dono seitō ni zokushite
imasu ka.*

RELIGION

Are you religious?

宗教を信仰していますか？
shūkyō o shinkō shiteimasu ka.

I'm _____ / I was
raised _____.

私は____です / 私は____として育ち
ました。
*watashi wa _____ desu / watashi
wa _____ toshite sodachi
mashita.*

Protestant

プロテスタント
purotesutanto

Catholic

カトリック
katorikku

Jewish

ユダヤ教徒
yudaya kyōto

Muslim

イスラム教徒
isuramu kyōto

Buddhist

仏教徒
bukkyōto

Greek Orthodox

ギリシャ正教徒
girisha seikyōto

Hindu

ヒンズー教徒
hinzū kyōto

agnostic

不可知論者
fuka chiron sha

atheist
無神論者
mu shinron sha

I'm spiritual but I don't attend services.
私は信心深いですが、教会の礼拝には参加しません。
watashi wa shinjin bukai desuga, kyōkai no reihai niwa sanka shimasen.

I don't believe in that.
それは信じません。
sore wa shinji masen.

That's against my beliefs.
それは私の信仰に反します。
sore wa watashi no shinkō ni hanshi masu.

I'd rather not talk about it.
そのことについては話したくありません。
sono koto ni tsuite wa hanashi taku arima sen.

MUSICAL TASTES

What kind of music do you like?
どのような音楽が好きですか？
dono yō na ongaku ga suki desu ka.

I like ____.
____が好きです。
____ ga suki desu.

rock music
ロック音楽
rokku ongaku

classic rock
クラシック ロック
kurashikku rokku

hip-hop
ヒップ ホップ
hippu hoppu

techno
テクノ
tekuno

soul
ソウル
sōru

classical
クラシック
kurashikku

jazz
ジャズ
jazu

country	カントリー音楽
	kantorī ongaku
reggae	レゲー
	regē
opera	オペラ
	opera
show-tunes / musicals	映画音楽 / ミュージカル
	eiga ongaku / myūjikaru
pop	ポップ
	Poppu

HOBBIES

What do you like to do in your spare time?	空いている時間には何をするのが好きですか？
	aite iru jigan niwa nani o suru noga suki desu ka.
I like ____.	____のが好きです。
	____ no ga suki desu.
playing the guitar	ギターを弾く
	gitā o hiku
playing the piano	ピアノを弾く
	piano o hiku

For other instruments, see the English / Japanese dictionary.

painting	絵を描く
	e o kaku
drawing	スケッチする
	sukecchi suru
dancing	ダンスをする
	dansu o suru
reading	本を読む
	hon o yomu
blogging	ブログを書く
	burogu o kaku
watching TV	テレビを見る
	terebi o miru

shopping	買い物をする *kaimono o suru*
going to the movies	映画を観に行く *eiga o mini iku*
hiking	ハイキングをする *haikingu o suru*
camping	キャンプをする *kyanpu o suru*
hanging out	ぶらぶらする *bura bura suru*
traveling	旅行する *ryokō suru*
eating out	外食する *gaishoku suru*
cooking	料理をする *ryōri o suru*
sewing	裁縫をする *saihō o suru*
sports	スポーツをする *supōtsu o suru*

For a full list of food types, see Dining in Chapter 4.

What kind of books do you like to read?	どんな本を読むのが好きですか? *donna hon o yomu noga suki desu ka.*
I like ____.	____が好きです。 *____ ga suki desu.*
mysteries	ミステリー *misuterī*
Westerns	西部劇物 *seibu geki mono*
dramas	劇の脚本 *geki no kyakuhon*
novels	小説 *shōsetsu*

classics	古典
	koten
biographies	伝記物
	denki mono
auto-biographies	自叙伝
	jijoden
romance	恋愛小説
	renai shōsetsu
history	歴史物
	rekishimono
memoirs	伝記
	denki
non-fiction	ノンフィクション
	non fikushon
What kind of movies do you like?	どんな映画が好きですか？
	donna eiga ga suki desu ka.
I like ____.	私は____が好きです。
	watashi wa ____ ga suki desu.
action films	アクション映画
	akushon eiga
thrillers	スリラー
	surirā
drama	ドラマ
	dorama
comedy	コメディ
	komedi
old movies	昔の映画
	mukashi no eiga
documentary films	ドキュメンタリー映画
	dokyumentarī eiga
Do you like to dance?	踊るのは好きですか？
	odoru nowa suki desu ka.
Would you like to go out?	外に出かけたいですか？
	soto ni dekake tai desu ka.

May I buy you dinner sometime?	いつか夕食をご馳走させてください。 *itsuka yūshoku o gochisō sasete kudasai.*
What kind of food do you like?	どんな料理が 好きですか？ *donna ryōri ga suki desu ka.*
Would you like to go ____?	____行きたいですか？ *____ ikitai desu ka.*
to a movie	映画を観に *eiga o mini*
to a concert	コンサートに *konsāto ni*
to the zoo	動物園に *dōbutsu en ni*
to the beach	ビーチに *bīchi ni*
to a museum	美術館に *bijutsu kan ni*
for a walk in the park	公園に散歩しに *kōen ni sanpo shini*
dancing	ダンスをしに *dansu o shini*
Would you like to get ____?	____に行きたいですか？ *____ ni ikitai desu ka.*
lunch	お昼ごはんを食べ *ohiru gohan o tabe*
coffee	コーヒーを飲み *kōhī o nomi*
dinner	夕食を食べ *yūshoku o tebe*

PARTING WAYS

Keep in touch.

連絡を取り合いましょう。
renraku o toriai mashō.

Please write or email.

手紙か E メールをください。
tegami ka E mēru o kudasai.

Here's my phone number /
e-mail.

これが私の電話番号 / E メールです。
*kore ga watashi no denwa bangō /
denshi mēru adoresu desu.*

Call me.

私に電話をください。
watashi ni denwa o kudasai.

May I have your phone
number / e-mail please?

あなたの電話番号 / E メール アドレス
をいただけますか?
*anata no denwa bangō / E mēru
adoresu o itadake masu ka.*

May I have your card?

あなたの名刺をいただけますか?
anata no meishi o itadake masu ka.

CHAPTER SIX

MONEY & COMMUNICATIONS

This chapter covers money, the mail, phone, Internet service, and other tools you need to connect with the outside world.

MONEY

I need to exchange money.	お金を両替する必要があります。 *okane o ryōgae suru hitsuyō ga arimasu.*
Do you accept ____ ?	____は使えますか? *____ wa tsukae masu ka.*
Visa / MasterCard / Discover / American Express / Diners' Club credit cards	ビザカード / マスターカード / ディスカバー / アメリカン エキスプレス / ダイナーズ クラブ クレジットカード *biza kādo / masutā kādo / disukabā / amerikan ekisupuresu / daināzu kurabu kurejitto kādo*
bills	紙幣 *shihei*
coins	硬貨 *kōka*
money transfers	振り込み *furikomi*
May I wire transfer funds here?	ここから電信振り込みできますか? *koko kara denshin furikomi deki masu ka.*
Would you please tell me where to find ____ ?	____はどこにありますか。 *____ wa doko ni arimasu ka.*
a bank	銀行 *ginkō*
a credit bureau	クレジット部 *kurejitto bu*
an ATM	ATM *ATM*

a currency exchange

両替所
ryōgae jo

A receipt, please.

レシートをください。
reshīto o kudasai.

Would you tell me _____?

_____は何ですか?
_____ wa nan desu ka.

the exchange rate for
dollars to yen

ドルから円への交換レート
doru kara en eno kōkan rēto

the exchange rate for
pounds to yen

ポンドから円への変換レート
pondo kara en eno kōkan rēto

Is there a service charge?

サービス料は取られますか?
sābisu ryō wa torare masu ka.

May I have a cash advance
on my credit card?

このクレジットカードでキャッシングで
きますか?
*kono kurejitto kādo de kyasshingu
deki masu ka.*

Will you accept a
credit card?

クレジットカードを使えますか?
kurejitto kādo o tsukae masu ka.

May I have smaller
bills, please?

小さい額のお札に両替してもらえ
ますか?
*chiisai gaku no osatsu ni ryōgae
shite morae masu ka.*

Can you make change?

小さい額のお札にお願いします。
*chiisai gaku no osatsu ni
onegaishimasu.*

I only have bills.

お札しかありません。
osatsu shika ari masen.

Some coins, please.

小銭もまぜてください。
kozeni mo mazete kudasai.

Listen Up: Bank Lingo

ここに署名してください。 *koko ni shomei shite kudasai.*	Please sign here.
レシートのお返しです。 *reshīto no okaeshi desu.*	Here is your receipt.
身分証明書を見せてください。 *mibun shōmeisho o misete kudasai.*	May I see your ID, please?
現金のみです。 *genkin nomi desu.*	Cash only.

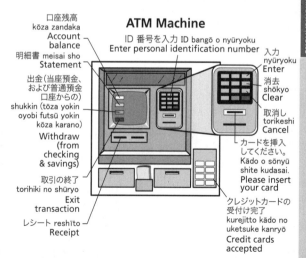

ATM Machine

口座残高
kōza zandaka
Account balance

明細書 meisai sho
Statement

出金(当座預金、および普通預金口座からの)
shukkin (tōza yokin oyobi futsū yokin kōza karano)
Withdraw (from checking & savings)

取引の終了
torihiki no shūryo
Exit transaction

レシート reshīto
Receipt

ID 番号を入力 ID bangō o nyūryoku
Enter personal identification number

入力
nyūryoku
Enter

消去
shōkyo
Clear

取消し
torikeshi
Cancel

カードを挿入してください。
Kādo o sōnyū shite kudasai.
Please insert your card

クレジットカードの受付け完了
kurejitto kādo no uketsuke kanryō
Credit cards accepted

PHONE SERVICE

Where can I buy a
SIM card?

SIM カードはどこで買うことができま
すか?
*SIM kādo wa doko de kau koto ga
deki masu ka.*

Where can I buy or rent a
cell phone?

携帯電話はどこで借りるか買うことが
できますか?
*keitai denwa wa dokode kariru ka
kau koto ga deki masu ka.*

What rate plans do you
have?

どんな料金プランがありますか?
donna ryōkin puran ga arimasu ka.

Is data included in the rate?

この料金にはデータが含まれていま
すか?
*kono ryōkin niwa dēta ga
fukumarete imasu ka.*

I'd like a pay-as-you-go
SIM card.

プリペイドの SIM カードを買いたい
です。
puripeido no SIM kādo o kaitai desu.

May I have a prepaid
calling card?

プリペイドのコーリングカードをくだ
さい。
*puripeido no kōringu kādo o
kudasai.*

May I add more minutes
to my phone card?

テレフォンカードにもっと時間を追加
できますか?
*terefon kādo ni motto jikan o tsuika
deki masu ka.*

MAKING A CALL

May I dial direct?

直通電話はできますか?
chokutsū denwa wa deki masu ka.

Operator please.

オペレーターをお願いします。
operētā o onegai shimasu.

I'd like to make an
international call.

国際電話をかけたいのですが。
kokusai denwa o kake tai no desuga.

I'd like to make a collect
call.

コレクトコールをお願いします。
korekuto kōru o onegai shimasu.

Listen Up: Telephone Lingo

お電話番号をお願いします。 *odenwa bangō o onegai shimasu.*	What number?
申し訳ございませんが、相手先の電話は話し中です。 *mōshiwake gozai masen ga, aite saki no denwa wa hanashi chū desu.*	I'm sorry, the line is busy.
一度切ってからまたおかけ直しください。 *ichido kitte kara mata okake naoshi kudasai.*	Please, hang up and redial.
申し訳ございませんが、どなたも電話にでられません。 *mōshiwake gozai masen ga, donata mo denwa ni derare masen.*	I'm sorry, nobody is answering.
カードの残り時間は10分です。 *kādo no nokori jikan wa juppun desu.*	Your card has ten minutes left.

MONEY & COMMUNICATIONS

I'd like to use a calling card.	コーリングカードを使います。 *kōringu kādo o tsukai masu.*
Bill my credit card.	私のクレジットカードに請求してください。 *watashi no kurejitto kādo ni seikyū shite kudasai.*
May I bill the charges to my room?	私の部屋に請求してもらえますか？ *watashi no heya ni seikyū shite morae masu ka.*
May I bill the charges to my home phone?	これはわたしの家の電話に請求していただけますか？ *kore wa watashi no ie no denwa ni seikyū shite itadake masu ka.*

Information, please.	インフォメーションをお願いします。
	infomēshon o onegai shimasu.
I'd like the number for ____.	____の番号をお願いします。
	____ no bangō o onegai shimasu.
I just got disconnected.	電話が切れてしまいました。
	denwa ga kirete shimai mashita.
The line is busy.	只今話し中です。
	tadaima hanashi chū desu.

INTERNET ACCESS

Where can I find an Internet café?	インターネットカフェはどこにありますか?
	intānetto kafe wa dokoni arimasu ka.
Is there Wi-Fi?	**Wi-Fi はありますか?**
	Wi-Fi wa arimasu ka.
How much do you charge per minute / hour?	1 分 / 1 時間いくらですか?
	ippun / ichi jikan ikura desu ka.
Can I print here?	ここで印刷できますか?
	koko de insatsu deki masu ka.
Would you please help me change the language preference to English?	言語を英語に変えるのを手伝っていただけませんか?
	gengo o eigo ni kaeru no o tetsudatte itadake masen ka.
May I scan something?	何かスキャンしてもいいですか?
	nanika sukyan shitemo ii desu ka.
Can I upload photos from my digital camera?	デジタルカメラから写真をアップロードできますか?
	dejitaru kamera kara shashin o appurōdo deki masu ka.
Do you have a computer with a USB port?	**USB ポート付きのコンピュータはありますか?**
	USB pōto tsuki no konpyūtā wa arimasu ka.
Do you have a Mac?	**Mac はありますか?**
	Makku wa arimasu ka.

Do you have a PC?

PC はありますか?
PC wa arimasu ka.

Do you have a newer
version of this software?

**このソフトウェアの新しいバージョンは
ありますか?**
*kono sofuto uea no atarashii bājon
wa arimasu ka.*

MAIL

Where is the post office?

郵便局はどこにありますか?
yūbin kyoku wa doko ni arimasu ka.

May I send an international
package?

外国に小包を送れますか?
*gaikoku ni kozutsumi o okure
masu ka.*

Do I need a customs form?

**関税申告用紙に記入しなければなり
ませんか?**
*kanzei shinkoku yōshi ni kinyū shi
nakere ba nari masen ka.*

Do you sell insurance for
packages?

小包に保険をかけられますか?
*kozutsumi ni hoken o kakerare
masu ka.*

Please, mark it fragile.

「割れ物注意」の印を付けてください。
*「waremono chūi」 no shirushi o
tsukete kudasai.*

Please, handle with care.

丁寧に扱ってください。
teinei ni atsukatte kudasai.

Do you have twine?	ひもはありますか？ *himo wa arimasu ka.*
Where is a DHL office?	**DHL はどこにありますか？** *DHL wa doko ni arimasu ka.*
Do you sell stamps?	切手を売っていますか？ *kitte o utte imasu ka.*
Do you sell postcards?	はがきを売っていますか？ *hagaki o utte imasu ka.*
May I send that first class?	それをファースト クラスで送れますか？ *sore o fāsuto kurasu de okure masu ka.*
How much to send that express / air mail?	それを 速達 / 航空便で送るといくらかかりますか？ *sore o sokutatsu / kōkū bin de okuru to ikura kakari masu ka.*
Do you offer overnight delivery?	翌日配達のサービスはありますか？ *yokujitsu haitatsu no sābisu wa arimasu ka.*
How long will it take to reach the United States?	何日くらいでアメリカに届きますか？ *nan nichi kurai de amerika ni todoki masu ka.*
I'd like to buy an envelope.	封筒を 1 枚ください。 *fūtō o ichi mai kudasai.*
May I send it airmail?	それを航空便で送ってください。 *sore o kōkū bin de okutte kudasai.*
I'd like to send it certified / registered mail.	それを配達証明郵便 / 書留郵便で送ってください。 *sore o haitatsu shōmei yūbin / kakitome yūbin de okutte kudasai.*

Listen Up: Postal Lingo

次の方どうぞ！ *tsugi no kata dōzo.*	Next!
ここに置いてください。 *koko ni oite kudasai.*	Please, set it here.
どのクラスですか？ *dono kurasu desu ka.*	Which class?
どのサービスになさいますか？ *dono sābisu ni nasai masu ka.*	What kind of service would you like?
ご用件をどうぞ。 *goyōken o dōzo.*	How can I help you?
持ち込み窓口 *mochikomi madoguchi*	dropoff window
引き取り窓口 *hikitori madoguchi*	pickup window

CHAPTER SEVEN

CULTURE

CINEMA

Is there a movie theater nearby?	この近くに映画館はありますか？ *kono chikakuni eiga kan wa arimasu ka.*
What's playing tonight?	今夜上映されるのは何ですか？ *kon ya jōei sareru nowa nan desu ka.*
Is that in English or Japanese?	それは英語ですか、それとも日本語ですか？ *sore wa eigo desuka, sore tomo nihongo desu ka.*
Are there English subtitles?	英語の字幕は出ますか？ *eigo no jimaku wa demasu ka.*
Is the theater air conditioned?	館内は冷房が効いていますか？ *kan nai wa reibō ga kiite imasu ka.*
How much is a ticket?	チケットはいくらですか？ *chiketto wa ikura desu ka.*
Do you have a ____ discount?	____割引きはありますか？ *____ waribiki wa arimasu ka.*
senior	高齢者 *kōreisha*
student	学生 *gakusei*
children's	児童 *jidō*
What time is the movie showing?	映画は何時に始まりますか？ *eiga wa nanji ni hajimari masu ka.*
How long is the movie?	上映時間はどのくらいですか？ *jōei jikan wa dono kurai desu ka.*
May I buy tickets in advance?	前もってチケットを買えますか？ *mae motte chiketto o kae masu ka.*

Is it sold out?
売り切れですか？
urikire desu ka.

When does it begin?
いつ始まりますか？
itsu hajimari masu ka.

PERFORMANCES

Are there any plays showing right now?
現在上演されている劇はありますか？
genzai jōen sarete iru geki wa arimasu ka.

Where can I buy tickets?
チケットはどこで買えますか？
chiketto wa doko de kae masu ka.

Are there student discounts?
学生割引きはありますか？
gakusei waribiki wa arimasu ka.

I need ____ seats.
____席ください。
____ seki kudasai.

For a full list of numbers, see p7.

An aisle seat.
通路側の座席。
tsūro gawa no zaseki.

An orchestra seat, please.
オーケストラ席をお願いします。
ōkesutora seki o onegai shimasu.

What time does the play start?
劇は何時に始まりますか？
geki wa nanji ni hajimari masu ka.

Is there an intermission?
途中で休憩はありますか？
tochū de kyūkei wa arimasu ka.

Is there an opera house nearby?
この近所にオペラハウスはありますか？
kono kinjo ni opera hausu wa arimasu ka.

Is there a local symphony?
地方交響楽団はありますか？
chihō kōkyō gakudan wa arimasu ka.

May I purchase tickets over the phone?
電話でチケットを買えますか？
denwa de chiketto o kae masu ka.

What time is the box office open?
チケット売り場は何時に開きますか？
chiketto uriba wa nanji ni hiraki masu ka.

CULTURE

Listen Up: Box Office Lingo

何をご覧になりますか？
nani o goran ni nari masu ka.

何枚ですか？
nan mai desu ka.

大人２枚ですか？
otona nimai desu ka.

ポップコーン？
poppukōn.

バターは？塩は？
batā wa? shio wa?

ほかにも何かございますか？
hoka nimo nani ka gozai masu ka.

What would you like to see?

How many?

For two adults?

Popcorn?

With butter? Salt?

Would you like anything else?

I need space for a wheelchair, please.	車椅子が入れるくらいの空間が必要です。 *kuruma isu ga haireru kurai no kūkan ga hitsuyō desu.*
Do you have private boxes available?	ボックス席はありますか？ *bokkusu seki wa arimasu ka.*
Is there a church that gives concerts?	コンサートを催す教会はありますか？ *konsāto o moyōsu kyōkai wa arimasu ka.*
A program, please.	プログラムをください。 *puroguramu o kudasai.*
Please show us to our seats.	座席まで案内していただけますか。 *zaseki made annai shite itadake masu ka.*

MUSEUMS, GALLERIES & ATTRACTIONS

Do you have a museum guide?	美術館ガイドはいますか？
	bijutsukan gaido wa imasu ka.
Do you have guided tours?	ガイドが付いて説明しますか？
	gaido ga tsuite setsumei shimasu ka.
What are the museum hours?	美術館の開館時間は何時から何時までですか？
	bijutsukan no kaikan jikan wa nanji kara nanji made desu ka.
Do I need an appointment?	予約が必要ですか？
	yoyaku ga hitsuyō desu ka.
What is the admission fee?	入場料はいくらですか？
	nyūjō ryō wa ikura desu ka.
Do you have ____?	____はありますか？
	____ wa arimasu ka.
student discounts	学生割引き
	gakusei waribiki
senior discounts	高齢者割引き
	kōreisha waribiki
Do you have services for the hearing impaired?	聴覚障害者のためのサービスはありますか？
	chōkaku shōgaisha no tame no sābisu wa arimasu ka.
Do you have audio tours in English?	英語の音声ガイドはありますか？
	eigo no onsei gaido wa arimasu ka.

CHAPTER EIGHT

SHOPPING

This chapter covers the phrases you'll need to shop in a variety of settings, from the mall to street vendors. We also threw in the terminology you'll need to visit the barber or hairdresser.

For coverage of food and grocery shopping, see p94.

GENERAL SHOPPING TERMS

Could you please tell me ____?	____を教えてください。 ____ o oshiete kudasai
how to get to a mall	ショッピングセンターへの行き方 shoppingu sentā eno iki kata
the best place for shopping	ショッピングに一番よいところ shoppingu ni ichiban yoi tokoro
how to get downtown	繁華街への行き方 hanka gai eno iki kata
Where can I find a ____?	____はどこにありますか? ____ wa doko ni arimasu ka.
shoe store	靴屋 kutsu ya
clothing store	服の店 no mise
designer fashion shop	デザイナー ブランドの店 dezaināー burando no mise
vintage clothing store	ビンテージ物を売っている洋服屋 bintēji mono o utteiru yōfuku ya
jewelry store	宝石店 hōseki ten
bookstore	本屋 hon ya
toy store	おもちゃ屋 omocha ya
stationery store	文房具店 bunbōgu ten

antique shop	骨董品店 *kottōhin ten*
cigar shop	タバコ屋 *tabako ya*
souvenir shop	お土産屋 *omiyage ya*
flea market	フリーマーケット *furī māketto*

CLOTHES SHOPPING

I'd like to buy ____.	____を買いたいのですが。 ____ *o kaitai no desuga.*
men's shirts	紳士用のシャツ *shinshi yō no shatsu*
women's shoes	婦人用の靴 *fujin yō no kutsu*
children's clothes	子供服 *kodomo fuku*
toys	オモチャ *omocha*

For a full list of numbers, see p7.

I'm looking for a size ____.	____サイズを探しています。 ____ *saizu o sagashite imasu.*
small	S *esu*
medium	M *emu*
large	L *eru*
extra-large	LL *eru eru*
I'm looking for ____.	____を探しています。 ____ *o sagashite imasu.*
a silk blouse	シルクのブラウス *shiruku no burausu*

earrings
イヤリング
iyaringu

watch
腕時計
ude dokei

dress
ワンピース
wan pīsu

shirt
シャツ
shatsu

tie
ネクタイ
nekutai

jacket
ジャケット
jaketto

belt
ベルト
beruto

pants
ズボン
zubon

shoe
靴
kutsu

cotton pants	コットンのズボン	*kotton no zubon*
a hat	帽子	*bōshi*
sunglasses	サングラス	*san gurasu*
underwear	下着	*shitagi*
cashmere	カシミヤの	*kashimiya no*
socks	靴下	*kutsu shita*
sweaters	セーター	*sētā*
a coat	コート	*kōto*
a swimsuit	水着	*mizugi*

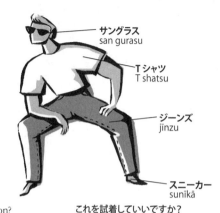

サングラス
san gurasu

T シャツ
T shatsu

ジーンズ
jīnzu

スニーカー
sunīkā

May I try it on?	これを試着していいですか？ *kore o shichaku shite ii desu ka?*
Do you have fitting rooms?	試着室はありますか？ *shichaku shitsu wa arimasu ka.*
Thanks, I'll take it.	ありがとうございます。これにします。 *arigatōgozaimasu. kore ni shimasu.*
Do you have that in ____?	これと同じで____はありますか？ *kore to onaji de ____ wa arimasu ka.*
a smaller / larger size	小さい / 大きいサイズ *chiisai / ōkii saizu*
a different color	違う色 *chigau iro*
How much is it?	それはいくらですか？ *sore wa ikura desu ka.*

ARTISAN MARKET SHOPPING

Is there ____?	____はありますか？ *____ wa arimasu ka.*
a craft market	工芸品市場 *kōgei hin ichiba*

an artisan market	伝統工芸品市場 *dentō kōgei hin ichiba*
a farmer's market	農産物市場 *nōsan butsu ichiba*
That's beautiful. May I look at it?	それはきれいですね。それを見せていただけますか？ *sore wa kirei desu ne. sore o misete itadake masu ka.*
When is the farmer's market open?	朝市は何時からですか？ *asaichi wa nanji kara desu ka.*
Is that open every day of the week?	それは毎日開いていますか？ *sore wa mai nichi aite imasu ka.*
How much does that cost?	それはいくらしますか？ *sore wa ikura shimasu ka.*
How much for two?	2つだといくらですか？ *futatsu dato ikura desu ka.*
Do I get a discount if I pay in cash?	現金で支払うと割引がありますか？ *genkin de shiharau to waribiki ga arimasu ka.*
No thanks, maybe I'll come back.	いいえ、いりません。でもまた後で戻ってくるかもしれません。 *iie, iri masen. demo mata ato de modotte kuru kamo shirema sen.*
Would you take ¥ ____?	____円で買えますか？ *____ en de kae masu ka.*

For a full list of numbers, see p7.

Do you have a less expensive one?	もう少し安いのはありますか？ *mō sukoshi yasui nowa arimasu ka.*
Is there tax?	税金はかかりますか？ *zeikin wa kakari masu ka.*
May I have the VAT forms?	VAT付加価値税用紙をください。 *VAT fuka kachi zei yōshi o kudasai.*

BOOKSTORE / NEWSSTAND SHOPPING

Is there _____ nearby?	この近くに_____はありますか？
	kono chikaku ni _____ wa arimasu ka.
a bookstore	本屋
	hon ya
a newsstand	新聞売り場
	shinbun uriba
Do you have _____ in English?	英語の_____はありますか？
	eigo no _____ wa arimasu ka.
books	本
	hon
newspapers	新聞
	shinbun
magazines	雑誌
	zasshi
books about local history	地方の歴史に関する本
	chihō no rekishi ni kansuru hon
picture books	絵本
	ehon

SHOPPING FOR ELECTRONICS

Can I play this in the _____?	これは_____でつかえますか？
	kore wa _____ de tsukae masu ka.
Will this game work on my game console in the _____?	このゲームは、_____にある私のゲーム機で使用できますか？
	kono gēmu wa, _____ ni aru watashi no gēmu ki de shiyō dekimasu ka.
Do you have this in a _____ market format?	これと同じもので_____対応のものがありますか？
	koreto onaji mono de _____ taiō no mono ga arimasu ka.
Can you convert this to a _____ market format?	これは_____の形式に変換できますか？
	kore wa _____ no keishiki ni henkan deki masu ka.

U.S.

アメリカ
amerika

U.K.

イギリス
igirisu

Is this DVD region encoded?

これは DVD のリージョンがエンコード
されていますか?
kono DVD no rījon wa enkōdo sarete imasu ka.

Will this work with a 110V AC adapter?

これは 110VのAC アダプターで動き
ますか?
kore wa hyaku jū boruto no AC adaputā de ugoki masu ka.

Do you have an adapter plug for 110 to 220?

110 から 220 に変換するアダプター プ
ラグはありますか?
hyaku jū kara ni hyaku ni jū ni henkan suru adaputā puragu wa arimasu ka.

Do you sell electronics adapters here?

電子アダプターは売っていますか?
denshi adaputā wa utte imasu ka.

Is it safe to use my laptop with this adapter?

このアダプターで私のラップトップを使
っても大丈夫ですか?
kono adaputā de watashi no rappu toppu o tsukattemo daijōbu desu ka.

If it doesn't work, may I return it?

もし使えなかった場合返品できます
か?
moshi tsukaenakatta baai henpin deki masu ka.

May I try it here in the store?

これをここで試してみることはできま
すか?
kore o koko de tameshite miru koto wa deki masu ka.

AT THE BARBER / HAIRDRESSER

May I make an appointment?	予約を取ることができますか? *yoyaku o toru koto ga deki masu ka.*
Do I need an appointment?	予約は必要ですか? *yoyaku wa hitsuyō desu ka.*
A trim, please.	髪をそろえてください。 *kami o soroete kudasai.*
Would you make the color ____?	____色に変えてください。 *____ iro ni kaete kudasai.*
darker	もっと濃い *motto koi*
lighter	もっと明るい *motto akarui*
I'd like it curled.	カールしてください。 *kāru shite kudasai.*
Please use low heat.	低温でお願いします。 *teion de onegai shimasu.*
Please don't blow dry it.	ブローしないでください。 *burō shinaide kudasai.*
Please dry it straight.	ストレートにドライしてください。 *sutorēto ni dorai shite kudasai.*
Would you fix my highlights?	ハイライトを直してください。 *hai raito o naoshite kudasai.*
Could you trim my bangs?	前髪を切りそろえてください。 *maegami o soroete kudasai.*
Do you offer waxes?	ックス脱毛はしていますか? *wakkusu datsumō wa shite imasu ka.*
I'd like a Brazilian wax.	ブラジリアンワックスをしたいです。 *burajirian wakkusu o shitai desu.*
Please wax my ____.	私の____をワックスしてください。 *watashi no ____ o wakkusu shite kudasai.*
legs	足 *ashi*

bikini line	ビキニの線
	bikini no sen
eyebrows	まゆ毛
	mayu ge
under my nose	鼻の下
	hana no shita
Please trim my beard.	ひげを揃えてください。
	hige o soroete kudasai.
A shave, please.	剃ってください。
	sotte kudasai.
Use a fresh blade please.	良く切れる刃を使ってください。
	yoku kireru ha o tsukatte kudasai.

CHAPTER NINE
SPORTS & FITNESS

GETTING FIT

Is there a gym nearby?
この近くにジムはありますか?
kono chikaku ni jimu wa arimasu ka.

Does the hotel have a gym?
ホテルにはジムがありますか?
hoteru niwa jimu ga arimasu ka.

Do you have free weights?
フリーウェイトはありますか?
furī ueito wa arimasu ka.

Is there a pool?
プールはありますか?
pūru wa arimasu ka.

Do I have to be a member?
会員でなければなりませんか?
kai in de nakere ba narima sen ka.

May I come here for one day?
一日ここに来ることはできますか?
ichi nichi koko ni kuru koto wa deki masu ka.

How much does a membership cost?
会員になるにはいくらかかりますか?
kaiin ni naru niwa ikura kakari masu ka.

I need to get a locker please.
ロッカーを使いたいのですが。
rokkā o tsukai tai no desuga.

Do you have a lock?
鍵はありますか?
kagi wa arimasu ka.

Do you have a treadmill?	トレッドミルはありますか?
	toreddo miru wa arimasu ka.
Do you have a stationary bike?	エアロ バイクはありますか?
	earo baiku wa arimasu ka.
May I have clean towels?	きれいなタオルをいただけますか。
	kirei na taoru o itadake masu ka.
Where are the showers / locker-rooms?	シャワー / ロッカールームはどこにありますか?
	shawā / rokkā rūmu wa doko ni arimasu ka.
Do you have aerobics classes?	エアロビクスのクラスはありますか?
	earobikusu no kurasu wa arimasu ka.

CATCHING A GAME

Where is the stadium?	スタジアムはどこですか?
	sutajiamu wa doko desu ka.
Who is playing?	誰がプレイしていますか?
	dare ga purē shite imasu ka.
Which is the best team?	最高のチームはどれですか?
	saikō no chīmu wa dore desu ka.
Where can I buy tickets?	チケットはどこで買えますか?
	chiketto wa doko de kae masu ka.
The best seats, please.	一番よい席をお願いします。
	ichiban yoi seki o onegai shimasu.
The cheapest seats, please.	一番安い席をお願いします。
	ichiban yasui seki o onegai shimasu.
May I have box seats?	ボックス シートをいただけますか?
	bokkusu shīto o itadake masu ka.
Wow! What a game!	うわぁ! すごい試合だ!
	uwa! sugoi shiai da.
Go go go!	行け、行け、行け!
	ike, ike, ike!
Oh no!	あ、だめだ!
	a, dame da!
Score!	入れろ!
	irero!

What's the score?	何点ですか？ *nan ten desu ka.*
Who's winning?	どっちが勝ってますか？ *docchi ga katte masu ka.*

HIKING

Where can I find a guide to hiking trails?	ハイキングトレイルのガイドはどこで見つけられますか？ *haikingu toreiru no gaido wa doko de mitsuke rare masu ka.*
Do we need to hire a guide?	ガイドを雇う必要がありますか？ *gaido o yatou hitsuyō ga arimasu ka.*
Where can I rent equipment?	装具はどこで借りられますか？ *sōgu wa doko de kari rare masu ka.*
Where can we go mountain climbing?	どこで登山ができますか？ *doko de tozan ga deki masu ka.*
Are the routes ____ ?	ルートは____されていますか？ *rūto wa ____ sarete imasu ka.*
well marked	標識が完備 *hyōshiki ga kanbi*
in good condition	整備 *seibi*
What is the altitude there?	標高はいくらですか？ *hyōkō wa ikura desu ka.*

How long will it take?	どのくらい時間がかかりますか？
	dono kurai jikan ga kakari masu ka.
Is it very difficult?	とても難しいですか？
	totemo muzukashii desu ka.
Can we camp off the trail?	トレイル外でキャンプはできますか？
	toreiru gai de kyanpu wa deki masu ka.
Is it okay to build fires here?	ここで火をおこしてもいいですか？
	koko de hi o okoshite mo ii desuka.
Do we need permits?	許可が要りますか？
	kyoka ga iri masu ka.

For more camping terms, see p74.

BOATING & FISHING

I'd like to go fishing.	魚釣りに行きたいです。
	sakana tsuri ni ikitai desu.
Can I rent a boat?	ボートをレンタルできますか？
	bōto o rentaru deki masu ka.
When do we sail?	いつ出航しますか？
	itsu shukkō shimasu ka.
How long is the trip?	航海は何日くらいですか？
	kokai wa nan nichi kurai desu ka
Where are the life preservers?	救命用具はどこにありますか？
	kyūmei yōgu wa doko ni arimasu ka.
Can I purchase bait?	えさを買えますか？
	esa o kae masu ka.

Can I rent a pole?	釣竿を借りられますか？ *tsurizao o kari rare masu ka.*
I got one!	かかった！ *kakatta!*
Help! Lifegard!	助けて！監視員さん！ *tasukete! kanshi in san!*
I can't swim.	泳げません。 *oyoge masen.*
Can we go ashore?	岸に上がれますか？ *kishi ni agare masu ka.*

For more boating terms, see p59.

DIVING

I'd like to go snorkeling.	スノーケルをしたいのですが。 *sunōkeru o shitai no desuga.*
I'd like to go scuba diving.	スキューバダイビングをしたいのですが。 *sukyūba daibingu o shitai no desuga.*
I have a NAUI / PADI certification.	私は NAUI / PADI の資格証明書を持っています。 *watashi wa NAUI / PADI no shikaku shōmei sho o motte imasu.*
I need to rent gear.	道具を借りる必要があります。 *dōgu o kariru hitsuyō ga arimasu.*
Are the currents strong?	潮の流れは強いですか？ *shio no nagare wa tsuyoi desu ka.*
How clear is the water?	海の中の透明度はどうですか？ *umi no naka no tōmeido wa dō desu ka.*

SURFING

I'd like to go surfing.

サーフィンをしたいのですが。
sāfin o shitai no desuga.

Are there any good beaches?

よいビーチはありますか？
yoi bīchi wa arimasu ka.

Can I rent a board?

ボードを借りることはできますか？
bōdo o karirukoto wa deki masu ka.

How are the currents?

潮の流れはどうですか？
shio no nagare wa dō desu ka.

How high are the waves?

波の高さはどれくらいですか？
nami no takasa wa dore kurai desu ka.

Are there facilities on that beach?

そのビーチにシャワーやトイレはありますか？
sono bīchi ni shawā ya toire wa arimasu ka.

Is there wind surfing there also?

そこにはウィンド サーフィンもありますか？
soko niwa uindo sāfin mo arimasu ka.

GOLFING

I'd like to reserve a tee-time, please.

ティー タイムの予約をお願いします。
tī taimu no yoyaku o onegai shimasu.

Do we need to be members to play?

会員でないとプレイできませんか？
kaiin de nai to purē deki masen ka.

How many holes is your course?

このコースは何ホールありますか？
kono kōsu wa nan hōru arimasu ka.

What is par for the course?

このコースのパーはいくつですか？
kono kōsu no pā wa ikutsu desu ka.

What is the dress code for players?	プレーヤのドレスコードは何ですか？ *purēyā no doresu kōdo wa nani desu ka?*
I need to rent clubs.	クラブを借りなければなりません。 *kurabu o kari nakereba narimasen.*
I need to purchase a sleeve of balls.	ボール一箱買わなければなりません。 *bōru hito hako kawa nakereba narimasen.*
Do you have carts?	カートはありますか？ *kāto wa arimasu ka.*
How much are the greens fees?	グリーン料金はいくらですか？ *gurīn ryōkin wa ikura desu ka.*

CHAPTER TEN

NIGHTLIFE

For coverage of movies and cultural events, see p124, Chapter Seven, "Culture."

CLUB HOPPING

Where can I find ____?
____はどこにありますか？
____ wa doko ni arimasu ka.

a good nightclub
よいナイトクラブ
yoi naito kurabu

a club with a live band
ライブ演奏のあるクラブ
raibu ensō no aru kurabu

a jazz club
ジャズ クラブ
jazu kurabu

a gay / lesbian club
ゲイ / レズビアン クラブ
gei / rezubian kurabu

the most popular club in town
街で一番人気があるクラブ
machi de ichiban ninki ga aru kurabu

the most upscale club
最高級バー
sai kōkyū bā

What's the cover charge?
カバー チャージはいくらですか？
kabā chāji wa ikura desu ka.

Do they have a dress code?
服装に規則はありますか？
fukusō ni kisoku wa arimasu ka.

Is it expensive?
値段は高いですか？
nedan wa takai desu ka.

What's the best time to go?
いつ行くのが一番いいですか？
itsu iku noga ichiban ii desu ka.

What kind of music do they play there?
どんな音楽を演奏していますか？
donna ongaku o ensō shite imasu ka.

Is it smoking?
タバコを吸えますか？
tabako o sue masu ka.

Is it nonsmoking?	禁煙ですか？
	kin en desu ka.
I'd like ____.	____ください。
	____ kudasai.
a drink, please	飲み物を
	nomi mono o
a bottle of beer, please	ビールを1本
	bīru o ippon
a beer on tap, please	生ビールを
	nama bīru o
a shot of ____, please	____を1杯
	____ o ippai

For a full list of drinks, see p81.

For a full list of drinks, see p81.

With ice, please.	氷を入れてください。
	kōri o irete kudasai.
How much for a glass of beer?	ビール1杯はいくらですか？
	bīru ippai wa ikura desu ka.
I'd like to buy a drink for that woman over there.	あちらの女性に飲み物を一杯おごります。
	achira no josei ni nomimono o ippai ogori masu.
I'd like to buy a drink for that man over there.	あちらの男性に飲み物を一杯おごります。
	achira no dansei ni nomimono o ippai ogori masu.
A pack of cigarettes, please.	タバコを1箱ください。
	tabako o hito hako kudasai.
Do you smoke?	タバコを吸いますか？
	tabako o suimasu ka.
Would you like a cigarette?	タバコ1本いかがですか？
	tabako ippon ikaga desu ka.
May I run a tab?	つけにしていいですか？
	tsuke ni shite ii desu ka.
What's the cover?	カバーチャージはいくらですか？
	kabā chāji wa ikura desu ka.

NIGHTLIFE

ACROSS A CROWDED ROOM

Excuse me; may I buy you a drink?	あのー、私のおごりで1杯いかがですか？
	anō, watashi no ogori de ippai ikaga desu ka.
You look amazing.	すてきですね。
	suteki desu ne.
I wanted to meet you.	私はあなたに会いたいです。
	watashi wa anata ni aitai desu.
Are you single?	あなたは独身ですか？
	anata wa dokushin desu ka.
Would you like to dance?	ダンスしませんか？
	dansu shima sen ka.
Give me your hand.	手をかしてください。
	te o kashite kudasai.
What would you like to drink?	飲み物は何がいいですか？
	nomi mono wa nani ga ii desu ka.
You're a great dancer.	踊りが上手ですね。
	odori ga jōzu desu ne.
Do you like this song?	この歌は好きですか？
	kono uta wa suki desu ka.
May I have your phone number / email address?	あなたの電話番号 / Eメールアドレスを教えてください。
	anata no denwa bangō / E mēru adoresu o oshiete kudasai.

Do You Mind if I Smoke?

タバコはありますか？	Do you have a cigarette?
tabako wa arimasuka.	
火はありますか？	Do you have a light?
hi wa arimasuka.	
火を貸しましょうか？	May I offer you a light?
hi o kashi mashō ka.	
禁煙です。	Smoking not permitted.
kin en desu.	

CHAPTER ELEVEN

HEALTH & SAFETY

This chapter covers the terms you'll need to maintain your health and safety—including the most useful phrases for the pharmacy, the doctor's office, and the police station.

AT THE PHARMACY

Please fill this prescription.
この薬を処方してください。
kono kusuri o shohō shite kudasai.

Do you have something for ____ ?
____に効く薬はありますか？
____ ni kiku kusuri wa arimasu ka.

a cold
カゼ
kaze

a cough
咳
seki

I need something ____.
____が欲しいのですが。
____ ga hoshii no desuga.

to help me sleep
眠れるようになるもの
nemureru yōni naru mono

to help me relax
気を静められるもの
ki o shizume rareru mono

I want to buy ____.
____をください。
____ o kudasai.

condoms
コンドーム
kondōmu

an antihistamine
抗ヒスタミン剤
kō hisutamin zai

antibiotic cream
抗生物質クリーム
kōsei busshitsu kurīmu

aspirin
アスピリン
asupirin

non-aspirin pain reliever
アスピリン以外の鎮痛剤
asupirin igai no chintsūzai

medicine with codeine	コデインを含む薬 *kodein o fukumu kusuri*
insect repellant	虫除けローション *mushi yoke rōshon*
I need something for ____.	____に効くものが欲しいのですが。 *____ ni kiku mono ga hoshii no desuga.*
congestion	充血 *jūketsu*
warts	いぼ *ibo*
constipation	便秘 *benpi*
diarrhea	下痢 *geri*
indigestion	消化不良 *shōka furyō*
nausea	吐き気 *hakike*
motion sickness	乗り物酔い *norimono yoi*
seasickness	船酔い *funayoi*

AT THE DOCTOR'S OFFICE

I would like to see ____.	____に診ていただきたいのですが。 *____ ni mite itadaki tai no desuga.*
a doctor	医者 *isha*
a chiropractor	カイロプラクター *kairo purakutā*
a gynecologist	婦人科医 *fujinka i*
an eye / ears & nose / throat specialist	眼科 / 耳鼻科 / 咽喉科医 *ganka / jibika / inkōka i*

a dentist	歯医者
	haisha
an optometrist	検眼師
	kenganshi
a dermatologist	皮膚科医
	hifu ka i
Do I need an appointment?	予約が必要ですか?
	yoyaku ga hitsuyō desu ka.
Do I have to pay up front?	先に支払わなければなりませんか?
	sakini shiharawa nakereba nari masen ka.
I have an emergency.	緊急なんです。
	kinkyū nan desu.
My prescription has run out and I need a refill.	薬がなくなってしまったので薬をいただきたいのですが。
	kusuri ga nakunatte shimatta node kusuri o itadakitai no desuga.

SYMPTOMS

For a full list of body parts, see the graphic on the next page.

My ＿＿ hurts.	＿＿が痛いんです。
	＿＿ *ga itain desu.*
My ＿＿ is stiff.	＿＿が凝っています。
	＿＿ *ga kotte imasu.*
I think I'm having a heart attack.	心臓発作を起こしたみたいです。
	shinzō hossa o okoshita mitai desu.
I think I'm having an allergic reaction.	アレルギー反応を起こしたと思います。
	arerugī hannō o okoshita to omoi masu.
I can't move.	動けません。
	ugoke masen.
I fell.	転びました。
	korobi mashita.
I fainted.	気を失いました。
	ki o ushinai mashita.

I have a cut on my ____.	____を切りました。
	____ o kiri mashita.
I have a headache.	頭痛がします。
	zutsū ga shimasu.
My vision is blurry.	物がぼやけて見えます。
	mono ga boyakete mie masu.
I feel dizzy.	めまいがします。
	memai ga shimasu.
I think I'm pregnant.	妊娠したみたいなんです。
	ninshin shita mitai nan desu.
I don't think I'm pregnant.	妊娠ではないと思います。
	ninshin dewa nai to omoi masu.
I think I have an infection.	感染したと思います。
	kansen shita to omoi masu.
I'm having trouble walking.	歩行が困難なんです。
	hokō ga konnan nan desu.

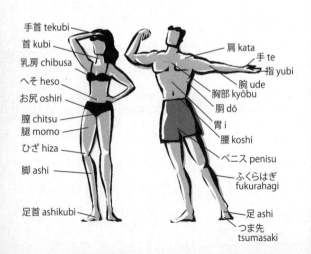

手首 tekubi
首 kubi
乳房 chibusa
へそ heso
お尻 oshiri
膣 chitsu
腿 momo
ひざ hiza
脚 ashi
足首 ashikubi

肩 kata
手 te
指 yubi
腕 ude
胸部 kyōbu
胴 dō
胃 i
腰 koshi
ペニス penisu
ふくらはぎ fukurahagi
足 ashi
つま先 tsumasaki

I can't get up.	立ち上がれません。
	tachi agare masen.
I was mugged.	襲われました。
	osoware mashita.
I was raped.	強姦されました。
	gōkan sare mashita.
A dog attacked me.	犬に襲われました。
	inu ni osoware mashita.
A snake bit me.	蛇にかまれました。
	hebi ni kamare mashita.
I can't move my ____	____を動かすと痛みます。
without pain.	*____ o ugokasu to itami masu.*
I think I sprained my ankle.	足首を捻挫したと思います。
	ashikubi o nenza shita to omoi masu.

MEDICATIONS

Please fill this prescription.	この処方箋の薬をください。
	Kono shohōsen no kusuri o kudasai.
I need a prescription for ____.	____の処方箋が必要です。
	____ no shohōsen ga hitsuyō desu.
I need morning-after pills.	モーニング アフター ピルが欲しいのですが。
	mōningu afutā piru ga hoshii no desuga.
I need birth control pills.	避妊薬が欲しいのですが。
	hinin yaku ga hoshii no desuga.
I lost my eyeglasses and need new ones.	眼鏡をなくしたので、新しいのが必要なんですが。
	megane o nakushita node, atarashii noga hitsuyō nan desuga.
I need new contact lenses.	新しいコンタクトレンズが必要なんですが。
	atarashii kontakuto renzu ga hitsuyō nan desuga.

I need erectile dysfunction pills.	勃起不全改善薬が欲しいのですが。
	bokki fuzen kaizen yaku ga hoshii no desuga.
I am allergic to ____.	私は____にアレルギーがあります。
	watashi wa____ ni arerugī ga arimasu.
penicillin	ペニシリン
	penishirin
antibiotics	抗生物質
	kōsei busshitsu
sulfa drugs	サルファー剤
	sarufā zai
steroids	ステロイド
	suteroido
I have asthma.	私は喘息を持っています。
	watashi wa zensoku o motte imasu.

DENTAL PROBLEMS

I have a toothache.	歯が痛みます。
	ha ga itami masu.
I chipped a tooth.	歯が欠けました。
	ha ga kake mashita.
My bridge came loose.	ブリッジがゆるんできました。
	burijji ga yurunde kimashita.
I lost a crown.	歯にかぶせていたものがとれてしまいました。
	ha ni kabusete ita mono ga torete shimai mashita.
I lost a denture plate.	義歯がとれてしまいました。
	gishi ga torete shimai mashita.

AT THE POLICE STATION

I'm sorry, did I do something wrong?	すみません、私がなにか悪いことをしましたか？
	sumima sen, watashi ga nani ka warui koto o shimashita ka.
I am ____.	私は____です。
	watashi wa ____ desu.
American	アメリカ人
	amerika jin
British	イギリス人
	igirisu jin
Canadian	カナダ人
	kanada jin
Irish	アイルランド人
	airurando jin
Australian	オーストラリア人
	ōsutoraria jin
a New Zealander	ニュージーランド人
	nyūjīrando jin
The car is a rental.	車はレンタ カーです。
	kuruma wa rentakā desu.
Do I pay the fine to you?	罰金を払うのですか？
	bakkin o harau no desu ka.
Do I have to go to court?	裁判所に行かなければなりませんか？
	saiban sho ni ikana kereba narima sen ka.
When?	いつですか？
	itsu desu ka.
I'm sorry, my Japanese isn't very good.	すみません、日本語はあまり上手に話せません。
	sumima sen, nihon go wa amari jōzuni hanase masen.
I need an interpreter.	通訳が必要です。
	tsūyaku ga hitsuyō desu.

Listen Up: Police Lingo

免許証、登録証、保険証を見せてください。 *menkyo shō, tōroku shō, hoken shō o misete kudasai.*	Your license, registration and insurance, please.
罰金は1000円です。私に直接払ってもかまいません。 *bakkin wa sen en desu. watashi ni chokusetsu harattemo kamai masen.*	The fine is ¥1000. You can pay me directly.
パスポートを見せてください。 *pasupōto o misete kudasai.*	Your passport please?
どこに行くんですか? *doko ni ikun desu ka.*	Where are you going?
なぜそんなに急いでいますか? *naze sonnani isoide imasu ka.*	Why are you in such a hurry?

I'm sorry, I don't understand the ticket.	すみません、このチケットの意味がわかりません。 *sumima sen, kono chiketto no imi ga wakari masen.*
May I call my embassy?	私の国の大使館に電話をかけてもいいですか? *watashi no kuni no taishi kan ni denwa o kaketemo ii desu ka.*
I was robbed.	強盗に遭いました。 *gōtō ni ai mashita.*
I was mugged.	襲われました。 *osoware mashita.*
I was raped.	強姦されました。 *gōkan sare mashita.*

Do I need to make a report?	警察に届け出る必要がありますか？ *keisatsu ni todokederu hitsuyō ga arimasu ka.*
Somebody broke into my room.	誰かが私の部屋に侵入しました。 *dareka ga watashi no heya ni shin nyū shima shita.*
Someone stole my ____.	私は____を盗まれました。 *watashi wa ____ o nusumare mashita.*
purse	ハンドバッグ *hando baggu*
wallet	財布 *saifu*
cell phone	携帯電話 *keitai denwa*
passport	パスポート *pasupōto*
laptop	ラップトップ *rapputoppu*
backpack	バックパック *bakkupakku*
camera	カメラ *kamera*

DICTIONARY KEY

n	noun	*s*	singular
v	verb	*pl*	plural
adj	adjective		
prep	preposition		
adv	adverb		

Japanese verbs are conjugated only to indicate tense (see p28). They are listed here in present tense form.

For food terms, see the Menu Reader (p85) and Grocery section (p94) in Chapter 4, Dining.

A

able, to be able to (can) *v* でき る dekiru

above *adj* 上の / 上に ue no / ue ni p6

accept, to accept *v* 受け入れる uke ireru

Do you accept credit cards? クレジットカードは使えます か? kurejitto kādo wa tsukae masu ka. p37

accident *n* 事故 jiko p54

I've had an accident. 事故に あいました。jiko ni ai mashita. p54

account *n* 口座 kōza

I'd like to transfer to / from my checking / savings account. 当座預金 / 普通預 金口座へ / から振り替えたい のですが。tōza-yokin / futsū-yokin e / kara furikaete tai no desuga.

acne *n* にきび nikibi

across *prep* の向こう側 no mukō gawa

across the street この道の向 こう側 kono michi no mukō gawa p6

action films アクション映画 akushon eiga p112

actual *adj* 実際の jissai no

adapter アダプター adaputā p70

adapter plug *n* アダプター プラ グ adaputā puragu

address *n* 住所 jūsho

What's the address? 住所は 何ですか? jūsho wa nan desu ka.

admission fee n 入場料 nyūjōryō p127

in advance 前もって mae motte p124

African-American *adj* アフリ カ系アメリカ人の afurika kei amerika jin no

afternoon *n* 午後 gogo / 昼間 hiruma p17

in the afternoon 午後に gogo ni

age *n* 歳 toshi
What's your age? 何歳です
か? nan sai desu ka.

agency *n* 会社 kaisha p48
car rental agency レンタ カー
会社 rentakā gaisha

agnostic *adj* 不可知論の
fukachiron no

air conditioning *n* 冷房 reibō
p58, 124 / エアコン eakon
p48, 65, 71
air conditioned rooms エアコ
ン付きの部屋 eakon tsuki no
heya p64
**Would you lower / raise the
air conditioning?** 冷房を
下げて / 上げていただけませ
んか? reibō o sagete / agete
itadake masen ka.

airport *n* 空港 kūkō
I need a ride to the airport.
空港まで乗って行く必要があ
ります。kūkō made notte iku
hitsuyō ga arimasu.
**How far is it from the
airport?** 空港からどのくらい
のところにありますか? kūkō
kara dono kurai no tokoro ni
arimasu ka.

airsickness bag *n* 飛行機酔い
の袋 hikōki yoi no fukuro p46

aisle *n* 通路 tsūro

action films アクション映画
akushon eiga p112

alarm clock *n* 目覚まし時計
mezamashi tokei dokei p71

alcoholic drink アルコール飲料
arukōru inryō
Do you serve alcohol? アル
コール飲料は出していますか?
arukōru wa dashite imasu ka.
I'd like nonalcoholic beer.
アルコール抜きのビールをく
ださい。arukōru nuki no bīru
o kudasai.

all *n* すべて subete p15

all *adj* すべての subete
no p15
all of the time いつも itsumo
That's all, thank you. 以上で
す。どうもありがとう。ijō desu.
dōmo arigatō.

allergic *adj* アレルギー体質の
arerugī taishitu no / アレル
ギー反応の arerugī han nō
no p71
I'm allergic to ____. 私は____
にアレルギーがあります。
watashi wa ____ ni arerugī ga
arimasu. p80, 152
See p80 and 152 for
common allergens.

altitude *n* 標高 hyōkō p139

aluminum *n* アルミニウム
aruminiumu

ambulance *n* 救急車 kyūkyūsha

American *adj* アメリカの、アメ
リカ人の amerika no, amerika
jin no p153

amount *n* 量 ryō

angry *adj* 怒った okotta

animal *n* 動物 dōbutsu

another *adj* 別の betsu no

answer n 答え kotae

answer, to answer (phone call, question) v 答える kotaeru

> **Answer me, please.** 答えてください。kotaete kudasai.

antibiotic n 抗生物質 kōsei busshitsu

> **I need an antibiotic.** 抗生物質をください。kōsei busshitsu o kudasai.

antihistamine n 抗ヒスタミン剤 kōhisutamin zai **p147**

anxious adj 心配な shinpai na / 心配している shinpai shiteiru **p104**

any adj 何か nanika / 何も nanimo

anything n 何でも nan demo

anywhere adv どこへも doko emo

April n 四月 shi gatsu **p19**

appointment n 予約 yoyaku **p127, 135, 149**

> **Do I need an appointment?** 予約が必要ですか? yoyaku ga hitsuyō desu ka. **p127, 135, 149**

are v See be, to be.

Argentinian adj アルゼンチンの、アルゼンチン人の aruzenchin no, aruzenchin jin no

arm n 腕 ude **p150**

arrive, to arrive v 到着する tōchaku suru

arrival(s) n 到着 tōchaku

animal n 動物 dōbutsu

art adj 芸術の geijutsu no

> **exhibit of art** 美術品の展示 bijutsu hin no tenji

art museum 美術館 bijutsu kan

artist n 芸術家 geijutsu ka

Asian adj アジアの、アジア人の ajia no, ajia jin no

ask a question v 質問する shitsumon suru

ask for (request) v 頼む tanomu

aspirin n アスピリン asupirin **p147**

assist v 手伝う tetsudau

assistance n 手伝い tetsudai / アシスタンス ashisutansu **p62**

asthma n 喘息 zensoku **p170**

> **I have asthma.** 喘息があります。zensoku ga arimasu. / 喘息を持っています。zensoku o motte imasu. **p152**

atheist n 無神論者 mushinron sha **p109**

ATM n ATM 機 ATM ki

> **I'm looking for an ATM.** ATM 機を探しています。ATM ki o sagashite imasu.

attend v 参加する sanka suru / 出席する shusseki suru

audio adj 音声の onsei no **p127**

August n 八月 hachi gatsu **p19**

aunt n おば oba / おばさん obasan **p100**

Australia n オーストラリア
ōsutoraria

Australian adj オーストラリ
アの、オーストラリア人の
ōsutoraria no, ōsutoraria jin
no p153

autumn n 秋 aki p19

available adj 使用可能な
shiyō kanō na

B

baby n 赤ちゃん aka chan p102
/ ベビー bebī

baby adj 赤ちゃんの aka chan
no

Do you sell baby food? ベ
ビーフードは売っていますか?
bebī fūdo wa utte imasu ka.

babysitter n ベビーシッター
bebī shittā

**Do you have babysitters
who speak English?** 英語を
話すベビーシッターはいます
か? eigo o hanasu bebī shittā
wa imasu ka.

back n 背中 senaka

My back hurts. 背中が痛みま
す。 senaka ga itami masu.

back rub n 背中をさする senaka
o sasuru

backed up (toilet) adj つまって
いる tsumatte iru

The toilet is backed up. トイ
レがつまっています。 toire ga
tsumatte imasu.

backward 後ろに ushiro ni

bag n 袋 fukuro

airsickness bag 飛行機酔いの
袋 hikōki yoi no fukuro p46

My bag was stolen. 私のバッ
クが盗まれました。 watashi no
baggu ga nusumare mashita.

I lost my bag. 私はバックを失
くしました。 watashi wa baggu
o nakushi mashita.

Open this bag, please かば
んを開けてください。 kaban o
akete kudasai. p41

backward n 後ろに ushiro ni p6

bag v 袋に入れる fukuro ni ireru

baggage n 手荷物
tenimotsu

baggage adj 手荷物の
tenimotsu no

baggage claim 手荷物引き渡
し所 tenimotsu hikiwatashi
jo p36

bait n えさ esa

balance (on bank account) n
残高 zandaka p117

balance v バランスを取る
baransu o toru

balcony n バルコニー
barukonī p65

ball (sport) n ボール bōru

ballroom dancing n 社交ダン
ス shakō dansu

band (musical ensemble) n
演奏 ensō p144

band-aid n バンドエイド
bando eido

bank n 銀行 ginkō p115

Can you help me find a bank? 銀行はどこにあるか教えていただけますか? ginkō wa doko ni aruka oshiete itadake masu ka.

bar *n* バー bā

barber *n* 理髪店 rihatsu ten

bass (instrument) *n* バス basu

bath *n* お風呂 ofuro

bathroom (restroom) *n* トイレ toire p59, 65, 74

Where is the nearest public bathroom? ここから一番近い公衆トイレはどこにありますか? koko kara ichiban chikai kōshū toire wa doko ni arimasu ka.

bathtub *n* 浴槽 yokusō p65

bathe, to bathe oneself *v* お風呂に入る ofuro ni hairu

battery (for flashlight) *n* 電池 denchi

battery (for car) *n* バッテリー batterī

bee *n* ハチ hachi

I was stung by a bee. ハチに刺されました。hachi ni sasare mashita.

be, to be (temporary state, condition, mood) *v* である de aru

be, to be (permanent quality) *v* である de aru

beach *n* ビーチ bīchi p63, 65, 113, 142

beach *v* ビーチに乗り上げる bīchi ni noriageru

beard *n* ひげ hige

beautiful *adj* きれいな kireina p137

bed *n* ベッド beddo p64, 66

beer *n* ビール bīru p45, 82, 145

beer on tap 生ビール nama bīru p145

begin *v* 始まる hajimaru p125

behave *v* 振る舞う furumau

behind *adv* 後ろの ushiro no p5

below *adv* 下の shita no p6

belt *n* ベルト beruto p43

conveyor belt ベルトコンベヤー beruto konbeyā

berth *n* 寝台 shindai

best 最高の saikō no

bet, to bet *v* かける kakeru

better より良い yori yoi

big *adj* 大きい ōkii p16

bilingual *adj* 二ヶ国語を話す ni kakoku go o hanasu

bill (currency) *n* 紙幣 shihei p115/ お札 osatsu p116

bill *v* 請求する seikyū suru p119

biography *n* 伝記 denki

biracial *adj* 人種の混じった jinshu no majitta

bird *n* 鳥 tori

birth control *n* 避妊 hinin

I'm out of birth control pills. 避妊薬がなくなりました。hinin yaku ga nakunari mashita.

I need more birth control pills. もっと避妊薬が必要です。motto hinin yaku ga hitsuyō desu.

bit (small amount) n 少し sukoshi

black adj 黒い kuroi / 黒人 koku jin p87

blanket n 毛布 mōfu p45

bleach n ブリーチ burīchi

blind adj 目の見えない me no mienai

I am blind / visually impaired. 私は、目が見えません / 目が不自由です。watashi wa me ga mie masen / me ga fujiyū desu. p62

block n 角 kado p6 / ブロック burokku

blogging ブログを書く burogu o kaku p110

blond(e) adj 金髪の kinpatsu no

blouse n ブラウス burausu p129

blue adj 青い aoi

blurry adj ぼやけた boyaketa p150

board n 搭乗 tōjō

on board 搭乗して tōjō shite

board v 入港する nyūkō suru

boarding pass n 搭乗券 tōjō ken p44

boat n ボート bōto

Bolivian adj ボリビアの、ボリ ビア人の boribia no, boribia jin no

bomb n 爆弾 bakudan

book n 本 hon p111, 133

bookstore n 本屋 hon ya p128

boss n 上司 jōshi

bottle n ビン bin

May I heat this (baby) bottle someplace? どこかで このビンを温めることができま すか? dokoka de kono bin o atatameru koto ga deki masu ka.

bottle opener 栓抜き sennuki p70

box (seat) n ボックス席 bokkusu seki p126 / ボックス シート bokkusu sīto p138

box office n チケット売り場 chiketto uriba

boy n 男の子 otoko no ko

boyfriend n ボーイフレンド bōi furendo p100

braid n 編んだ髪 anda kami

braille, American n 点字、アメ リカの tenji, amerika no

brake n ブレーキ burēki p52

emergency brake 非常ブレー キ hijō burēki

brake v ブレーキをかける burēki o kakeru

brandy n ブランデー burandē p84

bread n パン pan p83, 94

break v 壊れる kowareru

breakfast n 朝食 chōshoku p67

What time is breakfast? 朝 食は何時ですか? chōshoku wa nan ji desu ka.

bridge (across a river / dental) n 橋 hashi / 歯の矯正 ブリッジ ha no kyōsei burijji

briefcase *n* ブリーフケース burīfu kēsu **p47**

bright *adj* 明るい akarui

broadband *n* ブロードバンド burōdo bando

bronze *adj* ブロンズ製の buronzu sei no

brother *n* 兄弟 kyōdai／ご兄弟 go kyōdai **p100**

brown *adj* 茶色の cha iro no

brunette *n* ブルネット burunetto

Buddhist *n* 仏教徒 bukkyōto **p108**

budget *n* 予算 yosan

buffet *n* バイキング baikingu

bug *n* 虫 mushi

bull *n* 雄牛 oushi

bullfight *n* 闘牛 tōgyū

bullfighter *n* 闘牛士 tōgyū shi

burn *v* 焼く yaku／焼きつける yaki tsukeru

> **Can I burn a CD here?** こ こで CD に焼きつけ（書込 み）できますか? koko de CD ni yakitsuke (kakikomi) deki masu ka.

bus *n* バス basu **p55, 58**

> **Where is the bus stop?** バス 停はどこにありますか? basu tei wa doko ni arimasu ka.
> **Which bus goes to _____?**
> _____行きのバスはどれですか。
> _____ yuki no basu wa dore desu ka. **p58**

business *n* ビジネス bijinesu **p39, 69**

business *adj* 商用で shōyō de **p102**

> **business center** ビジネス セン ター bijinesu sentā **p71**

busy *adj* 客の多い kyaku no ōi (restaurant)、話し中で hanashi chū de (phone)

butter *n* バター batā **p81, 83**

buy, to buy *v* 買う kau **p118, 138**

C

café *n* 喫茶店 kissa ten **p36, 77, 120**

> **Internet café** インターネット カ フェ intānetto kafe **p120**

call, to call *v* 呼ぶ yobu (shout) 電話をかける denwa o kakeru (phone) **p67, 68, 69**

> **Call the police!** 警察を呼ん でください! keisatsu o yonde kudasai! **p7**
> **Call an ambulance.** 救急車を 呼んでください。kyūkyūsha o yonde kudasai. **p7**

camp, to camp *v* キャンプをす る kyanpu o suru **p111**

camper *n* キャンパー kyanpā **p74**

camping *adj* キャンプの kyanpu no

> **Do we need a camping permit?** キャンプをする許可 が必要ですか? kyanpu o suru kyoka ga hitsuyō desu ka.

campsite n キャンプサイト kyanpu saito

can n 缶詰 kanzume

can (able to) v できる dekiru

Canada n カナダ kanada

Canadian adj カナダの、カナダ人の kanada no, kanada jin no p153

cancel, to cancel v 取り消す tori kesu p41

My flight was canceled. 私のフライトはキャンセルされました。watashi no furaito wa kyanseru saremashita.

canvas n キャンバス kyanbasu (for painting) / キャンバス地 kyanbasu ji (material) p47

cappuccino n カプチーノ kapuchīno

car n 車 kuruma

car rental agency レンタカー会社 rentakā gaisha

I need a rental car. レンタカーが必要です。rentakā ga hitsuyô desu.

card n カード kādo p67

Do you accept credit cards? クレジットカードはは使えますか？kurejitto kādo wa tsukae masu ka. p67

May I have your business card? あなたの名刺をいただけますか？anata no meishi o itadake masu ka.

car seat (child's safety seat) n チャイルドシート chairudo shīto

Do you rent car seats for children? チャイルドシートをレンタルしていますか？chairudo shīto o rentaru shite imasu ka.

carsickness n 車酔い kuruma yoi

cash n 現金 genkin p132

cash only 現金のみ genkin nomi p117

cash, to cash v 現金に換える genkin ni kaeru

to cash out (gambling) 清算する seisan suru

cashmere n カシミヤ kashimiya

casino n カジノ kajino p59

cat n ねこ neko

Catholic adj カトリック教の katorikku kyō no p108

cavity (tooth cavity) n 虫歯 mushiba

I think I have a cavity. 虫歯があるようなんです。mushiba ga aru yô nandesu.

CD n CD p49

CD player n CDプレーヤー CD purēyā p49

celebrate, to celebrate v 祝う iwau

cell phone n 携帯電話 keitai denwa p118, 155

centimeter n センチメートル senchi mētoru p14

chamber music n 室内楽 shitsunai gaku

champagne シャンパン shanpan p82

change (money) *n* おつり otsuri

I'd like change, please. おつりをください。 otsuri o kudasai.

This isn't the correct change. このおつりは正しくありません。 kono otsuri wa tadashiku arimasen.

change (to change money, clothes) *v* 交換する kōkan suru

changing room *n* 更衣室 kōi shitsu

charge, to charge (money) *v* 請求する seikyū suru p119

charge, to charge (a battery) *v* 充電する jūden suru p62

charmed *adj* 魅了された miryō sareta

charred (meat) *adj* ベリーウェルで berī weru de p79

charter, to charter *v* チャーターする chātā suru

cheap *adj* 安い yasui

check *n* 小切手 kogitte / チェック chekku

check, to check *v* 調べる shiraberu

checked (pattern) *adj* チェックの chekku no

check-in *n* チェックイン chekku in p35

What time is check-in? チェックインは何時ですか? chekku in wa nan ji desu ka.

Is online check-in available? オンラインチェックインはできますか? onrain chekku in wa deki masu ka. p39

check-out *n* チェックアウト chekku auto

check-out time チェックアウトの時間 chekku auto no jikan

What time is check-out? チェックアウトは何時ですか? chekku auto wa nan ji desu ka.

check out, to check out *v* チェックアウトする chekku auto suru

cheese *n* チーズ chīzu p95

chicken *n* チキン chikin

child *n* 子供 kodomo p80

children *n* 子供たち kodomo tachi

Are children allowed? 子供もいいですか? kodomo mo ii desu ka.

Do you have children's programs? 子供用のプログラムはありますか? kodomo yō no puroguramu wa arimasu ka.

Do you have a children's menu? 子供用のメニューはありますか? kodomo yō no menyū wa arimasu ka.

Chinese *adj* 中国の、中国人の chūgoku no, chūgoku jin no

chiropractor *n* カイロプラクター kairo purakutā p148

church *n* 教会 kyōkai p126

cigar *n* 葉巻 hamaki

cigarette *n* タバコ tabako

a pack of cigarettes タバコ1箱 tabako hito hako

cinema *n* 映画館 eiga kan

city n 市 shi / 街 machi p65

claim n 請求 seikyū

I'd like to file a claim. 賠償を請求します。baishō o seikyū shimasu.

clarinet n クラリネット kurarinetto

class n クラス kurasu p39

business class ビジネス クラス bijinesu kurasu

economy class エコノミー クラス ekonomī kurasu

first class ファースト クラス fāsuto kurasu

classic rock n クラシック ロック kurashikku rokku p109

classical (music) adj クラシックの kurasshikku no

classics 古典 koten p112

clean adj 清潔な seiketsu na

clean, to clean v 掃除する sōji suru

Please clean the room today. 今日、部屋を掃除してください。kyō, heya o sōji shite kudasai.

clear v 明らかにする akiraka ni suru

clear adj 透明な tōmei na p141

climbing n 登山 tozan p139

climb, to climb v 登る noboru

to climb a mountain 山に登る yama ni noboru

to climb stairs 階段を昇る kaidan o noboru

close, to close v 閉じる tojiru

close (near) 近い chikai p5

closed adj 閉じた tojita

cloudy adj 曇った kumotta p107

clover n クローバー kurōbā

go clubbing, to go clubbing v クラブに踊りに行く kurabu ni odori ni iku

coat n コート kōto p130

cockfight n 闘鶏 tōkei

cocktail n カクテル kakuteru p83

coffee n コーヒー kōhī p113

iced coffee アイス コーヒー aisu kōhī

cognac n コニャック konyakku p84

coin n 硬貨 kōka

cold n カゼ kaze p97, 147

I have a cold. カゼを引きました。kaze o hiki mashita.

cold adj 寒い samui p72

I'm cold. 寒いです。samui desu.

It's cold out. 外は寒いです。soto wa samui desu.

coliseum n 大劇場 daigeki jō

collect adj 受信人払いの jushin nin barai no

I'd like to place a collect call. コレクト コールをお願いします。korekuto kōru o onegai shimasu.

collect, to collect v 集める atsumeru

college n 大学 daigaku

Colombian adj コロンビアの、コロンビア人の koronbia no, koronbia jin no

color n 色 iro

color v 色をぬる iro o nuru

comedy *n* コメディ komedi
p112

computer *n* コンピューター
konpyūtā

computer programmer コ
ンピューター プログラマー
konpyūtā puroguramā **p105**

concert *n* コンサート konsāto
p113

condition *n* 状態 jōtai

in good / bad condition 良
い / 悪い 状態 yoi / warui jōtai

condom *n* コンドーム kondōmu
p147

condor *n* コンドル kondoru

confirm, to confirm *v* 確認する
kakunin suru **p41**

I'd like to confirm my
reservation. 予約を確認した
いのですが。yoyaku o kakunin
shitai no desuga.

confused *adj* 混乱した konran
shita

congested *adj* 混雑した
konzatsu shita

connection speed *n* 回線速度
kaisen sokudo

constipated *adj* 便秘した benpi
shita

I'm constipated. 便秘していま
す。benpi shite imasu.

contact lens *n* コンタクト レンズ
kontakuto renzu

I lost my contact lens. コン
タクト レンズをなくしました。
kontakuto renzu o nakushi
mashita.

continue, to continue *v* 続け
る tsuzukeru

convertible *n* オープンカー
ōpun kā

cook, to cook *v* 料理する
ryōri suru

I'd like a room where I can
cook. 料理することができる部
屋をお願いします。ryōri suru
koto ga dekiru heya o onegai
shimasu.

cookie *n* クッキー kukkī **p95**

copper *adj* 銅製の dōsei no

corner *n* 隅 sumi

on the corner 隅の

correct *v* 直す naosu

correct *adj* 正しい tadashii

Am I on the correct train?
私は正しい電車に乗っていま
すか? watashi wa tadashii
densha ni notte imasu ka.

cost, to cost *v* 金額がかかる
kingaku ga kakaru

How much does it cost? そ
れはいくらしますか? sore wa
ikura shimasu ka. **p132**

Costa Rican *adj* コスタリカの、
コスタリカ人の kosutarika no,
kosutarika jin no

costume *n* 衣装 ishō

cotton *n* 綿 men / コットン
kotton **p130**

cough *n* 咳 seki **p165**

cough *v* 咳をする seki o suru

counter (in bar) *n* カウンター
kauntā **p77**

country music *n* カントリー音楽 kantorī ongaku

court (legal) *n* 裁判所 saiban sho p54, 153

court (sport) *n* コート kōto

courteous *adj* ていねいな teinei na / 親切な shinsetsuna p74

cousin *n* いとこ itoko

cover charge (in bar) *n* カバーチャージ kabā chāji p144

cow *n* 牛 ushi

crack (in glass object) *n* ヒビ 割れ hibi ware

craftsperson *n* 職人 shoku nin p109 / 工芸家 kōgeika

cream *n* クリーム kurimu p81, 147

credit card *n* クレジット カー ド kurejitto kādo p39, 69, 123, 124

Do you accept credit cards? クレジットカードを使えます か？ kurejitto kādo o tsukae masu ka. p37, 67, 115, 116

crib *n* ベビーベッド bebī beddo p66

crown (dental) *n* 歯にかぶせ ているもの ha ni kabusete iru mono

curb *n* 縁石 enseki

curl *n* カール kāru

curly *adj* カールした kāru shita

currency exchange *n* 両替 ryōgae p36, 115

Where is the nearest currency exchange? ここか ら一番近い両替所はどこにあ りますか？ koko kara ichiban chikai ryōgae jo wa doko ni arimasu ka.

current (water) *n* 潮の流れ shio no nagare

customs *n* 税関 zeikan p35, 38 / 関税 kanzei p121

cut (wound) *n* 切り傷 kiri kizu

I have a bad cut. 私はひどい 切り傷があります。 watashi wa hidoi kirikizu ga arimasu.

cut, to cut *v* 切る kiru

cybercafé *n* サイバー カフェ saibā kafe

Where can I find a cybercafé? サイバー カフェは どこにありますか？ saibā kafe wa doko ni arimasu ka.

D

damaged *adj* 損傷した sonshō shita p49

Damn! *expletive* しまった! shimatta / 残念! zan nen

dance *v* 踊る odoru p112 / ダン スをする dansu o suru

danger *n* 危険 kiken p54

dark *n* 暗がり kuragari

dark *adj* 暗い kurai

daughter *n* 娘 musume / お嬢 さん ojōsan p102

day *n* 日 hi

the day after tomorrow あさって asatte p4

the day before yesterday おととい ototoi p4

these last few days ここ2‐3日 koko nisan nichi

dawn n 夜明け yoake p17

at dawn 夜明けに yoake ni

deaf adj 耳が聞こえない mimi ga kikoenai

deal (bargain) n 取引き torihiki

What a great deal! なんてすばらしい取引だ! nante subarashii torihiki da.

deal (cards) v 配る kubaru

Deal me in. 私も入れてください。watashi mo irete kudasai.

December n 十二月 jū ni gatsu p19

declare v 申告する shinkoku suru p41, 43

I have nothing to declare. 申告するものはありません。shinkoku suru mono wa arimasen.

Do you have anything to declare? 申告する持ち物はありますか? shinkoku suru mochimono wa arimasu ka. p41

declined adj 拒否された kyohi sareta

Was my credit card declined? 私のクレジット カードが拒否されたのですか? watashi no kurejitto kādo ga kyohi saretano desu ka.

deep adj 深い fukai

delay n 遅れ okure p42

How long is the delay? どのくらいの遅れですか? dono kurai no okure desuka. p42

delighted adj 嬉しい ureshii

democracy n 民主主義 minshu shugi

dent v へこむ hekomu

He / She dented the car. 彼 / 彼女が車をへこませました。kare / kanojo ga kuruma o hekomase mashita.

dentist n 歯医者 haisha p149

denture n 義歯 gishi

denture plate 義歯 gishi

departure n 出発 shuppatsu

depressed 落ち込んだ気分の ochikonda kibun no p104

dermatologist 皮膚科医 hifu ka i p149

designer n デザイナー dezainā p104

dessert n デザート dezāto p84

dessert menu デザートのメニュー dezāto no menyū

destination n 行き先 yuki saki

diabetic adj 糖尿病の tōnyōbyō no

dial (a phone) v 電話をかける denwa o kakeru / ダイヤル daiyaru suru p118

dial direct 直通番号にかける chokutsū bangō ni kakeru

diaper n おむつ omutsu

ENGLISH—JAPANESE

Where can I change a diaper? おむつはどこで替えられますか? omutsu wa doko de kaerare masu ka.

diarrhea n 下痢 geri p148

dictionary n 辞書 jisho

different (other) adj 異なる kotonaru / 違う chigau p131 / 別の betsuno p72

difficult adj 困難な konnan na / 難しい muzukashii p140

dinner n 夕食 yūshoku p113

directory assistance (phone) n 番号案内 bangō annai

dirty adj 汚い kitanai p72

disability n 障害 shōgai

disappear v 消える kieru

disco n ディスコ disuco

disconnected adj 切断された setsudan sareta

Operator, I was disconnected. オペレータさん、電話が切れてしまいました。opērēta san, denwa ga kirete shimai mashita.

discount n 値引き nebiki

Do I qualify for a discount? 私は値引きの対象になりますか? watashi wa nebiki no taishō ni narimasuka.

dish n 料理 ryōri p80

dive v もぐる moguru

scuba dive スキューバダイブ sukyūba daibu p141

divorced adj 離婚した rikon shita

dizzy adj めまいがする memai ga suru p150

do, to do v する suru

doctor n 医者 isha p104, 148

I need a doctor. 医者をお願いします。isha o onegai shimasu. p7

doctor's office n 医院 iin

documentary films ドキュメンタリー映画 dokyumentarī eiga p112

dog n 犬 inu p151

service dog 介護犬 kaigo ken p42, 62, 66

dollar n ドル doru

door n ドア doa

double adj ダブルの daburu no p64

double bed ダブルベッド daburu beddo p64

double vision 二重映像 nijū eizō

down adj 下に shita ni

download v ダウンロードする daunrōdo suru

downtown n 繁華街 hanka gai p137

dozen n ダース dāsu p15

drain n 排水 haisui

drama n 劇の脚本 geki no kyakuhon

drama (film) ドラマ dorama p111

drawing (work of art) n 絵 e

dress (garment) n ドレス doresu

dress (general attire) n 服装 fukusō p144

What's the dress code? 服装の規則は何ですか? fukusō no kisoku wa nan desu ka.

dress v 着る kiru

Should I dress up for that affair? そこでは正装しなければなりませんか? soko dewa seisō shinakereba nari masen ka.

dressing (salad) n ドレッシング doressingu

dried adj 乾燥した kansō shita

drink n 飲み物 nomi mono p79, 145

I'd like a drink. 飲み物をください。 nomi mono o kudasai.

drink, to drink v 飲む nomu

drip v 滴る shitataru

drive v 運転する unten suru

driver n 運転手 unten shu p56

driving range n ゴルフ練習場 gorufu renshū jō

drum n ドラム doramu

dry adj 乾いた kawaita

This towel isn't dry. このタオルは乾いていません。 kono taoru wa kawaite imasen.

dry, to dry v 乾かす kawakasu

I need to dry my clothes. 私の服を乾かす必要があります。 watashi no fuku o kawakasu hitsuyō ga arimasu.

dry cleaner n ドライ クリーナー dorai kurīnā

dry cleaning n ドライ クリーニング dorai kurīningu

duck n アヒル ahiru

duty-free adj 免税の menzei no p36

duty-free shop n 免税店 menzei ten p36

DVD n DVD p49

Do the rooms have DVD players? その部屋には DVD プレーヤーがありますか? sono heya niwa DVD purēyā ga arimasu ka.

Where can I rent DVDs or videos? DVD またはビデオはどこで借りられますか? DVD matawa bideo wa doko de karirare masu ka.

E

earlier adj 前に mae ni p4

early adj 早い hayai p17

It's early. 早いです。 hayai desu.

eat v 食べる taberu

to eat out 外食する gaishoku suru

economy n エコノミー ekonomī

Ecuadorian adj エクアドルの、エクアドル人の ekuadoru no, ekuadoru jin no

editor n 編集者 henshū sha p104

educator n 教育者 kyōiku sha p105

eggs n 卵 tamago p95

eight n 八 hachi p7

eighteen n 十八 jū hachi p8

eighth n 8 番目の hachi banme no p12

eighty n 八十 hachi jū p8

election *n* 選挙 senkyo p108

electrical hookup *n* 電気接続部 denki setsuzoku bu p74

elevator *n* エレベーター erebētā p61, 66

eleven *n* 十一 jū ichi p7

e-mail *n* Eメール E mēru p114

May I have your e-mail address? あなたのEメールアドレスをいただけますか? anata no E mēru adoresu o itadake masu ka.

e-mail message Eメール メッセージ E ii- mēru messēji

e-mail, to send e-mail *v* Eメールする ii-mēru suru

embarrassed *adj* 恥ずかしい hazukashii

embassy *n* 大使館 taishi kan

emergency *n* 緊急 kinkyū

emergency brake *n* 非常ブレーキ hijō burēki

emergency exit *n* 非常用出口 hijōyō deguchi p40

employee *n* 従業員 jūgyō in

employer *n* 雇い主 yatoi nushi

engine *n* エンジン enjin p52

engineer *n* エンジニア enjinia p104

England *n* イギリス igirisu

English *adj* イギリス(の)、イギリス人(の) igirisu no, igirisu jin no

Do you speak English? 英語を話しますか? eigo o hanashi masu ka. p2

enjoy, to enjoy *v* 楽しむ tanoshimu

enter, to enter *v* 入る hairu

Do not enter. 進入禁止 shinyū kinshi

enthusiastic *adj* 熱心な nesshin na p104

entrance *n* 入口 iriguchi p38

envelope *n* 封筒 fūtō p122

environment *n* 環境 kankyō

escalator *n* エスカレーター esukarētā

espresso *n* エスプレッソ esupuresso

exchange rate *n* 交換レート kōkan rēto p116

What is the exchange rate for US / Canadian dollars? アメリカドル / カナダドルの交換レートは何ですか? amerika doru / kanada doru no kōkan rēto wa nan desu ka.

excuse (pardon) *v* すみません sumi masen p53, 83, 146

Excuse me. すみません sumi masen

exhausted *adj* 疲れた tsukareta

exhibit *n* 展示 tenji

exit *n* 出口 deguchi p40

not an exit 出口なし deguchi nashi

exit *v* 出る deru

expensive *adj* 高い takai p76, 132, 144

explain v 説明する setsumei suru

express adj 特急の tokkyū no

express check-in 特別優先チェックイン tokubetsu yūsen chekku in

extra (additional) adj 余分の yobun no

extra-large adj 特大の tokudai no / LL eru eru p129

eye n 目 me

eyebrow n まゆ毛 mayu ge

eyeglasses n 眼鏡 megane

eyelash n まつ毛 matsu ge

F

fabric n 布 nuno

face n 顔 kao

faint v 気を失う ki o ushinau p149

fall (season) n 秋 aki

fall v 落ちる ochiru

family n 家族 kazoku / ご家族 go kazoku p100

fan n 扇風機 senpūki

far adj 遠くに tōkuni / 遠い tōi p5

How far is it to ____? ____まではどれだけ遠く離れていますか? ____ made wa doredake tōku hanarete imasu ka.

fare n 料金 ryōkin

fast adj 速い hayai

fat adj 太った futotta p16

father n 父 chichi / お父さん otōsan p106

faucet n 蛇口 jaguchi

fault n 落ち度 ochido p55

I'm at fault. 私に落ち度があります。watashi ni ochido ga arimasu. p55

It was his fault. それは彼に落ち度があります。sore wa kare ni ochido ga arimasu.

fax n ファックス fakkusu

February n 二月 ni gatsu p19

fee n 料金 ryōkin

female adj 女性の josei no

fiancé(e) n 婚約者 konyaku sha p100

fifteen adj 十五の jūgo no p8

fifth adj 五番目の go banme no p13

fifty adj 五十の gojū no p8

find v 見つける mitsukeru

fine (for traffic violation) n 罰金 bakkin p54, 154

fine adj 元気な genki na p1

I'm fine. 私は元気です。watashi wa genki desu.

fire! n 火事だ! kaji da.

first adj 最初の saisho no

fishing pole n 釣竿 tsuri zao

fitness center n フィットネス センター fittonesu sentā / ジム jimu p63

fit (clothes) v ぴったり合う pittari au

Does this look like it fits? ぴったり合っているように見えますか? pittari atte iru yō ni miemasu ka.

fitting room n 試着室 shichaku shitsu

five adj 五つの itsutsu no p7

flight n フライト furaito / ＿＿便 ＿＿bin p37

> **Where do domestic flights arrive / depart?** 国内線の出発/到着場所はどこですか? kokunai sen no shuppatsu / tōchaku basho wa doko desu ka.
>
> **Where do international flights arrive / depart?** 国際線の出発/到着場所はどこですか? kokusai sen no shuppatsu / tōchaku basho wa doko desu ka.
>
> **What time does this flight leave?** このフライトは何時に出発しますか? kono furaito wa nan ji ni shuppatsu shimasu ka.

flight attendant n 飛行機の乗務員 hikōki no jōmuin

floor n 階 kai

> **ground floor** 1 階 ikkai p66
> **second floor** 2 階 ni kai

flower n 花 hana

flush (gambling) n フラッシュ furasshu

flush, to flush v 流れる、流す nagareru, nagasu

> **This toilet won't flush.** このトイレは流れません。kono toire wa nagare masen.

flute n フルート furūto

food n 食べ物 tabe mono

foot (body part, measurement) n 足フット ashi, futto

forehead n 額 hitai

fork フォーク fōku p83

formula n 粉ミルク kona miruku

> **Do you sell infants' formula?** ベビー用粉ミルクは売っていますか? bebī yō kona miruku wa utte imasu ka.

forty adj 四十の yonjū no p8

forward adj 先へ saki e / 前へ mae e p6

four adj 四つの yottsu no p7

fourteen adj 十四の jūyon no / 十四の jū shi no p8

fourth adj 四番目の yon banme no p13

> **one-fourth** 四分の一 yon bun no ichi

fragile adj 割れやすい ware yasui / 「割れ物注意」「waremono chūi」 p121

freckle n そばかす sobakasu

French adj フランスの、フランス人の furansu no, furansu jin no

fresh adj 新鮮な shinsen na p83, 96

Friday n 金曜日 kin yō bi p17

friend n 友人 yūjin / 友達 tomodachi p100

front adj 前方の zenpō no p40

> **front desk** フロント デスク furonto desuku p68

front door フロントドア furonto doa

frozen food n 冷凍食品 reitō shokuhin p94

fruit n 果物 kuda mono p95

fruit juice n フルーツ ジュース furūtsu jūsu

full, to be full (after a meal) adj 満腹になった manpuku ni natta

Full house! n フル ハウス! furu hausu.

fuse n ヒューズ hyūzu

G

gallon n ガロン garon p15

garlic n にんにく nin niku p102

gas n ガソリン gasorin p50

  gas gauge 燃料計 nenryō kei
  out of gas ガソリンが入っていない gasorin ga haitte inai

gate (at airport) n ゲート gēto p35

German adj ドイツの、ドイツ人の doitsu no, doitsu jin no

gift n 贈り物 okuri mono

gin n ジン jin p82

girl n 女の子 onna no ko

girlfriend n ガールフレンド gāru furendo p100

give, to give v あげる ageru

glass n グラス gurasu / コップ koppu p79, 84

  Do you have it by the glass? グラスでありますか? gurasu de arimasuka.

I'd like a glass please. グラスで一つお願いします。gurasu de hitotsu onegai shimasu.

glasses (eye) n 眼鏡 megane

I need new glasses. 新しい眼鏡が必要です。atarashii megane ga hitsuyō desu.

glove n 手袋 tebukuro

gluten-free グルテン抜きの料理 guruten nuki no ryōri p80

go, to go v 行く iku

goal (sport) n ゴール gōru

goalie n ゴールキーパー gōru kīpā p150

gold adj 金製の kin sei no

golf n ゴルフ gorufu p47

golf, to go golfing v ゴルフをする gorufu o suru

good adj よい yoi p63, 75

goodbye n さようなら sayōnara p104

government 政府 seifu p107

grade (school) n 学年 gakunen

gram n グラム guramu

grandfather n 祖父 sofu / お祖父さん ojīsan

grandmother n 祖母 sobo / お祖母さん obāsan

grandparent n 祖父母 sofubo

grape n ぶどう budō

gray adj 灰色の hai iro no

great adj 立派な rippa na

Greek adj ギリシャの、ギリシャ人の girisha no, girisha jin no

Greek Orthodox adj ギリシャ正教の girisha seikyō no p108

green *adj* 緑色の midori iro no

groceries *n* 食料品 shokuryō hin

group *n* グループ gurūpu p44, 155

grow, to grow (get larger) *v* 育つ sodatsu

> **Where did you grow up?** どこで育ちましたか? doko de sodachi mashita ka.

guard *n* ガード gādo

> **security guard** セキュリティガード sekyuritī gādo / 警備員 keibi in p36

Guatemalan *adj* グアテマラの、グアテマラ人の guatemara no, guatemara jin no

guest *n* お客 okyaku

guide (of tours) *n* ガイド gaido

guide (publication) *n* ガイドブック gaido bukku

guide, to guide *v* 案内する an nai suru

guided tour *n* ガイド付きツアー gaido tsuki tuā

guitar *n* ギター gitā p110

gym *n* ジム jimu p137

gynecologist *n* 婦人科医 fujinka i

H

hair *n* 髪の毛 kami no ke

haircut *n* ヘアーカット heā katto

> **I need a haircut.** 髪の毛を切りたいのですが。 kami no ke o kiri tai no desuga.

> **How much is a haircut?** カットはいくらですか? katto wa ikura desuka.

hairdresser *n* ヘアードレッサー heā doressā

hair dryer *n* ヘアードライヤー heā doraiyā p71

half *n* 半分 hanbun

> **one-half** 二分の一 ni bun no ichi

hallway *n* 廊下 rōka

hand *n* 手 te

handicapped-accessible *adj* 障害者に対応した shōgai sha ni taiō shita

handle, to handle *v* 扱う atsukau

handsome *adj* ハンサムな hansamu na p102

hangout (hot spot) *n* 溜まり場 tamari ba

hang out (to relax) *v* よく出入りする yoku deiri suru

hang up (to end a phone call) *v* 切る kiru p119

hanger *n* ハンガー hangā

happy *adj* 幸せな shiawase na / 嬉しい ureshii p103

hard *adj* 難しい muzukashii (difficult) / 硬い katai (firm) p47

hat *n* 帽子 bōshi

have *v* 持つ motsu

hazel *adj* 薄茶色の usu chairo no

headache *n* 頭痛 zutsu p150

headlight *n* ヘッドライト heddo raito

headphones *n* ヘッドホーン heddo hōn

hear *n* 聞く kiku

hearing-impaired *adj* 聴覚障害の chōkaku shōgai no

heart *n* 心臓 shinzō p149

heart attack *n* 心臓発作 shinzō hossa p149

hectare *n* ヘクタール hekutāru p14

hello *n* こんにちは kon nichi wa p1

Help! *n* 助けて! tasukete.

Can you help me? 助けてください。 tasukete kudasai. p7

help, to help *v* 助ける tasukeru

hen *n* 雌鶏 mendori

her *adj* 彼女の kanojo no p26

herb *n* ハーブ hābu

here *n* ここ koko p5

high *adj* 高い takai

highlights (hair) *n* ハイライト hairaito p135

highway *n* 高速道路 kōsoku dōro

hike, to hike *v* ハイキングをする haikingu o suru

him *pron* 彼 kare o p26

Hindu *adj* ヒンズー教の、ヒンズー人の hinzū kyō no, hinzū jin no p108

hip-hop *n* ヒップホップ hippu hoppu

his *adj* 彼の kare no

historical *adj* 歴史的な rekishi teki na

history *n* 歴史 rekishi

hobby *n* 趣味 shumi

hold, to hold *v* 抱く daku

to hold hands 手を握る te o nigiru

Would you hold this for me? これを持っていただけませんか? kore o motte itadake masen ka.

hold, to hold (to pause) *v* 待つ matsu

Hold on a minute! ちょっと待って! chotto matte.

I'll hold. パスします。 pasu shimasu.

hold, to hold (gambling) *v* パスする pasu suru

holiday *n* 休日 kyūjitsu

home *n* 家 ie

homemaker *n* 主婦 shufu

Honduran *adj* ホンジュラスの、ホンジュラス人の honjurasu no, honjurasu jin no

horn *n* 角 tsuno

horse *n* 馬 uma

hostel *n* ホステル hosuteru p63

hot *adj* 熱い atsui

hot chocolate *n* ホット チョコレート hotto chokorēto p82

hotel *n* ホテル hoteru p55, 63

Do you have a list of local hotels? 地元のホテルの一覧表はありますか? jimoto no hoteru no ichiran hyō wa arimasu ka.

hour *n* 時間 jikan p120, 127

hours (at museum) *n* 時間 jikan

how *adv* いくら ikura (how much), いくつ ikutsu (how many) p3, 37, 39

humid *adj* 湿気のある shikke no aru p107

hundred *n* 百 hyaku

hurry *v* 急ぐ

> **I'm in a hurry.** 私は急いでいます。watashi wa isoide imasu.
> **Hurry, please!** 急いでください! isoide kudasai.

hurt, to hurt *v* 痛む itamu p149

> **Ouch! That hurts!** 痛い! itai. 痛いです! itai desu.

husband *n* 夫 otto / 主人 shujin / ご主人 go shujin p99

I

I *pron* 私は watashi wa

ice *n* 氷 kōri p145

identification *n* 身分証明書 mibun shōmei sho p44

immigration 入国審査 nyūkoku shinsa p35

inch *n* インチ inchi p14

indigestion *n* 消化不良 shōka furyō

inexpensive *adj* 高くない takaku nai p76

infant *n* 赤ちゃん akachan

> **Are infants allowed?** 赤ちゃんもいいですか? Akachan mo ii desu ka.

information *n* 情報 jōhō

information booth *n* 案内所 an nai jo

injury *n* けが kega

insect repellent *n* 虫除け mushi yoke p148

inside *n* 内部 naibu / 中 naka p77

insult *v* 侮辱する bujoku suru

insurance *n* 保険 hoken p50, 121

interest rate *n* 金利 kinri

intermission *n* 休憩 kyūkei

Internet *n* インターネット intānetto p65,71,120

> **High-speed Internet** 高速インターネット kōsoku intānetto
> **Do you have Internet access?** インターネットに接続できますか? intānetto ni setsuzoku deki masu ka.
> **Where can I find an Internet café?** インターネットカフェはどこにありますか? intā netto kafe wa doko ni arimasu ka.

interpreter *n* 通訳 tsūyaku p153

> **I need an interpreter.** 通訳が必要です。tsūyaku ga hitsuyō desu.

introduce, to introduce *v* 紹介する shōkai suru p99

> **I'd like to introduce you to ____.** あなたを____に紹介します。anata o ____ ni shōkai shimasu.

Ireland *n* アイルランド airurando

Irish *adj* アイルランドの、アイルランド人の airurando no, airurando jin no

is *v* See **be (to be)**.

Italian *adj* イタリアの、イタリア人の itaria no, itaria jin no p106

J

jacket *n* 上着 uwagi p43, 78

January *n* 一月 ichi gatsu p19

Japanese *adj* 日本の、日本人の nihon no, nihon jin no p106

jazz *n* ジャズ jazu p109

Jewish *adj* ユダヤ教の、ユダヤ人の yudaya kyō no, yudaya jin no p108

jog, to run *v* ジョギングをする joggingu o suru

juice *n* ジュース jūsu p45

June *n* 六月 roku gatsu p19

July *n* 七月 shichi gatsu p19

K

keep, to keep *v* 保つ tamotsu

kid *n* 子供 kodomo

Are kids allowed? 子供もいいですか? kodomo mo ii desu ka.

Do you have kids' programs? 子供用のプログラムはありますか? kodomo yō no puroguramu wa arimasu ka.

Do you have a kids' menu? 子供用のメニューはありますか? kodomo yō no menyū wa arimasu ka.

kilo *n* キログラム kiro guramu

kilometer *n* キロメートル kiro mētoru p14

kind *n* 種類 shurui (type)

What kind is it? それはどんな種類ですか? sore wa donna shurui desu ka.

kiss *n* キス kisu

kitchen *n* キッチン kicchin

knife ナイフ naifu p83

know, to know (something) *v* 知っている shitte iru

know, to know (someone) *v* 知っている shitte iru

L

land, to land *v* 着陸する chakuriku suru / 着く tsuku p45

landscape *n* 景色 keshiki

language *n* 言語 gengo

laptop *n* ラップトップ rappu toppu p144

large *adj* 大きい ōkii p131

last, to last *v* 続く tsuzuku

last *adv* 最後に saigo ni

late *adj* 遅い osoi p17

Please don't be late. どうか遅れないでください。dōka okure naide kudasai.

later *adv* あとで ato de

See you later. それじゃ、また後で。soreja, mata ato de.

laundry *n* 洗濯 sentaku / ランドリー randorī p70

lavender *adj* ラベンダー色の rabendā iro no

law *n* 法律 hōritsu

lawyer *n* 弁護士 bengo shi p104

least *n* 最小 saishō

least *adj* 最も小さい、最も少な
  い mottomo chiisai, mottomo
  sukunai

leather *n* 皮 kawa p47

leave, to leave (depart) *v* 出
  発する shuppatsu suru
  p37

left *adj* 左の hidari no p5
  on the left 左に hidari ni

leg *n* 脚 ashi

lemonade *n* レモネード
  remonēdo

less *adj* もっと少ない motto
  sukunai

lesson *n* レッスン ressun

license *n* 免許証 menkyo shō
  p154
  driver's license 運転免許証
  unten menkyo shō

life preserver *n* 救命用具
  kyūmei yōgu

light (lamp) *n* ランプ ranpu
  p52

light (for cigarette) *n* 火 hi
  p146
  May I offer you a light? 火を
  貸しましょうか？ hi o kashima
  shō ka.

lighter (cigarette) *n* ライタ
  ー raitā

like, desire *v* 望む、nozomu
  I would like ____. ____が好き
  です。____ ga suki desu.

like, to like *v* 好きである suki
  de aru

I like this place. 私はここが好
  きです。watashi wa koko ga
  suki desu.

limo *n* リムジン rimujin p55

liquor *n* 酒 sake p43

liter *n* リットル rittoru p14

little *adj* 小さい chiisai (size)、少
  し sukoshi (amount)

live, to live *v* 住む sumu
  Where do you live? あなたは
  どこに住んでいますか？ anata
  wa doko ni sunde imasu ka.

living *n* 生活 seikatsu
  **What do you do for a
  living?** 何をして生活してい
  ますか？ nani o shite seikatsu
  shite imasu ka.

local *adj* 地方の chihō no p50

lock *n* 鍵 kagi p137

lock, to lock *v* 鍵をかける kagi
  o kakeru
  I can't lock the door. ドアに
  鍵をかけることができません。
  doa ni kagi o kakeru koto ga
  dekima sen.
  I'm locked out. ドアに鍵がか
  かってしまい部屋に入ること
  ができません。doa ni kagi ga
  kakatte shimai heya ni hairu
  koto ga deki masen.

locker *n* ロッカー rokkā p137
  storage locker 保管ロッカー
  hokan rokkā
  locker room ロッカールーム
  rokkā rūmu p138

long *adv* 長く nagaku

For how long? どれくらい長く? dore kurai nagaku.

long *adj* 長い nagai p15

look, to look (to observe) *v* 見る miru

I'm just looking. ただ見ているだけです。 tada miteiru dake desu.

Look here! ここを見て! koko o mite.

look, to look (to appear) *v* のように見える no yō ni mieru

How does this look? これはどう見えますか? kore wa dō mie masu ka.

look for, to look for (to search) *v* 探す sagasu

I'm looking for a porter. ポーターを探しています。 pōtā o sagashite imasu.

loose *adj* ゆるい yurui

lose, to lose *v* 失くす nakusu

I lost my passport. 私はパスポートを失くしました。 watashi wa pasupōto o nakushi mashita.

I lost my wallet. 私は財布を失くしました。 watashi wa saifu o nakushi mashita.

I'm lost. 道に迷いました。 michi ni mayoi mashita.

loud *adj* うるさい urusai

loudly *adv* うるさく urusaku

lounge *n* ラウンジ raunji

lounge, to lounge *v* くつろぐ kutsurogu

love *n* 愛 ai

love, to love *v* 愛する ai suru

to love (family) 愛する ai suru

to love (a friend) 愛する ai suru

to love (a lover) 愛する ai suru

low *adj* 低い hikui

lunch *n* 昼食 chūshoku / ランチ ranchi p76

luggage *n* 荷物 nimotsu p36, 55 / 旅行カバン ryokō kaban

Where do I report lost luggage? 旅行カバンの紛失はどこに報告しますか? ryokō kaban no funshitsu wa doko ni hōkoku shimasu ka.

Where is the lost luggage claim? 紛失した旅行カバンを受け取る場所はどこですか? funshitsu shita ryokō kaban o uketoru basho wa doko desu ka.

M

machine *n* 機械 kikai

made of ____ *adj* ____から作られた ____kara tsuku rareta

magazine *n* 雑誌 zasshi

maid (hotel) *n* メード mēdo

maiden *adj* 未婚の mikon no

That's my maiden name. それは私の旧姓です。 sore wa watashi no kyūsei desu.

mail *n* 郵便 yūbin / 手紙 tegami p71

air mail 航空便 kōkūbin

registered mail 書留 kakitome

mail *v* 郵便で出す yūbin de dasu

make, to make v 作る tsukuru

makeup n 化粧 keshō

make up, to make up (apologize) v 埋め合せをする ume awase o suru

make up, to make up (apply cosmetics) v 化粧をする keshō o suru

male n 男性 dansei

male adj 男性の dansei no

mall n ショッピングセンター shoppingu sentā p128

man n 男 otoko

manager n マネージャー manējā

manual (instruction booklet) n マニュアル manyuaru p50

many adj 多い ōi / 沢山の takusan no p15

map n 地図 chizu p53

March (month) n 三月 san gatsu p19

market n マーケット māketto / 市場 ichiba p129

flea market フリーマーケット furii māketto p129

open-air market 青空市場 aozora ichiba

married adj 既婚の kikon no / 結婚している kekkon shite iru p101

marry, to marry v 結婚する kekkon suru

massage n マッサージ massāji p69

match (sport) n 試合 shiai

match n マッチ macchi n

book of matches マッチ macchi

match, to match v 調和する chōwa suru

Does this ＿＿ match my outfit? この＿＿は私の服と合いますか kono ＿＿ wa watashi no fuku to aimasu ka?

May (month) n 五月 go gatsu p19

may v aux してよい shite yoi May I ＿＿? ＿＿してもよいですか? ＿＿ shitemo yoi desu ka.

meal n 食事 shokuji p40, 42, 45

meat n 肉 niku p84, 95

meatball n ミートボール mīto bōru

medication n 薬物治療 yakubutsu chiryō

medium (size) adj ミディアム midiamu

medium rare (meat) adj ミディアム レア midiamu rea p79

medium well (meat) adj ミディアム ウェル midiamu weru p79

member n 会員 kai in

memoirs 伝記 denki. p112

menu n メニュー menyū p77, 79

May I see a menu? メニューを見せていただけませんか? menyū o misete itadake masen ka.

children's menu 子供用のメニュー kodomo yō no menyū

diabetic menu 糖尿病患者用の tōnyōbyō kanja yō no menyū

kosher menu コーシャ料理の kōsha ryōri no menyū

metal detector *n* 金属探知機 kinzoku tanchi ki

meter *n* メートル mētoru p14

Mexican *adj* メキシコの、メキシコ人の mekishiko no, mekishiko jin no

middle *adj* 中間の chūkan no

midnight *n* 真夜中 mayonaka

mile *n* マイル mairu p11

military *n* 軍 gun

milk *n* 牛乳 gyūnyū / ミルク miruku p83

milk shake ミルクセーキ miruku sēki

milliliter *n* ミリリットル miri rittoru

millimeter *n* ミリメートル miri mētoru

minute *n* 分 fun

in a minute すぐに sugu ni

miss, to miss (a flight) *v* 乗りそこなう / 乗り遅れる nori sokonau / nori okureru p42

missing *adj* 見つからない mitsukara nai

My child is missing. 私の子供が迷子になりました。watashi no kodomo ga maigo ni nari mashita. p7

mistake *n* 間違い machigai p73

moderately priced *adj* 手頃な値段の tegoro na nedan no p63

mole (facial feature) *n* ほくろ hokuro

Monday *n* 月曜日 getsu yō bi p17

money *n* お金 okane

money transfer 振込 furikomi

month *n* See months of the year p19

last month 先月 sengetsu p4

next month 来月 raigetsu p4

morning *n* 朝 asa / 午前 gozen p17, 70

in the morning 午前 gozen

mosque *n* モスク mosuku

mother *n* 母 haha / お母さん okāsan p100

mother, to mother *v* 世話をする sewa o suru

motorcycle *n* バイク baiku

mountain *n* 山 yama

mountain climbing 登山 tozan p139

mouse *n* ねずみ nezumi

mouth *n* 口 kuchi

move, to move *v* 動く ugoku

movie *n* 映画 eiga p111, 112, 124

much *n* 多量 taryō / 沢山の takusan no p15

mug, to mug (someone) *v* 襲う osou

mugged *adj* 襲われた osowareta

museum *n* 美術館 bijutsu kan p127

music *n* 音楽 ongaku p109
  live music 生演奏 nama ensō
musician *n* ミュージシャン myūjishan p105
Muslim *adj* イスラム教の isuramu kyō no p108
mustache *n* 口ひげ kuchi hige
mystery (novel) *n* ミステリー misuterī

N

name *n* 名前 namae p1
  My name is ___. 私は___と申します。watashi wa ___ to mōshimasu. p1
  What's your name? あなたの名前は何ですか? anata no namae wa nan desu ka.
napkin *n* ナプキン napukin
narrow *adj* 狭い semai p16
nationality *n* 国籍 kokuseki
nausea *n* 吐き気 hakike p148
near *adj* 近い chikai p5
nearby *adj* 近くに chikaku ni p76
neat (tidy) *adj* きちんとした kichin to shita
need, to need *v* 欲しい hoshii
neighbor *n* 近所の人 kinjo no hito / ご近所の方 kinjo no kata p100
nephew *n* おい oi / 甥御さん oigo san p100
network *n* ネットワーク nettowāku
new *adj* 新しい atarashii p151
newspaper *n* 新聞 shinbun

newsstand *n* 新聞売り場 shinbun uriba p133
New Zealand *n* ニュージーランド nyūjīrando
New Zealander *adj* ニュージーランドの、ニュージーランド人の nyūjīrando no, nyūjīrando jin no p153
next *prep* 次 tsugi
  next to の次 no tsugi
  the next station 次の駅 tsugi no eki
Nicaraguan *adj* ニカラグアの、ニカラグア人の nikaragua no, nikaragua jin no
nice *adj* すてきな suteki na
niece *n* めい mei / 姪御さん meigo san p100
night *n* 夜 yoru p17
  at night 夜に yoru ni
  per night 一泊当たり ippaku atari p67
nightclub *n* ナイトクラブ naito kurabu
nine *adj* 九つの kokonotsu no p7
nineteen *adj* 十九の jūkyū no p8
ninety *adj* 九十の kyūjū no p8
ninth *adj* 九番目の kyū banme no p14
no *adv* でない de nai
noisy *adj* 音がうるさい oto ga urusai
nonalcoholic drink *n* ノンアルコールの to ノンアルコール飲料 non arukōru inryō

non-fiction n ノンフィクション non fikushon p112

none n 何もない nanimo nai / 少しもない sukoshi mo nai、全くない mattaku nai p15

nonsmoking adj 禁煙 kin en

nonsmoking area 禁煙場所 kin en basho

nonsmoking room 禁煙室 kin en shitsu

noon n 正午 shōgo p17

nose n 鼻 hana p136

novel n 小説 shōsetsu

November n 十一月 jū ichi gatsu p19

now adv 今 ima p3

number n 数字 sūji / 番号 bangō p57

Which room number? 部屋は何番?heya wa nan ban.

May I have your phone number? あなたの電話番号を教えていただけますか? anata no denwa bangō o oshiete itadake masu ka.

nurse n 看護師 kango shi p105

nurse v 授乳する junyū suru

Do you have a place where I can nurse? 授乳できる場所はありますか? junyū dekiru basho wa arimasu ka.

nursery n 託児所 takuji sho

Do you have a nursery? 託児所はありますか? takuji sho wa arimasu ka.

nuts n ナッツ類 nattsu rui

O

o'clock adv 時 ji p4

two o'clock 2 時 ni ji

October n 十月 jū gatsu p19

offer, to offer v 提供する teikyō suru

officer n 係員 kakari in p44

oil n 油 abura p80, 83

okay adv オッケー okkē

old adj 古い furui / ＿歳の ＿ sai no p102

old movies 昔の映画 mukashi no eiga p112

olive n オリーブ orību

one adj 一つの hitotsu no p7

one way (traffic sign) adj 一方通行 ippō tsūkō

open (business) adj 営業中 eigyō chū

Are you open? 営業していますか? eigyō shite imasu ka.

opera n オペラ opera p110

operator (phone) n オペレーター operētā

optometrist n 検眼師 kengan shi

orange (color) adj オレンジ色の orenji iro no

orange juice n オレンジジュース orenji jūsu p45

order, to order (demand) v 注文する chūmon suru

order, to order (request) v 頼む tanomu

organic adj 有機の yūki no

Ouch! 痛い! itai.

outside n 外 soto p77

overcooked *adj* 焼き(煮)すぎた yaki (ni) sugita

overheat, to overheat *v* オーバーヒートする ōbāhīto suru

The car overheated. 車がオーバーヒートしました。kuruma ga ōbāhīto shimashita.

overflowing *adv* あふれて afurete

oxygen tank *n* 酸素タンク sanso tanku

P

package *n* 小包み kozutsumi p121

pacifier *n* おしゃぶり oshaburi

page, to page (someone) *v* 呼び出す yobidasu p37

paint, to paint *v* 塗る nuru

painting *n* 絵 e

pale *adj* 青白い ao jiroi

Panamanian *adj* パナマの、パナマ人の panama no, panama jin no

paper *n* 紙 kami

parade *n* パレード parēdo

Paraguayan *adj* パラグアイの、パラグアイ人の paraguai no, paraguai jin no

parent *n* 親 oya

park *n* 公園 kōen p113

park, to park *v* 駐車する chūsha suru

no parking 駐車禁止 chūsha kinshi p54

parking fee 駐車料金 chūsha ryōkin p54

parking garage 車庫 shako p54

partner *n* パートナー pātonā

party *n* 団体 dantai

party *n* パーティー pātī

political party 政党 seitō

pass, to pass *v* パスする pasu suru

I'll pass. パスします。pasu shimasu.

passenger *n* 乗客 jōkyaku

passport *n* パスポート pasupōto

I've lost my passport. 私はパスポートを失くしました。watashi wa pasupōto o nakushi mashita.

Your passport, please. パスポートをお願いします。pasupōto o onegai shimasu. p41

pay, to pay *v* 支払う shiharau

peanut *n* ピーナッツ pīnattsu

pedestrian *adj* 歩行者用の hokōsha yō no

pediatrician *n* 小児科医 shōnika i

Can you recommend a pediatrician? お勧めの小児科医はいますか? osusume no shōnika i wa imasu ka.

permit *n* 許可 kyoka

Do we need a camping permit? キャンプをする許可が必要ですか? kyanpu o suru kyoka ga hitsuyō desu ka.

permit, to permit *v* 許可する kyoka suru

Peruvian *adj* ペルーの、ペルー人の perū no, perū jin no

phone *n* 電話 denwa p65

May I have your phone number? あなたの電話番号を教えていただけますか? anata no denwa bangō o oshiete itadake masu ka.

Where can I find a public phone? 公衆電話はどこにありますか? kōshū denwa wa doko ni arimasu ka.

phone operator 電話オペレーター denwa operêtâ

Do you sell prepaid phones? プリペイド電話を売っていますか? puripeido denwa o utte imasu ka.

phone *adj* 電話の denwa no

Do you have a phone directory? 電話帳はありますか? denwa chō wa arimasu ka.

phone call *n* 電話 denwa

I need to make a collect phone call. コレクト コールをしたいのですが。korekuto kōru o shitai no desuga.

an international phone call 国際電話 kokusai denwa

photocopy, to photocopy *v* コピーを取る kopī o toru / コピーする kopī suru

piano *n* ピアノ piano p110

pillow *n* 枕 makura p45, 70, 71

down pillow 羽毛の枕 umō no makura p71

pink *adj* ピンクの pinku no

pint *n* パイント painto p15

pizza *n* ピザ piza p75

place, to place *v* 置く oku

plastic *n* プラスチック purasuchikku p47

plate お皿 osara p84

play *n* プレイ purei

play, to play (a game) *v* プレイする purei suru

play, to play (an instrument) *v* 演奏する ensō suru / 弾く hiku p110

playground *n* 遊び場 asobi ba

Do you have a playground? 遊び場はありますか? asobi ba wa arimasu ka.

please (polite entreaty) *adv* どうぞ dōzo

please, to be pleasing to *v* 喜ばせる yorokobaseru

pleasure *n* 喜び yorokobi

It's a pleasure. 嬉しいです。ureshii desu.

plug *n* コンセント konsento

plug, to plug *v* 差し込む sashi komu

point, to point *v* 指す sasu p2

Would you point me in the direction of___? ___の方向に指し示していただけませんか? ___ no hōkō ni sashi shimeshite itadake masen ka.

police *n* 警察 keisatsu p36

police station *n* 警察署 keisatsu sho / 警察の派出所 keisatsu no hashutsu sho p36

ENGLISH–JAPANESE

pool *n* プール pūru p63

pool (the game) *n* ビリヤード biriyādo

popcorn ポップコーン poppukōn p126

pop music *n* ポップ ミュージック poppu myūjikku

popular *adj* 人気がある ninki ga aru p159

port (beverage) *n* ポートワイン pōto wain

port (for ship) *n* 港 minato

porter *n* ポーター pōtā p35

portion *n* 部分 bubun

portrait *n* 肖像画 shōzō ga

postcard *n* ポストカード posuto kādo

post office *n* 郵便局 yūbin kyoku

   Where is the post office?
   郵便局はどこにありますか?
   yūbin kyoku wa doko ni
   arimasu ka.

poultry *n* 家禽 kakin

pound *n* ポンド pondo

prefer, to prefer *v* の方を好む no hō o konomu

pregnant *adj* 妊娠した ninshin shita

prepared *adj* 準備された junbi sareta

prescription *n* 処方箋 shohōsen p151／処方薬 shohōyaku p44

price *n* 価格 kakaku

print, to print *v* 印刷する insatsu suru p120

private berth / cabin *n* 個人客室 kojin kyakushitsu ／ キャビンkyabin

problem *n* 問題 mondai

process, to process *v* 処理する shori suru

product *n* 製品 seihin

professional *adj* プロフェッショナルな purofesshionaru na

program *n* プログラム puroguramu

   May I have a program? プログラムをいただけますか?
   puroguramu o itadake
   masu ka.

Protestant *n* プロテスタント purotesutanto

publisher *n* 出版社 shuppansha

Puerto Rican *adj* プエルトリコの、プエルトリコ人の puerutoriko no, puerutoriko jin no

pull, to pull *v* 引く hiku p38

pump *n* ポンプ ponpu

purple *adj* 紫の murasaki no

purse *n* 財布 saifu

push, to push *v* 押す osu p38

put, to put *v* 置く oku

Q

quarter *adj* 四分の一 yonbun no ichi

   one-quarter 四分の一 yon
   bun no ichi

quiet *adj* 静かな shizuka na p77

R

rabbit n うさぎ usagi

radio n ラジオ rajio

  satellite radio 衛星ラジオ eisei rajio

rain, to rain v 雨が降る ame ga furu

  Is it supposed to rain? 雨が降る予定ですか? ame ga furu yotei desuka.

rainy adj 雨の ame no

  It's rainy. 雨です。ame desu.

ramp, wheelchair n スロープ、車椅子 surōpu, kuruma isu p63

rare (meat) adj レアの rea no p81

rate (for car rental, hotel) n 料金 ryōkin p49, 67

  Do you have a monthly rate? 月額料金はありますか? getsugaku ryōkin wa arimasu ka. p67

  Do you have a weekend rate? 週末料金はありますか? shūmatsu ryōkin wa arimasu ka. p67

  What's the rate per day? 一日当たりの料金はいくらですか? ichi nichi atari no ryōkin wa ikura desu ka.

  What's the rate per week? 一週間当たりの料金はいくらですか? isshūkan atari no ryōkin wa ikura desu ka.

rate plan (cell phone) n 料金プラン ryōkin puran

rather adv むしろ mushiro

read, to read v 読む yomu

really adv 本当に hontō ni

receipt n レシート reshīto p116

receive, to receive v 受け取る uketoru

recommend, to recommend v 勧める susumeru

red adj 赤の aka no

redhead n 赤毛 akage

reef n さんご礁 sango shō

refill (of beverage) n el お替わり okawari

refill (of prescription) n 補充 hojū

reggae adj レゲー regē p110

relative (family) n 親戚 shinseki

remove, to remove v 取り除く torinozoku / 脱ぐ nugu p43

rent, to rent v 借りる kariru

  I'd like to rent a car. 車を借りたいのですが。kuruma o karitai no desuga. p48

repeat, to repeat v 繰り返す kuri kaesu p2

  Would you please repeat that? もう一度繰り返していただけますか? mō ichido kuri kaeshite itadake masu ka. p2

reservation n 予約 yoyaku

  I'd like to make a reservation for ____. ____の予約をしたいのですが。____ no yoyaku o shitai no desuga. See p7 for numbers.

restaurant n レストラン
resutoran p36

Where can I find a good restaurant? よいレストランはどこにありますか? yoi resutoran wa doko ni arimasu ka.

restroom n トイレ toire p36, 40, 61

Do you have a public restroom? 公衆トイレはありますか? kōshū toire wa arimasu ka.

return, to return (to a place) v 戻る modoru

return, to return (something to a store) v 返品する henpin suru p134

ride, to ride v 乗っていく notte iku

right adj 右の migi no p5, 53

It is on the right. 右側にあります。 migi gawa ni arimasu. p53

Turn right at the corner. 角を右に曲がります。 kado o migi ni magari masu.

rights n pl 権利 kenri

civil rights 市民の権利 shimin no kenri

river n 川 kawa

road n 道路 dōro

road closed sign n 道路閉鎖中 dōro heisa chū p54

rob, to rob v 奪う ubau

I've been robbed. 強盗に遭いました。 gōtō ni aimashita.

rock music ロック音楽 rokku ongaku p109

rock climbing n ロッククライミング rokku kuraimingu

rocks (ice) n ロック rokku p81

I'd like it on the rocks. ロックでお願いします。 rokku de onegai shimasu.

romance (novel) n 恋愛小説 ren ai shōsetsu

romantic adj ロマンチックな romanchikku na

room (hotel) n 部屋 heya

room for one / two 1人／2人部屋 hitori / futari beya

room service ルーム サービス rūmu sābisu

rope n ロープ rōpu

rose n バラ bara

royal flush n ロイヤル フラッシュ roiyaru furasshu

rum n ラム酒 ramu shu p82

run, to run v 走る hashiru

S

sad adj 悲しい kanashii p103

safe (for storing valuables) n 金庫 kinko

Do the rooms have safes? 部屋には金庫がありますか。 heyaniwa kinko ga arimasu ka.

safe (secure) adj 安全な anzen na

Is this area safe? この地域は安全ですか? kono chiiki wa anzen desu ka.

sail n 航海 kōkai

sail, to sail v 航海する kōkai suru

When do we sail? いつ出航しますか? itsu shukkō shimasu ka. p140

salad n サラダ sarada

salesperson n 販売員 hanbai in p104

salt n 塩 shio p87

Is that low-salt? それは減塩ですか? sore wa gen en desu ka.

Salvadorian adj サルバドルの、サルバドル人の sarubadoru no, sarubadoru jin no

satellite n 衛星 eisei p65

satellite tracking 衛星追跡 eisei tsuiseki

Saturday n 土曜日 do yō bi p17

sauce n ソース sōsu

say, to say v 言う iu p99

scan, to scan v (document) スキャンする sukyan suru p120

schedule n スケジュール sukejūru

school n 学校 gakkō

scooter n スクーター sukūtā p48

score n 得点 tokuten

Scottish adj スコットランドの、スコットランド人の sukottorando no, sukottorando jin no

scratched adj 傷のある kizu no aru p50

scratched surface 擦り傷のある表面 suri kizu no aru hyōmen

scuba dive, to scuba dive v スキューバダイブをする sukyūba daibingu o suru p141

sculpture n 彫刻 chōkoku

seafood n シーフード shifūdo p80/ 魚介類 gyokai rui

search n 検査 kensa

hand search 手で検査する te de kensa suru

search, to search v 調べる shiraberu

seasick adj 船酔い funa yoi p59

I am seasick. 船酔いしました。 funa yoi shimashita.

seasickness pill n 船酔いに効く薬 funa yoi ni kiku kusuri

seat n 座席 zaseki p39, 40 / 席 seki

child seat チャイルドシート chairudo shiito p49

second adj 二番目の niban me no p13

security 荷物検査 nimotsu kensa p35

security checkpoint セキュリティ チェックポイント sekyuritī chekku pointo

security guard セキュリティ ガード sekyuritī gādo / 警備員 keibi in p36

sedan n セダン sedan

see, to see v 見る miru

May I see it? 見せていただけますか? misete itadake masu ka.

self-serve *adj* セルフサービスの serufu sābisu no

sell, to sell *v* 売る uru

seltzer *n* ソーダ水 sōda sui p82

send, to send *v* 送る okuru p121, 122

separated (marital status) *adj* 別れた wakareta / 別居している bekkyo shite iru p101

September *n* 九月 ku gatsu p19

serve, to serve *v* 出す dasu

service *n* サービス sābisu

out of service 非稼働中 hikadocyu

services (religious) *n* 奉仕 hōshi / 礼拝 reihai p109

service charge *n* サービス料 sābisu ryō p67, 116

seven *adj* 七つの nanatsu no p7

seventy *adj* 七十の nana jū no p8

seventeen *adj* 十七の jūshichi no p8

seventh *adj* 七番目の nana ban me no p13

sew, to sew *v* 縫う nuu / 裁縫をする saihō o suru p111

sex (gender) *n* 性別 seibetsu

shallow *adj* 浅い asai

shampoo *n* シャンプー shanpū

sheet (bed linen) *n* シーツ shītsu

shellfish *n* 貝類 kai rui p80

ship *n* 船 fune p59

ship, to ship *v* 船で運ぶ fune de hakobu

How much to ship this to ___? これを___まで船で送るにはいくらかかりますか? kore o ___ made fune de okuru niwa ikura kakari masu ka.

shipwreck *n* 難破船 nanpa sen

shirt *n* シャツ shatsu

shoe *n* 靴 kutsu p43,128

shop *n* 店 mise

shop *v* 買い物をする kaimono o suru p111

I'm shopping for mens' clothes. 紳士服を買いに来ました。shinshi fuku o kai ni kimashita.

I'm shopping for womens' clothes. 婦人服を買いに来ました。fujin fuku o kai ni kimashita.

I'm shopping for childrens' clothes. 子供服を買いに来ました。kodomo fuku o kai ni kimashita.

short *adj* 短い mijikai p15

shorts *n* 半ズボン han zubon p78

shot (liquor) *n* 一杯 ippai

shout *v* 大声で呼ぶ ōgoe de yobu

show (performance) *n* ショー shō

What time is the show?
ショーは何時ですか? shō wa nanji desuka?

show, to show v 見せる miseru

Would you show me? 見せていただけませんか? misete itadake masen ka.

shower n シャワー shawā p65

Does it have a shower? それにはシャワーが付いていますか? sore niwa shawā ga tsuite imasu ka.

shower, to shower v シャワーを浴びる shawā o abiru

shrimp n 海老えび ebi p90

shuttle bus n シャトル バス shatoru basu

sick adj 病気の byōki no

I feel sick. 気分が悪いです。 kibun ga warui desu.

side n 添え物 soe mono

on the side (e.g., salad dressing) 横に添えて yoko ni soete p81

sidewalk n 歩道 hodō

sightseeing n 観光 kankō

sightseeing bus n 観光バス kankō basu

sign, to sign v 署名 shomei

Where do I sign? どこに署名すればいいですか? doko ni shomei sureba ii desu ka.

silk n シルク shiruku p129

silver adj 銀製の gin sei no

sing, to sing v 歌う utau

single (unmarried) adj 独身の dokushin no p101

Are you single? あなたは独身ですか? anata wa dokushin desu ka.

single (one) adj 一つの hitotsu no

single bed シングル ベッド shinguru beddo

sink n 洗面台 senmen dai

sister n 姉妹 shimai / ご姉妹 go shimai p100

sit, to sit v 座る suwaru

six adj 六つの muttsu no p7

sixteen adj 十六の jūroku no p8

sixty adj 六十の rokujū no p8

size (clothing, shoes) n サイズ saizu p129

skin n 皮膚 hifu

sleeping berth n 寝台 shindai

slow adj 遅い osoi

slow, to slow v 速度を落とす sokudo o otosu p56

Slow down! 速度を落としてください! sokudo o otoshite kudasai. p56

slow(ly) adv ゆっくり yukkuri

Speak more slowly. もっとゆっくり話してください。 motto yukkuri hanashite kudasai. p98

slum n スラム街 suramu gai

small adj 小さい chiisai p15

smell, to smell v 匂いをかぐ nioi o kagu

smoke, to smoke v タバコを吸う tabako o suu p145

smoking n 喫煙 kitsu en p36

smoking area 喫煙所 kitsu en jo p36

No Smoking 禁煙 kin en p38

snack n 軽食 keishoku p94

Snake eyes! n スネークアイだ! sunēku ai da.

snorkel n スノーケル sunōkeru

soap n 石鹸 sekken

sock n 靴下 kutsu shita

soda n ソーダ sōda p45

diet soda ダイエットソーダ daietto sōda

soft adj 柔らかい yawarakai

software n ソフトウェア sofuto uea

sold out adj 売り切れ urikire

some adj いくつかの ikutsukano

someone adj 誰か dare ka p44

something n 何か nani ka / 何 nani p78, 80

son n 息子 musuko / 息子さん musuko san p102

song n 歌 uta p146

sorry adj すみません sumi masen.

I'm sorry. すみません。 sumi masen.

soup n スープ sūpu

spa n スパ supa p63

Spain n スペイン supein

Spanish adj スペインの、スペイン人の supein no, supein jin no

ENGLISH–JAPANESE

spare tire n スペアタイヤ supea taiya

speak, to speak v 話す hanasu p2

Do you speak English? 英語を話しますか? eigo o hanashi masu ka. p2

Would you speak louder, please? もっと大きな声で話してください。 motto ōkina koe de hanashite kudasai. / もっと大きな声で話していただけませんか。 motto ōkina koe de hanashite itadake masen ka. p2

Would you speak slower, please? もっとゆっくり話してください。 motto yukkuri hanashite kudasai. / もっとゆっくり話していただけませんか。 motto yukkuri hanashite itadake masen ka. p2

special (featured meal) n スペシャル supesharu

specify, to specify v 具体的に述べる gutai teki ni noberu

speed limit n 制限速度 seigen sokudo p54

What's the speed limit? 制限速度は何キロですか? seigen sokudo wa nan kiro desu ka. p54

speedometer n 速度計 sokudo kei

spell, to spell v つづる tsuzuru p99

How do you spell that? つづりを言ってください。tsuzuri o itte kudasai. / つづりを言ってもらえますか。tsuzuri o itte morae masu ka.

spice n スパイス supaisu

spill, to spill v こぼす kobosu p46

split (gambling) n 分ける wakeru

spoon スプーン supūn p83

sports n スポーツ supōtsu p111

spring (season) n 春 haru p19

stadium n スタジアム sutajiamu p138

staff (employees) n スタッフ sutaffu p76

stamp (postage) n 切手 kitte

stair n 階段 kaidan

Where are the stairs? 階段はどこですか? kaidan wa doko desu ka.

Are there many stairs? 階段の数は多いですか? kaidan no kazu wa ōi desu ka.

stand, to stand v 立つ tatsu

start, to start (commence) v 始まる hajimaru

start, to start (a car) v 発車させる hassha saseru

state n 状況 jōkyō

station n 駅 eki p55, 56, 57, 60

Where is the nearest____? こ こから一番近い____はどこで すか? koko kara ichiban chikai ____ wa doko desu ka.

gas station ガソリン スタンド gasorin sutando

bus station バス停 basu tei

subway station 地下鉄の駅 chikatetsu no eki

train station 駅 eki

stay, to stay v 泊る tomaru / 滞在する taizai suru p67, 103

How long will you be staying? 滞在は何日間です か? taizai wa nan nichi kan desu ka. p41

Where are you staying? どこ に滞在しますか? doko ni taizai shimasu ka. p41

We'll be staying for ____ nights. ____日間滞在する予 定です。____ nichi kan taizai suru yotei desu. p67 For full coverage of numbers, see p7

steakhouse n ステーキ ハウス sutēki hausu p75

steal, to steal v 盗む nusumu

stolen adj 盗まれた nusumareta p47

stop n 駅 eki / 停車駅 teisha eki p57, 58, 61

Is this my stop? ここは私が 降りる駅ですか? koko wa watashi ga oriru eki desu ka.

I missed my stop. 私は乗り過 ごしてしまいました。watashi wa nori sugoshite shimai mashita.

stop, to stop v 停まる tomaru
  Please stop. 停まってくださ
  い。tomatte kudasai.
  STOP (traffic sign) 止まれ
  tomare
  Stop, thief! 止まれ、泥棒!
  tomare, dorobō.
store n 店 mise
straight (hair) adj ストレート
  の sutorēto no p135／直毛
  chokumō
  straight ahead ここをまっすぐ
  koko o massugu p5
  straight (drink) ストレートで
  sutorēto de p81
  **Go straight. (giving
  directions)** まっすぐ行きます。
  massugu ikimasu. p53
straight (gambling) n ストレー
  ト sutorēto
street n 道 michi p6
  across the street この道の向
  こう側 kono michi no mukō
  gawa p6
  down the street この道(の先)
  kono michi (no saki) p6
  Which street? どの道? dono
  michi.
  How many more streets?
  あと何本の道がありますか?
  ato nan bon no michi ga
  arimasuka?
stressed adj ストレスを感じてい
  る sutoresu o kanjite iru
striped adj 縞の shima no
stroller n ベビーカー bebī kā

Do you rent baby strollers?
  ベビーカーはレンタルできま
  すか? bebī kā wa rentaru deki
  masu ka.
substitution n 替わりのもの
  kawari no mono
suburb n 郊外 kōgai
subway n 地下鉄 chikatetsu
  p60
  subway line 地下鉄の路線
  chikatetsu no rosen
  subway station 地下鉄の駅
  chikatetsu no eki
  **Which subway do I take for
  ___?** ___へはどの地下鉄
  で行けばよいですか?___ewa
  dono chikatetsu de ikeba yoi
  desu ka.
subtitle n 字幕 jimaku
suitcase n スーツケース sūtsu
  kēsu p47
suite n スーツ sūtsu
summer n 夏 natsu p19
sun n 太陽 taiyō
sunburn n 日焼け hiyake
  I have a bad sunburn. 私は
  ひどく日焼けしました。watashi
  wa hidoku hiyake shimashita.
Sunday n 日曜日 nichi yō bi
  p17
sunglasses n サングラス
  sangurasu
sunny adj 晴れた hareta
  p105
  It's sunny out. 外は晴れてい
  ます。soto wa harete imasu.
sunroof n サンルーフ san rūfu

sunscreen n 日焼け止めクリーム hiyake dome kurīmu

> **Do you have sunscreen SPF ____?** SPF ____の日焼け止めクリームはありますか? SPF ____ no hiyake dome kurīmu wa arimasu ka.

supermarket n スーパーマーケット sūpā māketto

surf v サーフィンする sāfin suru p142

surfboard n サーフボード sāfu bōdo

suspiciously adv 怪しそうに ayashisō ni / 様子が変 yōsu ga hen p46

swallow, to swallow v 飲み込む nomi komu

sweater n セーター sētā p43, 130

swim, to swim v 泳ぐ oyogu p141

> **Can one swim here?** ここでは泳げますか? koko dewa oyoge masu ka.

swimsuit n 水着 mizugi

swim trunks n 水泳パンツ suiei pantsu

symphony n 交響楽団 kōkyō gakudan

T

table n テーブル tēburu p77

> **table for two** 2人用のテーブル futari yō no tēburu

tailor n 仕立て屋 shitate ya p70

> **Can you recommend a good tailor?** よい仕立て屋を勧めていただけませんか?yoi shitate ya o susumete itadake masen ka.

take, to take v 連れて行く tsureteiku

> **Take me to the station.** 駅まで連れて行ってください。eki made tsurete itte kudasai.

> **How much to take me to ____?** ____まで行くにはいくらかかりますか? ____ made iku niwa ikura kakari masu ka

take out menu n 持ち帰り用のメニュー mochi kaeri yō no menyū

talk, to talk v 話す hanasu

tall adj 高い takai / 背が高い se ga takai

tanned adj 日焼けした hiyake shita

taste (flavor) n 味 aji

taste (discernment) n 好み konomi

taste, to taste v 味見する ajimi suru

tax n 税金 zeikin p67, 132

> **value-added tax (VAT)** 付加価値税 fuka kachi zei p132

taxi n タクシー takushī p38, 55

> **Taxi!** タクシー! takushī.

> **Would you call me a taxi?** タクシーを呼んでいただけませんか? takushī o yonde itadake masen ka.

tea *n* お茶 ocha / 茶 cha **p83**

team *n* チーム chīmu **p138**

Techno *n* テクノ tekuno **p109**

television *n* テレビ terebi

temple *n* 寺院 jiin

ten *adj* 十の jū no **p7**

tennis *n* テニス tenisu
p63

　tennis court テニス コート
　tenisu kōto **p65**

tent *n* テント tento

tenth *adj* 十番目の jū ban me
no **p14**

terminal *n* (airport) ターミナル
tāminaru **p38**

Thank you. どうもありがとう。
dōmo arigatō **p1**

that (near) *adj* その sono

that (far away) *adj* あの ano

theater *n* 劇場 gekijō

them (m / f) *pron* 彼ら (に、を)
karera (ni, o) **p3**

there (demonstrative) *adv* そ
こに soko ni (nearby)、あそこに
asoko ni (far)

　Is / Are there ? ありますか?
　arimasu ka.

　over there あそこに asoko ni

these *adj* これらの korera no
p6

thick *adj* 厚い atsui

thief! 泥棒! dorobō! **p7**

thin *adj* 薄い usui

third *adj* 3番目の san banme no

thirteen *adj* 十三の jū san
no **p8**

thirty *adj* 三十の sanjū no **p8**

this *adj* この kono

those *adj* それらの sorerano

thousand 千 sen **p8**

three 三 san **p7**

thriller スリラー surirā **p112**

Thursday *n* 木曜日 moku yō
bi **p17**

ticket *n* 切符 kippu **p56, 60** / チ
ケット chiketto **p35, 58**

　ticket counter 切符売り場
　kippu uriba / チケットカウン
　ター chiketto kauntā

　one-way ticket 片道切符
　katamichi kippu **p56**

　round-trip ticket 往復切符
　ōfuku kippu **p56**

tight *adj* きつい kitsui

time *n* 時間 jikan

　Is it on time? それは定刻通り
　ですか? sore wa teikoku dōri
　desu ka.

　At what time? 何時に? nan ji
　ni.

　What time is it? 何時ですか?
　nan ji desu ka.

timetable *n* (train) 時刻表
jikoku hyō

tip (gratuity) *n* チップ chippu

tire *n* タイヤ taiya **p52**

　I have a flat tire. タイヤがパ
　ンクしました。taiya ga panku
　shima shita.

tired *adj* 疲れた tsukareta / 疲れ
ている tsukarete iru **p104**

today *n* 今日 kyō

toilet *n* トイレ toire

The toilet is overflowing. トイレの水が溢れているんです。 toire no mizu ga afurete irun desu. p72

The toilet is backed up. トイレがつまっています。 toire ga tsumatte imasu.

toilet paper *n* トイレット ペーパー toiretto pēpā

You're out of toilet paper. トイレット ペーパーがなくなりました。 toiretto pēpā ga naku nari mashita.

toiletries *n* 洗面用品 senmen yōhin p94

toll *n* 使用料 shiyōryō

tomorrow *n* 明日 ashita p4

ton *n* トン ton

too (excessively) *adv* 〜過ぎる 〜sugiru

too (also) *adv* 〜も 〜mo

tooth *n* 歯 ha p152

I lost my tooth. 歯が1本抜けました。 ha ga ippon nuke mashita.

toothache *n* 歯痛 haita

I have a toothache. 歯が痛みます。 ha ga itami masu.

toothbrush *n* 歯ブラシ haburashi p70

toothpaste 歯磨き粉 hamigakiko p70

total *n* 合計 gōkei

What is the total? 合計でいくらですか？ gōkei de ikura desu ka.

tour *n* ツアー tsuā

Are guided tours available? ガイド付きツアーはありますか？ gaido tsuki tsuā wa arimasu ka.

Are audio tours available? 音声ガイド付きツアーはありますか？ onsei gaido tsuki tsuā wa arimasu ka.

towel *n* タオル taoru

May we have more towels? もっとタオルをいただけますか？ motto taoru o itadake masu ka.

toy *n* おもちゃ omocha

toy store *n* おもちゃ屋 omocha ya

Do you have any toys for the children? 子供のおもちゃはありますか？ kodomo no omocha wa arimasu ka.

traffic *n* 交通 kōtsū

How's traffic? 交通状態はどうですか？ kōtsū jōtai wa dō desu ka.

traffic rules 交通規則 kōtsū kisoku

trail *n* 登山道 tozan dō / トレイル toreiru p139, 140

Are there trails? 登山道はありますか？ tozan dō wa arimasuka.

train *n* 列車 ressha / 電車 densha p55, 56

express train 特急列車 tokkyū ressha

local train 普通列車 futsū ressha

Does the train go to ____? この電車は____へ行きますか? kono densha wa ____ e ikimasu ka.

May I have a train schedule? 電車の時刻表をいただけますか? densha no jikokuhyō o itadake masu ka.

Where is the train station? 駅はどこにありますか? eki wa doko ni arimasuka.

train, to train v 訓練する kunren suru

transfer, to transfer v 移す utsusu

I need to transfer funds. 振込したいのですが。furikomi shitai no desuga.

transmission n 変速機 hensoku ki

automatic transmission オートマチック ōto machikku

standard transmission マニュアル manyuaru

travel, to travel v 旅行する ryokō suru p40, 42

trim, to trim (hair) v 切りそろえる kiri soroeru / そろえる soroeru p135

trip n 旅行 ryokō p97

triple adj 3 倍の san bai no adj triple

trumpet n トランペット tranpetto

trunk n 旅行カバン ryokō kaban / 荷物 nimotsu (luggage) p47 トランク toranku (in car)

try, to try (attempt) v 試す tamesu

try, to try on (clothing) v 試着する shichaku suru

try, to try (food) v 試食する shishoku suru

Tuesday n 火曜日 ka yō bi p17

turkey n 七面鳥 shichimenchō

turn, to turn v 曲がる magaru p53

to turn left / right 左 / 右に曲がる hidari / migi ni magaru p53

to turn off / on 消す / 付ける kesu / tsukeru

twelve adj 十二の jūni no p8

twenty adj 二十の nijū no p8

twine n 麻ひも asa himo / ひも himo p122

two adj 二つの futatsu no p12

U

umbrella n 傘 kasa f

uncle n おじ oji / おじさん ojisan p100

undercooked adj 完全に煮えていない kanzen ni niete iai

understand, to understand v 理解する rikai suru

I don't understand. わかりません。wakari masen. p2, 98

Do you understand? わかりますか? wakari masu ka.

underwear n 下着 shitagi

university n 大学 daigaku

up *adv* 上に ue ni p5

update, to update *v* 更新する kōshin suru

upgrade *n* アップグレード appugurēdo p49

upload, to upload *v* アップロードする appurōdo suru p120

upscale *adj* 高級な kōkyūna

Uruguayan *adj* ウルグアイの、ウルグアイ人の uruguai no, uruguai jin no

us *pron* 私達(に、を) watashi tachi (ni, o) p3

USB port *n* USB ポート USB pōto

use, to use *v* 使う tsukau

V

vacation *n* バケーション bakēshon / 休暇 kyūka p43

　on vacation 休暇で kyūka de

　to go on vacation バケーションに出かける bakēshon ni dekakeru

vacancy *n* 空き室 aki shitsu

van *n* バン ban

VCR *n* ビデオデッキ bideo dekki

　Do the rooms have VCRs? 部屋にはビデオデッキが置いてありますか? heya niwa bideo dekki ga oite arimasu ka.

vegan *adj* ベーガン料理 bēgan ryōri

vegetable *n* 野菜 yasai

vegetarian *n* ベジタリアン bejitarian p40

vending machine *n* 自動販売機 jidō hanbai ki

Venezuelan *adj* ベネズエラの、ベネズエラ人の benezuera no, benezuera jin no

version *n* バージョン bājon

very *adv* とても totemo p73, 74

video *n* ビデオ bideo

　Where can I rent videos or DVDs? DVD またはビデオはどこで借りられますか? DVD matawa bideo wa doko de karirare masu ka.

view *n* 眺め nagame

　beach view ビーチの眺め bīchi no nagame

　city view 市街の眺め shigai no nagame

vineyard *n* ぶどう園 budō en

vinyl *n* ビニール binīru p47

violin *n* バイオリン baiorin

visa *n* ビザ biza

　Do I need a visa? ビザが必要ですか? biza ga hitsuyō desu ka.

vision *n* 視力 shiryoku

visit, to visit *v* 訪ねる tazuneru

visually-impaired *adj* 視覚障害の shikaku shōgai no

　What is the purpose of your visit? 訪問の目的は何ですか? hōmon no mokuteki wa nani desu ka. p41

vodka *n* ウオッカ uokka p82

voucher *n* 利用券 riyōken p42

W

wait, to wait *v* 待つ matsu p77

Please wait. どうかお待ちください。dōka omachi kudasai.

How long is the wait? どのくらい待ちますか? dono kurai machi masu ka. p77

waiter *n* ウエイター ueitā

waiting area *n* 待合室 machiai shitu p35

wake-up call *n* ウェークアップコール ueku appu kōru

wallet *n* 財布 saifu p44

I lost my wallet. 私は財布を失くしました。watashi wa saifu o nakushi mashita.

Someone stole my wallet. 誰かに財布を盗まれました。dareka ni saifu o nusumare mashita. p44

walk, to walk *v* 歩く aruku

walker (ambulatory device) *n* 歩行器 hokōki p41

walkway *n* 歩道 hodō

moving walkway 自動移動通路 jidō idō tsūro

want, to want *v* 欲しい hoshii

war *n* 戦争 sensō p108

warm *adj* 暖かい atatakai p107

watch, to watch *v* 観察する kansatsu suru

water *n* 水 mizu p45

Is the water potable? この水は飲めますか? kono mizu wa nome masu ka.

Is there running water? ここに水道水はありますか? koko ni suidōsui wa arimasu ka. p74

wave, to wave *v* 振る furu

waxing *n* ワックス wakkusu

weapon *n* 武器 buki

wear, to wear *v* 着る kiru

weather forecast *n* 天気予報 tenki yohō

web designer ウェッブデザイナー webbu dezainā p105

Wednesday *n* 水曜日 sui yō bi p17

week *n* 週 shū p4

this week 今週 konshū

last week 先週 senshū

next week 来週 raishū

weigh *v* 重い omoi

I weigh ____. 私は体重が ____ あります。watashi wa taijyū ga ____ arimasu.

It weighs ____. これは____の重さがあります。kore wa ____ no omosa ga arimasu. See p7 for numbers.

weights *n* 重さ omosa

welcome *adv* ようこそ yōkoso

You're welcome. どういたしまして。dō itashi mashite.

well *adv* よく yoku

well done (meat) ウェル ダン weru dan

well done (task) よくやった yoku yatta

I don't feel well. 気分がよくありません。kibun ga yoku arimasen.

western *adj* ウェスタンの uesutan no

whale *n* 鯨 kujira

what *adv* 何の nan no / 何 nani p2

What sort of ____? どんな種 類の____? donna shurui no ____.

What time is ____? ____は何 時? ____ wa nan ji. p16

wheelchair *n* 車椅子 kuruma isu p41

wheelchair access 車椅子で のアクセス kurumaisu deno akusesu

wheelchair ramp 車椅子用ス ロープ kuruma isu yō surōpu

power wheelchair 電動車椅 子 dendō kuruma isu

wheeled (luggage) *adj* 車輪付 き sharin tsuki

when *adv* いつ itsu p3
See p2 for questions.

where *adv* どこ doko p3

Where is it? それはどこにあ りますか? sore wa doko ni arimasu ka.

which *adv* どれ dore p3

Which one? どっち? docchi

white *adj* 白い shiroi

white (Caucasian) 白人 haku jin

who *adv* 誰 dare p2

whose *adj* 誰の dare no

wide *adj* 広い hiroi p16

widow, widower *n* 未亡人 mibō jin, やもめ yamome p101

wife *n* 妻 tsuma / 奥さん okusan p102

wi-fi *n* ワイファイ wai fai

window *n* 窓 mado

windshield *n* フロントガラス furonto garasu

windshield wiper *n* ワイパー waipā

windy *adj* 風が強い kaze ga tsuyoi p115

wine *n* ワイン wain p45

winter *n* 冬 fuyu p19

wiper *n* ワイパー waipā

with ____ *prep* ____と一緒に ____ to issho ni

withdraw *v* 引く hiku

I need to withdraw money. お金を引き出したいのです が。okane o hiki dashi tai no desuga.

without____ *prep* ____なしで ____nashi de

woman *n* 女性 josei

work, to work *v* 機能する kinō suru

This doesn't work. これは 機能しません。kore wa kinō shimasen.

workout *n* ワークアウト wāku auto

worse than ____ ____よりも悪 い ____yori mo warui

worst *adj* 最悪 sai aku

write, to write *v* 書く kaku

Would you write that down for me? 紙に書いていただけますか？ kami ni kaite itadakemasu ka.

writer *n* 作家 sakka p104

X

x-ray machine *n* レントゲン rentogen

Y

yellow *adj* 黄色い kiiroi

Yes. *adv* はい。hai.

yesterday *n* 昨日 kinō p4

the day before yesterday おととい ototoi p4

yield sign *n* 優先標識 yūsen hyōshiki

you *pron* あなた、あなた達 anata, anata tachi p3

your, yours *adj* あなたの、あなた達の anata no, anata tachi no

young *adj* 若い wakai p102

Z

zoo *n* 動物園 dōbutsu en p113

A

abura 油 *oil* n p80, 83

adaputā アダプター *adapter* n p70, 134

adaputā puragu アダプター プラグ *adapter plug* n

afurete あふれて *overflowing* adv

afurika kei amerika jin no アフリカ系アメリカ人の *African-American* adj

ageru あげる *give, to give* v

ahiru アヒル *duck* n

ai suru 愛する *love, to love* v

ai suru 愛する *to love (family)*

ai suru 愛する *to love (a friend)*

ai suru 愛する *to love (a lover)*

ai 愛 *love* n

airurando no, airurando jin no アイルランドの、アイルランド人の *Irish* adj

airurando アイルランド *Ireland* n

aji 味 *taste (flavor)* n

ajia no, ajia jin no アジアの、アジア人の *Asian* adj

ajimi suru 味見する *taste, to taste* v

aka chan no 赤ちゃんの *baby* adj

bebī fūdo wa utte imasu ka. ベビー フードは売っていますか? *Do you sell baby food?*

aka chan 赤ちゃん p102 / bebī ベビー *baby* n

aka no 赤の *red* adj

akage 赤毛 *redhead* n

akarui 明るい *bright* adj

aki shitsu 空き室 *vacancy* n

aki 秋 *autumn / fall (season)* n p19

akushon eiga アクション映画 *action films* n p112

akiraka ni suru 明らかにする *clear* v

ame ga furu 雨が降る *rain, to rain* v

ame ga furu yotei desuka. 雨が降る予定ですか? *Is it supposed to rain?*

ame no 雨の *rainy* adj

ame desu. 雨です。 *It's rainy.*

amerika no, amerika jin no アメリカの、アメリカ人の *American* adj

an nai jo 案内所 *information booth* n

an nai suru 案内する *guide, to guide* v

anata no, anata tachi no あなたの、あなた達の *your, yours* adj

anata, anata tachi あなた、あなた達 *you* pron p3

ano あの *that (far away)* adj

anzen na 安全な *safe (secure)* adj

kono chiiki wa anzen desu ka. この地域は安全ですか? *Is this area safe?*

ao jiroi 青白い *pale* adj

aoi 青い *blue* adj

appugurēdo アップグレード *upgrade* n p51

appurōdo suru アップロードする *upload, to upload* v p120

are v See be, to be.

arerugī taishitsu no アレルギー体
質の / arerugī han nō noアレ
ルギー反応の allergic adj

watashi wa ____ ni arerugī ga
arimasu. 私は____にアレル
ギーがあります。 I'm allergic
to ____ p80,152. See p80
and p152 for common
allergens.

arukōru inryō アルコール飲料
alcoholic drink n

arukōru wa dashite imasu ka.
アルコールは出していますか?
Do you serve alcohol?

arukōru nuki no bīru o kudasai.
アルコール抜きのビールをくだ
さい。 I'd like nonalcoholic
beer.

aruku 歩く walk, to walk v

aruminiumu アルミニウム
aluminum n

aruzenchin no, aruzenchin jin no
アルゼンチンの、アルゼンチン
人の Argentinian adj

asa himo 麻ひも / himo ひも
twine n p122

asa 朝 / gozen 午前 morning n
p17, 70

asatte あさって the day after
tomorrow p4

gozen 午前 in the morning

asai 浅い shallow adj

ashi 脚 leg n

ashi, futto 足、フット foot (body
part, measurement) n

ashita 明日 tomorrow n p4

asobi ba 遊び場 playground n

asobi ba wa arimasu ka. 遊び場
はありますか? Do you have
a playground?

asupirin アスピリン aspirin n
p147

atarashii 新しい new adj

atatakai 暖かい warm adj p107

ATM ki ATM 機 ATM n

ATM ki o sagashite imasu.
ATM 機を探しています。 I'm
looking for an ATM.

ato de あとで later adv

soreja, mata ato de. それじゃ、ま
た後で。 See you later.

atsui 厚い thick adj

atsui 熱い hot adj

atsukau 扱う handle,
to handle v

atsumeru 集める collect,
to collect v

ayashisō ni 怪しそうに / yōsu ga
hen 様子が変 suspiciously
adv p46

B

bā バー bar n

baikingu バイキング buffet n

baiku バイク motorcycle n

baiorin バイオリン violin n

bājon バージョン version n

bakēshon / 休暇 kyūka バケーシ
ョン vacation n p43

kyūka de 休暇で on vacation
bakēshon ni dekakeru バケー
ションに出かける to go on
vacation

bakkin 罰金 *fine (for traffic violation)* n p54, 153

bakudan 爆弾 *bomb* n

ban バン *van* n

bangō annai 番号案内 *directory assistance (phone)* n

bara バラ *rose* n

baransu o toru バランスを取る *balance* v

barukonī バルコニー *balcony* n p65

basu バス *bass (instrument)* n

basu バス *bus* n p55, 57

basu tei wa doko ni arimasu ka. バス停はどこにありますか? *Where is the bus stop?*

_____ **yuki no basu wa dore desu ka.** _____行きのバスはどれですか。 *Which bus goes to _____?* p58

batā バター *butter* n p81, 83

batterī バッテリー *battery (for car)* n

bebī beddo ベビーベッド *crib* n p66

bebī kā ベビーカー *stroller* n

bebī kā wa rentaru deki masu ka. ベビーカーはレンタルできますか。 *Do you rent baby strollers?*

bebī shittā ベビーシッター *babysitter* n

eigo o hanasu bebī shittā wa imasu ka. 英語を話すベビーシッターはいますか? *Do you have babysitters who speak English?*

beddo ベッド *bed* n p64, 66

bēgan ryōri ベーガン料理 *vegan* adj

bejitarian ベジタリアン *vegetarian* n p42

benezuera no, benezuera jin no ベネズエラの、ベネズエラ人の *Venezuelan* adj

bengo shi 弁護士 *lawyer* n p104

benpi shita 便秘した *constipated* adj

benpi shite imasu. 便秘しています。 *I'm constipated.*

berī weru de ベリーウェルで *charred (meat)* adj p79

beruto ベルト *belt* n p130

beruto konbeyā ベルトコンベヤー *conveyor belt*

betsu no 別の *another* adj

bīchi ni noriageru ビーチに乗り上げる *beach* v

bīchi ビーチ *beach* n p63, 65, 113

bideo dekki ビデオデッキ *VCR* n

heya niwa bideo dekki ga oite arimasu ka. 部屋にはビデオデッキが置いてありますか? *Do the rooms have VCRs?*

bideo ビデオ *video* n

DVD matawa bideo wa doko de karirare masu ka. DVDまたはビデオはどこで借りられますか? *Where can I rent videos or DVDs?*

bijinesu ビジネス *business* n p42, 102

bijutsu kan 美術館 *museum n* p113, 127

bin ビン *bottle n*

dokoka de kono bin (honyubin) o atatameru koto ga deki masu ka. どこかでこのビン (哺乳瓶) を温めることができますか? *May I heat this (baby) bottle someplace?*

binīru ビニール *vinyl n* p47

biriyādo ビリヤード *pool (the game) n*

bīru ビール *beer n* p45, 82, 145

nama bīru 生ビール *beer on tap* p145

biza ビザ *visa n*

biza ga hitsuyō desu ka. ビザが必要ですか? *Do I need a visa?*

bōi furendo ボーイフレンド *boyfriend n* p100

bokkusu seki ボックス席 / bokkusu sīto ボックスシート p138 *box (seat) n*

boribia no, boribia jin no ボリビアの、ボリビア人の *Bolivian adj*

bōru ボール *ball (sport) n*

bōshi 帽子 *hat n*

bōto ボート *boat n*

boyaketa ぼやけた *blurry adj* p150

bubun 部分 *portion n*

budō en ぶどう園 *vineyard n*

budō ぶどう *grape n*

bujoku suru 侮辱する *insult v*

buki 武器 *weapon n*

bukkyōto 仏教徒 *Buddhist n* p108

burandē ブランデー *brandy n* p82

burausu ブラウス *blouse n* p129

burēki o kakeru ブレーキをかける *brake v*

burēki ブレーキ *brake n* p52

hijō burēki 非常ブレーキ *emergency brake*

burīchi ブリーチ *bleach n*

burīfu kēsu ブリーフケース *briefcase n* p47

burogu o kaku ブログを書く *blogging v* p110

burōdo bando ブロードバンド *broadband n*

buronzu sei no ブロンズ製の *bronze adj*

burunetto ブルネット *brunette n*

byōki no 病気の *sick adj*

kibun ga warui desu. 気分が悪いです。*I feel sick.*

C

CD *CD n* p49

CD purēyā CD プレーヤー *CD player n* p49

cha iro no 茶色の *brown adj*

chairudo shīto チャイルドシート *car seat (child's safety seat) n*

chairudo shīto o rentaru shite imasu ka. チャイルドシートをレンタルしていますか? *Do you rent car seats for children?*

chakuriku suru 着陸する / tsuku 着く *land, to land v* p45

chātā suru チャーターする
charter, to charter v

chekku auto suru チェックアウト
する *check out, to check
out* v

chekku auto チェックアウト
check-out n

chekku auto no jikan チェックア
ウトの時間 *check-out time*

chekku auto wa nan ji desu ka.
チェックアウトは何時ですか?
What time is check-out?

chekku in チェックイン *check-in*
n p35

chekku in wa nan ji desu ka.
チェックインは何時ですか?
What time is check-in?

onrain chekku in wa deki masu
ka. オンラインチェックインはで
きますか? *Is online check-in
available?*

chekku no チェックの *checked
(pattern)* adj

chichi 父 / otōsan お父さん
father n p100

chihō no 地方の *local* adj p50

chiisai 小さい *little* adj (size)
sukoshi、少し *(amount)*

chiisai 小さい *small* adj p15

chikai 近い *close (near)* p5

chikaku ni 近くに *nearby* adj
p76

chikatetsu 地下鉄 *subway* n
p60

chikatetsu no rosen 地下鉄の路
線 *subway line*

chikatetsu no eki 地下鉄の駅
subway station

_____ ewa dono chikatetsu de
ikeba yoi desu ka. _____へど
の地下鉄で行けばよいですか?
*Which subway do I take
for _____?*

chiketto uriba チケット売り場
box office n

chikin チキン *chicken* n

chīmu チーム *team* n p138

chippu チップ *tip (gratuity)*

chīzu チーズ *cheese* n p95

chizu 地図 *map* n p53

chōkaku shōgai no 聴覚障害の
hearing-impaired adj

chōkoku 彫刻 *sculpture* n

chōshoku 朝食 *breakfast* n p67

chōshoku wa nan ji desu ka. 朝
食は何時ですか? *What time
is breakfast?*

chōwa suru 調和する *match, to
match* v

kono _____ wa watashi no fuku
to aimasu ka? この_____は私
の服と合いますか *Does this
_____ match my outfit?*

chūgoku no, chūgoku jin no 中
国の、中国人の *Chinese* adj
p106

chūkan no 中間の *middle* adj

chūmon suru 注文する *order, to
order (demand)* v

chūsha suru 駐車する *park, to
park* v

chūsha kinshi 駐車禁止 *no
parking* p54

chūsha ryōkin 駐車料金
parking fee p54

shako 車庫 *parking garage* p56

chūshoku 昼食 / ranchi ランチ *lunch* n p76

D

daburu no ダブルの *double adj* p64

daburu beddo ダブル ベッド *double bed* p64

nijū eizō 二重映像 *double vision*

daigaku 大学 *college* n

daigaku 大学 *university* n

daigeki jō 大劇場 *coliseum* n

daku 抱く *hold, to hold* v

te o nigiru 手を握る *to hold hands*

kore o motte itadakemasen ka. これを持っていただけませんか? *Would you hold this for me?*

dansei no 男性の *male adj*

dansei 男性 *male* n

dantai 団体 *party* n

dare ka 誰か *someone* n p37, 44

dare no 誰の *whose adj*

dare 誰 *who adv* p2

dāsu ダース *dozen* n p15

dasu 出す *serve, to serve* v

de aru である *be, to be (temporary state, condition, mood)* v

de nai でない *no adv*

deguchi 出口 *exit* n p38

deguchi nashi 出口なし *not an exit*

dekiru できる *able, to be able to (can)* v

dekiru できる *can (able to)* v

denchi 電池 *battery (for flashlight)* n

denki setsuzoku bu 電気接続部 *electrical hookup* n p74

denki 伝記 *memoirs* n p112

denwa no 電話の *phone adj*

denwa chō wa arimasu ka. 電話帳はありますか? *Do you have a phone directory?*

denwa o kakeru 電話をかける / daiyaru suru ダイヤルする *dial (a phone)* v p118

chokutsū bangō ni kakeru 直通番号にかける *dial direct*

denwa 電話 *phone call* n

korekuto kōru o shitai no desuga. コレクト コールをしたいのですが。 *I need to make a collect phone call.*

kokusai denwa 国際電話 *an international phone call*

denwa 電話 *phone* n p65

anata no denwa bangō o oshiete itadake masu ka. あなたの電話番号を教えていただけますか? *May I have your phone number?*

kōshū denwa wa doko ni arimasu ka. 公衆電話はどこにありますか? *Where can I find a public phone?*

denwa operêtā 電話オペレーター *phone operator* n

puripeido denwa o utte imasu ka. プリペイド電話を売っていますか? *Do you sell prepaid phones?*

deru 出る *exit v*

dezainā デザイナー *designer n* p104

dezāto デザート *dessert n*

  dezāto no menyū デザートのメニュー *dessert menu* p84

do yō bi 土曜日 *Saturday n* p17

doa ドア *door n*

dorobō! 泥棒! *Thief*

dōbutsu en 動物園 *zoo n* p113

dōbutsu 動物 *animal n*

  bijutsu hin no tenji 美術品の展示 *exhibit of art*

doitsu no, doitsu jin no ドイツの、ドイツ人の *German adj*

doko demo どこでも *anywhere adv*

doko どこ *where adv* p3

  sore wa doko ni arimasu ka. それはどこにありますか? *Where is it?*

dokushin no 独身の *single (unmarried) adj* p101

  anata wa dokushin desu ka? あなたは独身ですか? *Are you single?*

dokyumentarī eiga ドキュメンタリー映画 *documentary films n* p112

dōmo arigatō どうもありがとう。 *Thank you.* p1

dorai kurīnā ドライ クリーナー *dry cleaner n*

dorai kurīningu ドライ クリーニング *dry cleaning n*

dorama ドラマ *drama (movie) n* p112

doramu ドラム *drum n*

dore どれ *which adv* p3

  docchi どっち? *Which one?*

doressingu ドレッシング *dressing (salad) n*

doresu ドレス *dress (garment) n*

dōro heisa chū 道路閉鎖中 *road closed sign n* p54

dōro 道路 *road n*

dorobō! 泥棒! *Thief! n* p7

doru ドル *dollar n*

dōsei no 銅製の *copper adj*

dōzo どうぞ *please (polite entreaty) adv*

DVD DVD *n* p49

  sono heya niwa DVD purēyā ga arimasu ka. その部屋にはDVD プレーヤーがありますか? *Do the rooms have DVD players?*

  DVD matawa bideo wa doko de karirare masu ka. DVD またはビデオはどこで借りられますか? *Where can I rent DVDs or videos?*

E

E mēru Eメール *e-mail n* p114

  anata no E mēru adoresu o itadake masu ka. あなたのEメールアドレスをいただけますか? *May I have your e-mail address?*

  ii mēru messēji Eメール メッセージ *e-mail message*

e 絵 *drawing (work of art), painting n*

ebi えび *shrimp* n p90

eiga kan 映画館 *cinema* n

eiga 映画 *movie* n p111, 112, 124

eigyō chū 営業中 *open (business)* adj

eigyō shite imasu ka. 営業していますか? *Are you open?*

eki 駅 / teisha eki 停車駅 *stop* n p54, 57, 61

koko wa watashi ga oriru eki desu ka. ここは私が降りる駅ですか? *Is this my stop?*

watashi wa nori sugoshite shimai mashita. 私は乗り過ごしてしまいました。 *I missed my stop.*

eki 駅 *station* n p55, 56, 57, 60

koko kara ichiban chikai ____ wa doko desu ka. ここから一番近い____はどこですか? *Where is the nearest ____?*

gasorin sutando ガソリン スタンド *gas station*

basu tei バス停 *bus station*

chikatetsu no eki 地下鉄の駅 *subway station*

eki 駅 *train station*

ekonomī エコノミー *economy* n

ekuadoru no, ekuadoru jin no エクアドルの、エクアドル人の *Ecuadorian* adj

enjin エンジン *engine* n p52

enjinia エンジニア *engineer* n p104

enseki 縁石 *curb* n

ensō suru 演奏する / hiku 弾く *play, to play (an instrument)* v p110

ensō 演奏 *band (musical ensemble)* n p144

erebētā エレベーター *elevator* n p61, 66

esa えさ *bait* n

esukarētā エスカレーター *escalator* n

esupuresso エスプレッソ *espresso* n

F

fittonesu sentā フィットネス センター / jimu ジム *fitness center* n p65

fōku フォーク *fork* n p83

fujinka i 婦人科医 *gynecologist* n

fukachiron no 不可知論の *agnostic* adj

fukai 深い *deep* adj

fukuro ni ireru 袋に入れる *bag* v

fukuro 袋 *bag* n

hikōki yoi no fukuro 飛行機酔いの袋 *airsickness bag* p46

watashi no baggu ga nusumare mashita. 私のバッグが盗まれました。 *My bag was stolen.*

watashi wa baggu o nakushi mashita. 私はバッグを失くしました。 *I lost my bag.*

fukusō 服装 *dress (general attire)* n

fukusō no kisoku wa nan desu ka. 服装の規則は何ですか？ *What's the dress code?*

fun 分 *minute n*

sugu ni すぐに *in a minute*

funa yoi 船酔い *seasick adj p59*

funa yoi shimashita. 船酔いしました。 *I am seasick.*

funa yoi ni kiku kusuri 船酔いに効く薬 *seasickness pill n*

fune de hakobu 船で運ぶ *ship, to ship v*

kore o ＿＿＿ made fune de okuru niwa ikura kakari masu ka? これを＿＿＿まで船で送るにはいくらかかりますか？ *How much to ship this to ＿＿＿?*

fune 船 *ship n p59*

furaito フライト / ＿＿bin ＿＿便 *flight n p37*

kokunai sen no tōchaku / shuppatsu basho wa doko desu ka. 国内線の到着/出発場所はどこですか？ *Where do domestic flights arrive / depart?*

kokusai sen no tōchaku / shuppatsu basho wa doko desu ka. 国際線の到着/出発場所はどこですか？ *Where do international flights arrive / depart?*

kono furaito wa nan ji ni shuppatsu shimasu ka. このフライトは何時に出発しますか？ *What time does this flight leave?*

furansu no, furansu jin no フランスの、フランス人の *French adj*

furasshu フラッシュ *flush (gambling) n*

furikomi 振り込み *money transfer*

furu hausu. フル ハウス！ *Full house!*

furu 振る *wave, to wave v*

furui 古い *old adj*

furumau 振る舞う *behave v*

furūto フルート *flute n*

furūtsu jūsu フルーツ ジュース *fruit juice n*

futatsu no 二つの *two adj p7*

fūtō 封筒 *envelope n p122*

futotta 太った *fat adj p16*

fuyu 冬 *winter n p19*

G

gādo ガード *guard n*

gaido bukku ガイドブック *guide (publication) n*

gaido tsuki tuā ガイド付きツアー *guided tour n*

gaido ガイド *guide (of tours) n*

gakkō 学校 *school n*

gakunen 学年 *grade (school) n*

garon ガロン *gallon n p15*

gāru furendo ガールフレンド *girlfriend n p100*

gasorin ガソリン *gas n p52*

nenryō kei 燃料計 *gas gauge*

gasorin ga haitte inai ガソリン が入っていない *out of gas*

geijutsu ka 美術家 *n artist*

geijutsu no 芸術の *art adj*

geki no kyakuhon 劇の脚本 *drama n*

gekijō 劇場 *theater n*

gengo 言語 *language n*

genki na 元気な *fine* p1

watashi wa genki desu. 私は元 気です。 *I'm fine.*

genkin ni kaeru 現金に換える *cash, to cash v*

seisan suru 清算する *to cash out (gambling)*

genkin 現金 *cash n*

genkin nomi 現金のみ *cash only* p54

geri 下痢 *diarrhea n* p148

gēto ゲート *gate (at airport) n* p34

getsu yō bi 月曜日 *Monday n* p17

getsugaku ryōkin 月額料金 *monthly rate* p49

gin sei no 銀製の *silver adj*

ginkō 銀行 *bank n* p115

ginkō wa doko ni aruka oshiete itadake masu ka. 銀行はどこ にあるか教えていただけます か? *Can you help me find a bank?*

girisha no, girisha jin no ギリシャ の、ギリシャ人の *Greek adj*

girisha seikyō no ギリシャ正教の *Greek Orthodox adj* p108

gishi 義歯 *denture n*

gishi 義歯 *denture plate*

gitā ギター *guitar n* p110

go banme no 五番目の *fifth adj*

go gatsu 五月 *May (month) n* p19

gogo 午後 *afternoon n* p17

gogo ni 午後に *in the afternoon*

gojū no 五十の *fifty adj* p8

gōkei 合計 *total n*

合計でいくらですか? gōkei de ikura desu ka. *What is the total?*

gōru kīpā ゴールキーパー *goalie n*

gōru ゴール *goal (sport) n*

gorufu o suru ゴルフをする *golf, to go golfing v*

gorufu renshū jō ゴルフ練習場 *driving range n*

gorufu ゴルフ *golf n*

guatemara no, guatemara jin no グアテマラの、グアテマラ人の *Guatemalan adj*

gun 軍 *military n*

guramu グラム *gram n*

gurasu グラス *glass* p79, 84

gurasu de arimasuka. グラスで ありますか? *Do you have it by the glass?*

gurasu de hitotsu onegai shimasu. グラスで一つお願いし ます。 *I'd like a glass please.*

guruten nuki no ryōri グルテン 抜きの料理 *gluten-free adj* p40, 80

gurūpu グループ *group n*

gutai teki ni noberu 具体的に述 べる *specify, to specify v*

gyūnyū 牛乳 / miruku ミルク
milk n p83

miruku sēki ミルクセーキ
milk shake

H

ha 歯 *tooth* n p152

ha ga ippon nuke mashita.
歯が1本抜けました。*I lost
my tooth.*

ha ni kabusete iru mono
歯にかぶせているもの *crown
(dental)* n

haburashi 歯ブラシ *toothbrush*
n p70

hābu ハーブ *herb* n

hachi banme no 8番目の
eighth n

hachi gatsu 八月 *August* n
p19

hachi jū 八十 *eighty* n p8

hachi ハチ *bee* n

hachi ni sasare mashita. ハチに
刺されました。*I was stung
by a bee.*

hachi 八 *eight* n p7

haha 母 / okāsan お母さん
mother n p100

hai iro no 灰色の *gray* adj

hai. はい。*Yes.* adv

haikingu o suru ハイキングをする
hike, to hike v

hairaito ハイライト *highlights
(hair)* n p135

hairu 入る *enter, to enter* v

shinyū kinshi 進入禁止 *Do
not enter.*

haisha 歯医者 *dentist* n p149

haisui 排水 *drain* n

haita 歯痛 *toothache* n

ha ga itami masu. 歯が痛みま
す。*I have a toothache.*

hajimaru 始まる *begin, start, to
start (commence)* v p125

hakike 吐き気 *nausea* n p148

haku jin 白人 *white
(person)* n

hamaki 葉巻 *cigar* n

hamigakiko 歯磨き粉
toothpaste n p70

han zubon 半ズボン *shorts*
n p78

hana 花 *flower* n

hana 鼻 *nose* n p136

hanasu 話す *speak, to
speak* v p2

eigo o hanashi masu ka? 英語
を話しますか？*Do you speak
English?* p2

motto ōkina koe de hanashite
kudasai. もっと大きな声で話し
てください。/ motto ōkina koe
de hanashite itadake masen
ka. もっと大きな声で話してい
ただけませんか。*Would you
speak louder, please?* p2

motto yukkuri hanashite
kudasai. もっとゆっくり話し
てください。/ motto yukkuri
hanashite itadake masen ka.
もっとゆっくり話していただけ
ませんか。*Would you speak
slower, please?* p2

hanasu 話す *talk, to talk* v

hanbai in 販売員 *salesperson*
n p104

hanbun 半分 *half* n

ni bun no ichi 二分の一 *one-half*

hangā ハンガー *hanger* n

hanka gai 繁華街 *downtown* n p128

hansamu na ハンサムな *handsome* adj p102

hareta 晴れた *sunny* adj p105

soto wa harete imasu. 外は晴れています。*It's sunny out.*

haru 春 *spring (season)* n p19

hashi 橋 / burijji ブリッジ ha no kyōsei burijji 歯の矯正ブリッジ *bridge (across a river / dental)* n

hashiru 走る *run, to run* v

hassha saseru 発車させる *start, to start (a car)* v

hayai 早い *early* adj p17

hayai desu. 早いです。*It's early.*

hayai 速い *fast* adj

hazukashii 恥ずかしい *embarrassed* adj

heā doraiyā ヘアードライヤー *hair dryer* n p71

heā doressā ヘアードレッサー *hairdresser* n

heā katto ヘアーカット *haircut* n

kami no ke o kiri tai no desuga. 髪の毛を切りたいのですが。*I need a haircut.*

katto wa ikura desuka. カットはいくらですか? *How much is a haircut?*

heddo hōn ヘッドホーン *headphones* n

heddo raito ヘッドライト *headlight* n

hekomu へこむ *dent* v

kare / kanojo ga kuruma o hekomase mashita. 彼 / 彼女が車をへこませました。*He / She dented the car.*

hekutāru ヘクタール *hectare* n p14

henkandekiru 変換できる *convertible* n

henpin suru 返品する *return, to return (something to a store)* v p134

henshū sha 編集者 *editor* n p104

hensoku ki 変速機 *transmission* n

ōto machikku オートマチック *automatic transmission*

manyuaru マニュアル *standard transmission*

heya 部屋 *room (hotel)* n

hitori / futari beya 1人 / 2人部屋 *room for one / two*

rūmu sābisu ルームサービス *room service*

hi 日 *day* n

ototoi おととい *the day before yesterday* p4

koko nisan nichi ここ 2 - 3日 *these last few days*

hi 火 *light (for cigarette)* n p146

hi o kashima shō ka. 火を貸しましょうか? *May I offer you a light?*

raitā ライター *lighter (cigarette)* n

hibi ware ヒビ割れ *crack (in glass object)* n

hidari no 左の *left* adj p5

hidari ni 左に *on the left*

hifu 皮膚 *skin* n

hifu ka i 皮膚科医 *dermatologist* n p149

hige ひげ *beard* n

hijō burēki 非常ブレーキ *emergency brake* n

hijō deguchi 非常出口 *emergency exit* n p40

hikōki no jōmuin 飛行機の乗務員 *flight attendant*

hikōki yoi no fukuro 飛行機酔いの袋 *airsickness bag* n p46

hiku 引く *pull, to pull* v p38

hiku 引く *withdraw* v

okane o hiki dashi tai no desuga. お金を引き出したいのですが。*I need to withdraw money.*

hikui 低い *low* adj

hinin 避妊 *birth control* n

hinin yaku ga nakunari mashita. 避妊薬がなくなりました。*I'm out of birth control pills.*

motto hinin yaku ga hitsuyō desu. もっと避妊薬が必要です。*I need more birth control pills.*

hinzū kyō no, hinzū jin no ヒンズー教の、ヒンズー人の *Hindu* adj p108

hippu hoppu ヒップホップ *hip-hop* n

hiroi 広い *wide* adj p16

hitai 額 *forehead* n

hitotsu no 一つの *one* adj p7, *single (one)* adj

shinguru beddo シングルベッド *single bed*

hiyake dome kurīmu 日焼け止めクリーム *sunscreen* n

SPF ____ no hiyake dome kurīmu wa arimasu ka. SPF ____の日焼け止めクリームはありますか？*Do you have sunscreen SPF ____?* See numbers p7.

hiyake shita 日焼けした *tanned* adj

hiyake 日焼け *sunburn* n

watashi wa hidoku hiyake shimashita. 私はひどく日焼けしました。*I have a bad sunburn.*

hodō 歩道 *sidewalk* n

hodō 歩道 *walkway* n

jidō idō tsūro 自動移動通路 *moving walkway*

hojū 補充 *refill (of prescription)* n

hoken 保険 *insurance* n p50, 154

hokōki 歩行器 *walker (ambulatory device)* n p41

hokōsha yō no 歩行者用の *pedestrian* adj

hokuro ほくろ *mole (facial feature)* n

hōmon no mokuteki wa nani desu ka. 訪問の目的は何ですか？*What is the purpose of your visit?* p41 hon ya 本屋 *bookstore* n p128

hon 本 *book* n p111, 133

honjurasu no, honjurasu jin no ホンジュラスの、ホンジュラス人 の *Honduran* adj

hontō ni 本当に *really* adv

hōritsu 法律 *law* n

hōshi 奉仕 / reihai 礼拝 *services (religious)* n p109

hoshii 欲しい *need, want* v

hosuteru ホステル *hostel* n p63

hoteru ホテル *hotel* n p63

jimoto no hoteru no ichiran hyō wa arimasu ka. 地元のホ テルの一覧表はありますか? *Do you have a list of local hotels?*

hotto chokorēto ホット チョコレー ト *hot chocolate* n p82

hyaku 百 *hundred* n

hyōkō 標高 *altitude* n p139

hyūzu ヒューズ *fuse* n

I

ichi gatsu 一月 *January* n p19

ie 家 *home* n

igirisu jin, igirisu no, igirisu jin no イギリス(の)、イギリス人(の) *English* n, adj

eigo o hanashi masu ka. 英語 を話しますか? *Do you speak English?* p2

igirisu イギリス *England* n

ii mēru suru Eメールする *e-mail, to send e-mail* v

iin 医院 *doctor's office* n

iku 行く *go, to go* v

ikura いくら *how* adv *(how much)*, ikutsu いくつ *(how many)* p37, 39

ikutsukano いくつかの *some* adj

ima 今 *now* adv p3

inchi インチ *inch* n p14

insatsu suru 印刷する *print, to print* v p120

intānetto インターネット *Internet* n p65, 71, 120

kōsoku intānetto 高速インター ネット *High-speed Internet*

intānetto ni setsuzoku deki masu ka. インターネットに接 続できますか? *Do you have Internet access?*

intā netto kafe wa doko ni arimasu ka. インターネットカ フェはどこにありますか? *Where can I find an Internet café?*

inu 犬 *dog* n p151

kaigo ken 介護犬 *service dog* p42, 62, 66

ippai 一杯 *shot (liquor)* n

ippō tsūkō 一方通行 *one way (traffic sign)* adj

iriguchi 入口 *entrance* n p38

iro o nuru 色をぬる *color* v

iro 色 *color* n

isha 医者 *doctor* n p104, 148

isha o onegai shimasu. 医者 をお願いします。 *I need a doctor.* p7

ishō 衣装 *costume* n

isogu 急ぐ *hurry* v

watashi wa isoide imasu. 私は 急いでいます。 *I'm in a hurry.*

isoide kudasai. 急いでください!
Hurry, please!

isuramu kyō no イスラム教の
Muslim adj p108

itai. 痛い! *Ouch!*

itamu 痛む *hurt, to hurt v*
p149

itai. 痛いです! itai desu. 痛い!
Ouch! That hurts!

itaria no, itaria jin no イタリアの、
イタリア人の *Italian adj*
p106

itoko いとこ *cousin n*

itsu いつ *when adv* p3

itsutsu no 五つの *five adj* p7

iu 言う *say, to say v* p99

iwau 祝う *celebrate, to
celebrate v*

J

jaguchi 蛇口 *faucet n*

jazu ジャズ *jazz n* p109

ji 時 *o'clock adv* p4

ni ji 2時 *two o'clock*

jidō hanbai ki 自動販売機
vending machine n

jiin 寺院 *temple n*

jikan 時間 *hour n* p120, 127

jikan 時間 *hours (at
museum) n*

jikan 時間 *time n*

sore wa teikoku dōri desu ka.
それは定刻通りですか? *Is it
on time?*

nan ji ni. 何時に? *At what
time?*

nan ji desu ka. 何時ですか?
What time is it?

jiko 事故 *accident n* p54

jiko ni ai mashita. 事故にあいま
した。 *I've had an accident.*
p54

jimaku 字幕 *subtitle n*

jimu ジム *gym n* p137

jin ジン *gin n* p82

jinshu no majitta 人種の混じった
biracial adj

jisho 辞書 *dictionary n*

jissai no 実際の *actual adj*

joggingu o suru ジョギングをする
jog, to run v

jōhō 情報 *information n*

jōkyaku 乗客 *passenger n*

jōkyō 状況 *state n*

josei no 女性の *female adj*

josei 女性 *woman n*

jōshi 上司 *boss n*

jōtai 状態 *condition n*

yoi / warui jōtai 良い / 悪い状態
in good / bad condition

jū ban me no 十番目の *tenth
adj*

jū gatsu 十月 *October n* p19

jū hachi 十八 *eighteen n* p8

jū ichi gatsu 十一月 *November
n* p19

jū ichi 十一 *eleven n* p7

jū ni gatsu 十二月 *December
n* p19

jū no 十の *ten adj* p7

jū san no 十三の *thirteen
adj* p7

jūden suru 充電する *charge, to
charge (a battery) v* p62

jūgo no 十五の *fifteen adj* p8

jūgyō in 従業員 *employee* n

jūkyū no 十九の *nineteen* adj p8

junbi sareta 準備された *prepared* adj

jūni no 十二の *twelve* adj p7

junyū suru 授乳する *nurse* v

junyū dekiru basho wa arimasu ka. 授乳できる場所はありますか? *Do you have a place where I can nurse?*

jūroku no 十六の *sixteen* adj p8

jūshichi no 十七の *seventeen* adj p8

jushin nin barai no 受信人払いの *collect* adj

korekuto kōru o onegai shimasu. コレクトコールをお願いします。*I'd like to place a collect call.*

jūsu ジュース *juice* n p94

jūyon no 十四の / jū shi no 十四の *fourteen* adj p7

K

ka yō bi 火曜日 *Tuesday* n p17

kabā chāji カバーチャージ *cover charge (in bar)* n p144

kaban o akete kudasai. かばんを開けてください。*Open this bag, please.* p41

kādo カード *card* n

kurejitto kādo wa tsukae masu ka. クレジットカードは使えますか? *Do you accept credit cards?* p37

anata no meishi o itadake masu ka. あなたの名刺をいただけますか? *May I have your business card?*

kado 角 / burokku ブロック *block* n

kagi o kakeru 鍵をかける *lock, to lock* v

doa ni kagi o kakeru koto ga dekima sen. ドアに鍵をかけることができません。*I can't lock the door.*

doa ni kagi ga kakatte shimai heya ni hairu koto ga deki masen. ドアに鍵がかかってしまい部屋に入ることができません。*I'm locked out.*

kagi 鍵 *lock* n p137

kai in 会員 *member* n

kai rui 貝類 *shellfish* n p80

kai 階 *floor* n

ikkai 1階 *ground floor* p66

ni kai 2階 *second floor*

kaidan 階段 *stair* n

kaidan wa doko desu ka. 階段はどこですか? *Where are the stairs?*

kaidan no kazu wa ōi desu ka. 階段の数は多いですか? *Are there many stairs?*

kaimono o suru 買い物をする *shop* v

shinshi fuku o kai ni kimashita. 紳士服を買いに来ました。*I'm shopping for mens' clothes.*

fujin fuku o kai ni kimashita. 婦人服を買いに来ました。*I'm shopping for womens' clothes.*

kodomo fuku o kai ni kimashita. 子供服を買いに来ました。*I'm shopping for childrens' clothes.*

kairo purakutā カイロプラクター *chiropractor n* p148

kaisen sokudo 回線速度 *connection speed n*

kaisha 会社 *agency n* p48

rentakā gaisha レンタカー会社 *car rental agency*

kaji da. 火事だ！*fire! n*

kajino カジノ *casino n* p63

kakaku 価格 *price n*

kakari in 係員 *officer n* p44

kakeru かける *bet, to bet v*

kakin 家禽 *poultry n*

kaku 書く *write, to write v*

kami ni kaite itadake masu ka. 紙に書いていただけますか？*Would you write that down for me?*

kakunin suru 確認する *confirm, to confirm v* p41

yoyaku o kakunin shitai no desuga. 予約を確認したいのですが。*I'd like to confirm my reservation.*

kakuteru カクテル *cocktail n* p81

kami no ke 髪の毛 *hair n*

kami 紙 *paper n*

kanada no, kanada jin no カナダの、カナダ人の *Canadian adj*

kanada カナダ *Canada n*

kanashii 悲しい *sad adj* p103

kango shi 看護師 *nurse n* p105

kankō basu 観光バス *sightseeing bus n*

kankō 観光 *sightseeing n*

kankyō 環境 *environment n*

kanojo no 彼女の *her adj* p25

kansatsu suru 観察する *watch, to watch v*

kansō shita 乾燥した *dried adj*

kantorī ongagu カントリー音楽 *country music n*

kanzen ni niete iai 完全に煮えていない *undercooked adj*

kanzume 缶詰 *can n*

kao 顔 *face n*

kapuchīno カプチーノ *cappuccino n*

kara tsuku rareta ～から作られた *made of ～ adj*

kare no 彼の *his adj*

kare o 彼を *him pron* p25

karera/kanojyora (ni, o)彼ら/彼女ら(に、を) *them (m / f)* p25

kariru 借りる *rent, to rent v*

kuruma o karitai no desuga. 車を借りたいのですが。*I'd like to rent a car.*

kāru shita カールした *curly adj*

kāru カール *curl n*

kasa 傘 *umbrella n*

kashimiya カシミヤ *cashmere n*

katorikku kyō no カトリック教の *Catholic adj* p108

kau 買う *buy, to buy v* p129, 138, 147

kauntā カウンター *counter (in bar) n* p77

kawa 川 *river n*

kawa 皮 *leather n* p47

kawaita 乾いた *dry*

kono taoru wa kawaite imasen. このタオルは乾いていません。 *This towel isn't dry.*

kawakasu 乾かす *dry, to dry v*

watashi no fuku o kawakasu hitsuyō ga arimasu. 私の服を乾かす必要があります。 *I need to dry my clothes.*

kawari no mono 替わりのもの *substitution n*

kaze ga tsuyoi 風が強い *windy adj* p115

kaze カゼ *cold n* p72, 84

kaze o hiki mashita. カゼを引きました。 *I have a cold.*

kazoku 家族 / go kazoku ご家族 *family n* p100

kega けが *injury n*

keisatsu sho 警察署 / keisatsu no hashutsu sho 警察の派出所 *police station n* p36

keisatsu o yonde kudasai! 警察を呼んでください! *Call the police!* p7

keisatsu 警察 *police n* p7

keishoku 軽食 *snack n* p94

keitai denwa 携帯電話 *cell phone n* p118, 155

kekkon suru 結婚する *marry, to marry v*

kengan shi 検眼師 *optometrist n*

kenri 権利 *rights n pl*

shimin no kenri 市民の権利 *civil rights*

kensa 検査 *search n*

te de kensa suru 手で検査する *hand search*

keshiki 景色 *landscape n*

keshō o suru 化粧をする *make up, to make up (apply cosmetics) v*

keshō 化粧 *makeup n*

kesu / tsukeru 消す / 付ける *to turn off / on*

ki o ushinau 気を失う *faint v* p149

kicchin キッチン *kitchen n*

kichin to shita きちんとした *neat (tidy) adj*

kieru 消える *disappear v*

kiiroi 黄色い *yellow adj*

kiken 危険 *danger n* p54

kikon no 既婚の / kekkon shite iru 結婚している *married adj* p101

kiku 聞く *hear v*

kin en no 禁煙の *non-smoking adj*

kin en shitsu 禁煙室 *non-smoking room*

kin sei no 金製の *gold adj*

kin yō bi 金曜日 *Friday n* p17

kingaku ga kakaru 金額がかかる *cost, to cost v*

sore wa ikura shimasu ka. それはいくらしますか? *How much does it cost?* p132 kinjo no hito 近所の人 / kinjo no kata ご近所の方 *neighbor* n p100

kinko 金庫 *safe (for storing valuables)* n

shitsu nai ni kinko wa arimasu ka. 室内に金庫はありますか? *Do the rooms have safes?*

kinkyū 緊急 *emergency* n

kinō suru 機能する *work, to work* v

kore wa kinō shimasen. これは機能しません。 *This doesn't work.*

kinō 昨日 *yesterday* n p4

ototoi おととい *the day before yesterday* p4

kinpatsu no 金髪の *blond(e)* adj

kinzoku tanchi ki 金属探知機 *metal detector* n

kippu 切符 / chiketto チケット *ticket* n p35, 37, 39, 56, 58

kippu uriba 切符売り場 / chiketto kauntā チケットカウンター *ticket counter*

kaban o akete kudasai. かばんを開けてください。 *Open this bag, please.*

katamichi kippu 片道切符 *one-way ticket* p56

ōfuku kippu 往復切符 *round-trip ticket* p56

kireina きれいな *beautiful* adj p102

kiri kizu 切り傷 *cut (wound)* n

watashi wa hidoi kirikizu ga arimasu. 私はひどい切り傷があります。 *I have a bad cut.*

kiri soroeru 切りそろえる / soroeru そろえる *trim, to trim (hair)* v p135

kiro guramu キログラム *kilo* n

kiro mētoru キロメートル *kilometer* n p14

kiru 切る *cut, hang up (to end a phone call)* v p119

kiru 着る *dress, wear* v

soko dewa seisō shinakereba nari masen ka. そこでは正装しなければなりませんか? *Should I dress up for that affair.*

kissa ten 喫茶店 *café* n p36, 77, 120

intānetto kafe インターネットカフェ *Internet café* p120

kisu キス *kiss* n

kitanai 汚い *dirty* adj p72

kitsu en 喫煙 *smoking* n p36

kitsu en jo 喫煙所 *smoking area* p36

kin en 禁煙 *No Smoking* p38

kitsui きつい *tight* adj

kitte 切手 *stamp (postage)* n

kizu no aru 傷のある *scratched* adj p50

suri kizu no aru hyōmen 擦り傷のある表面 *scratched surface*

kobosu こぼす *spill, to spill* v p46

kodomo 子供 *child, kid* n p100

kodomo mo ii desu ka. 子供もいいですか? *Are kids allowed?*

kodomo yō no puroguramu wa arimasu ka. 子供用のプログラムはありますか? *Do you have kids' programs?*

kodomo yō no menyū wa arimasu ka. 子供用のメニューはありますか? *Do you have a kids' menu?*

kodomo tachi 子供たち *children* n p102

kodomo mo ii desu ka. 子供もいいですか? *Are children allowed?*

kodomo yō no puroguramu wa arimasu ka. 子供用のプログラムはありますか? *Do you have children's programs?*

kodomo yō no menyū wa arimasu ka. 子供用のメニューはありますか? *Do you have a children's menu?*

kōen 公園 *park* n p113

kōgai 郊外 *suburb* n

kogitte 小切手 / chekku チェック *check* n

kōhī コーヒー *coffee* n p83

aisu kōhī アイス コーヒー *iced coffee*

kōhisutamin zai 抗ヒスタミン剤 *antihistamine* n p147

kōi shitsu 更衣室 *changing room* n

kojin kyakushitsu 個人客室 / kyabin キャビン *private berth* / *cabin* n

kōka 硬貨 *coin* n

kōkai 航海 *sail* n

kōkai suru 航海する *sail, to sail* v

itsu shukkō shimasu ka. いつ出航しますか? *When do we sail?* p140

kōkan rēto 交換レート *exchange rate* n p116

amerika doru / kanada doru no kōkan rēto wa nan desu ka. アメリカドル / カナダドルの交換レートは何ですか? *What is the exchange rate for US / Canadian dollars?*

kōkan suru 交換する *change (to change money, clothes)* v

koko ここ *here* n p5

kokonotsu no 九つの *nine* adj p7

kokuseki 国籍 *nationality* n

kōkyō gakudan 交響楽団 *symphony* n

kōkyūna 高級な *upscale* adj

komedi コメディ *comedy (movie)* n p112

kon nichi wa こんにちは *hello* n p1

kona miruku 粉ミルク *formula* n

bebī yō kona miruku wa utte imasu ka. ベビー用粉ミルクは売っていますか? *Do you sell infants' formula?*

kondoru コンドル *condor* n

konnan na 困難な / muzukashii 難しい *difficult* adj p140

kono この *this* adj

konomi 好み *taste (discernment)* n

konpyūtā コンピューター
computer n

konpyūtā puroguramā コン
ピューター プログラマー
computer programmer
n p105

konran shita 混乱した
confused adj

konsāto コンサート *concert*
n p113

kontakuto renzu コンタクト レン
ズ *contact lens* n

kontakuto renzu o nakushi
mashita. コンタクト レンズをな
くしました。 *I lost my contact
lens.*

konyakku コニャック *cognac*
n p82

konyaku sha 婚約者 *fiancé(e)*
n p100

konzatsu shita 混雑した
congested adj

koppu コップ *glass* n p79, 84

korera no これらの *these* adj p6

kōri 氷 *ice* n p70, 81

koronbia no, koronbia jin no コ
ロンビアの、コロンビア人の
Colombian adj

kōsei busshitsu 抗生物質
antibiotic n

kōsei busshitsu o kudasai. 抗
生物質をください。 *I need an
antibiotic.*

kōsha ryōri コーシャ料理 *kosher*
adj p80

kōshin suru 更新する *update,
to update* v

kōsoku dōro 高速道路
highway n

kosutarika no, kosutarika jin no
コスタリカの、コスタリカ人の
Costa Rican adj

kotae 答え *answer* n

kotaeru 答える *answer, to
answer (phone call,
question)* v

kotaete kudasai. 答えてくださ
い。 *Answer me, please.*

koten 古典 *classics* n p112

kōto コート *coat* n p130

kōto コート *court (sport)* n

kotonaru 異なる / chigau 違
う / betsuno 別の *different
(other)* adj p72, 131

kōtsū 交通 *traffic* n

kōtsū jōtai wa dō desu ka. 交
通状態はどうですか? *How's
traffic?*

kōtsū kisoku 交通規則 *traffic
rules*

kowareru 壊れる *break* v

kōza 口座 *account* n

tōza-yokin / futsū-yokin e /
kara furikaete tai no desuga.
当座預金 / 普通預金口座
へ / から振り替えたいのです
が。 *I'd like to transfer to /
from my checking / savings
account.*

kozutsumi 小包み *package* n
p121

ku gatsu 九月 *September* n
p19

kubaru 配る *deal (cards)* v

watashi mo irete kudasai. 私も入れてください。 *Deal me in.*

kuchi hige 口ひげ *mustache n*

kuchi 口 *mouth n*

kuda mono 果物 *fruit n* p95

kujira 鯨 *whale n*

kukkī クッキー *cookie n* p95

kūkō 空港 *airport n*

kūkō made notte iku hitsuyō ga arimasu. 空港まで乗って行く必要があります。 *I need a ride to the airport.*

kūkō kara dono kurai no tokoro ni arimasu ka. 空港からどのくらいのところにありますか? *How far is it from the airport?*

kumotta 曇った *cloudy adj* p107

kunren suru 訓練する *train, to train v*

kurabu ni odori ni iku クラブに踊りに行く *go clubbing, to go clubbing v*

kuragari 暗がり *dark n*

kurai 暗い *dark adj*

kurarinetto クラリネット *clarinet n*

kurashikku rokku クラシック ロック *classic rock* p109

kurasshikku no クラシックの *classical (music) adj*

kurasu クラス *class n*

bijinesu kurasu ビジネス クラス *business class*

ekonomī kurasu エコノミークラス *economy class*

fāsuto kurasu ファースト クラス *first class*

kurejitto kādo クレジット カード *credit card n* p37, 60, 115, 116

kurejitto kādo wa tsukae masu ka. クレジットカードは使えますか? *Do you accept credit cards?* p37, 67

kuri kaesu 繰り返す *repeat, to repeat v* p2

mō ichido kuri kaeshite itadake masu ka. もう一度繰り返していただけますか? *Would you please repeat that?* p2

kurimu クリーム *cream n* p81, 147

kurōbā クローバー *clover n*

kuroi 黒い / koku jin 黒人 *black adj*

kuruma isu 車椅子 *wheelchair n* p41, 61

kurumaisu deno akusesu 車椅子でのアクセス *wheelchair access*

kuruma isu yō surōpu 車椅子用スロープ *wheelchair ramp*

dendō kuruma isu 電動車椅子 *power wheelchair*

kuruma yoi 車酔い *carsickness n*

kuruma 車 *car n*

rentakā gaisha レンタ カー会社 *car rental agency*

rentakā ga hitsuyō desu. レンタ カーが必要です。 *I need a rental car.*

kurumi クルミ *walnut n*

kutsu shita 靴下 *sock n*

kutsu 靴 *shoe n* p130

kutsurogu くつろぐ *lounge, to lounge v*

kyaku no ōi 客の多い (restaurant), hanashi chū de 話し中で (phone) *busy adj*

kyanbasu キャンバス (for painting) / kyanbasu ji キャンバス地 (material) *canvas n* p47

kyanpā キャンパー *camper n* p74

kyanpu no キャンプの *camping adj*

kyanpu o suru kyoka ga hitsuyō desu ka. キャンプをする許可が必要ですか？ *Do we need a camping permit?*

kyanpu o suru キャンプをする *camp, to camp v* p111

kyanpu saito キャンプサイト *campsite n*

kyō 今日 *today n*

kyōdai 兄弟 / go kyōdai ご兄弟 *brother n* p100

kyohi sareta 拒否された *declined adj*

watashi no kurejitto kādo ga kyohi saretano desu ka. 私のクレジットカードが拒否されたのですか？ *Was my credit card declined?*

kyōiku sha 教育者 *educator n* p105

kyoka suru 許可する *permit, to permit v*

kyoka 許可 *permit n*

kyanpu o suru kyoka ga hitsuyō desu ka. キャンプをする許可が必要ですか？ *Do we need a camping permit?*

kyōkai 教会 *church n* p126

kyū banme no 九番目の *ninth adj*

kyūjitsu 休日 *holiday n*

kyūjū no 九十の *ninety adj* p8

kyūkei 休憩 *intermission n*

kyūkyūsha 救急車 *ambulance n*

kyūmei yōgu 救命用具 *life preserver n*

M

macchi マッチ *match n*

macchi マッチ *book of matches*

machiai shitu 待合室 *waiting area n* p35

machigai 間違い *mistake n* p73

mado 窓 *window n*

mae motte 前もって *in advance* p124

mae ni 前に *earlier adv* p4

magaru 曲がる *turn, to turn v* p53

hidari / migi ni magaru 左 / 右に曲がる *to turn left / right* p53

mairu マイル *mile n* p14

māketto マーケット / ichiba 市場 *market n* p129, 132

furii māketto フリーマーケット *flea market* p129

aozora ichiba 青空市場 *open-air market*

makura 枕 *pillow n* p45, 70, 71

umō no makura 羽毛の枕 *down pillow* p71

manējā マネージャー *manager n*

manpuku ni natta 満腹になった *full, to be full (after a meal) adj*

manyuaru マニュアル *manual (instruction booklet) n* p50

massāji マッサージ *massage n* p69

matsu ge まつ毛 *eyelash n*

matsu 待つ *hold, wait, to hold (to pause) v*

chotto matte. ちょっと待って! *Hold on a minute!*

pasu shimasu. パスします。 *I'll hold.*

dōka omachi kudasai. どうかお待ちください。 *Please wait.*

dono kurai machi masu ka. どのくらい待ちますか。 *How long is the wait?* p77

mayonaka 真夜中 *midnight n*

mayu ge まゆ毛 *eyebrow n*

me 目 *eye n*

me no mienai 目の見えない *blind adj*

watashi wa me ga mie masen / me ga fujiyū desu. 私は、目が見えません / 目が不自由です。 *I am blind / visually impaired.*

mēdo メード *maid (hotel) n*

megane 眼鏡 *eyeglasses n*

megane 眼鏡 *glasses (eye) n*

atarashii megane ga hitsuyō desu. 新しい眼鏡が必要です。 *I need new glasses.*

mei めい / meigo san 姪御さん *niece n* p100

mekishiko no, mekishiko jin no メキシコの、メキシコ人の *Mexican adj*

memai ga suru めまいがする *dizzy adj* p150

men 綿 / kotton コットン *cotton n* p130

mendori 雌鶏 *hen n*

menkyo shō 免許証 *license n* p154

unten menkyo shō 運転免許証 *driver's license*

menyū メニュー *menu n* p77, 79

menyū o misete kudasai メニューを見せてください？ *May I see a menu?*

kodomo yō no menyū 子供用のメニュー *children's menu*

tōnyōbyō kanja yō no menyū 糖尿病患者用のメニュー *diabetic menu*

kōsha ryōri no menyū コーシャ料理のメニュー *kosher menu*

menzei no 免税の *duty-free adj* p36

menzei ten 免税店 *duty-free shop n* p36

mētoru メートル *meter n* p14

mezamashi dokei 目覚まし時計 *alarm clock n* p71

mibō jin 未亡人, yamome やもめ
widow, widower n p101

mibun shōmei sho 身分証明書
identification n p44

michi 道 *street n* p6

kono michi no mukō gawa こ
の道の向こう側 *across the
street* p6

michi ni mayoi mashita. 道に迷
いました。*I'm lost.* p7

kono michi (no saki) この道(の
先) *down the street* p6

dono michi. どの道? *Which
street?*

ato nan bon no michi ga
arimasuka? あと何本の道があ
りますか? *How many more
streets?*

midiamu rea ミディアム レア
*medium rare (meat)
adj* p79

midiamu weru ミディアム ウェ
ル *medium well (meat)
adj* p79

midiamu ミディアム *medium
(size) adj*

midori iro no 緑色の *green adj*

migi no 右の *right adj* p5, 53

migi gawa ni arimasu. 右側に
あります。*It is on the right.*
p53

kado o migi ni magari masu. 角
を右に曲がります。*Turn right
at the corner.*

mijikai 短い *short adj* p15

mikon no 未婚の *maiden adj*

sore wa watashi no kyūsei
desu. それは私の旧姓です。
That's my maiden name.

mimi ga kikoenai 耳が聞こえない
deaf adj

minato 港 *port (for ship) n*

minshu shugi 民主主義
democracy n

miri mētoru ミリメートル
millimeter n

miri rittoru ミリリットル*milliliter
n*

miru 見る *look, to look (to
observe) v*

tada miteiru dake desu. ただ
見ているだけです。*I'm just
looking.*

koko o mite. ここを見て! *Look
here!*

miru 見る *see, to see v*

misete itadake masu ka? 見せて
いただけますか? *May I see
it?*

miryō sareta 魅了された
charmed adj

mise 店 *shop, store n*

miseru 見せる *show, to show v*

misete itadake masen ka. 見せ
ていただけませんか? *Would
you show me?*

misuterī ミステリー *mystery
(novel) n*

mīto bōru ミートボール
meatball n

mitsukara nai 見つからない
missing adj

watashi no kodomo ga maigo ni nari mashita. 私の子供が迷子になりました。 *My child is missing.* p7

mitsukeru 見つける *find* v

mizu 水 *water* n p45

kono mizu wa nome masu ka. この水は飲めますか? *Is the water potable?*

koko ni suidōsui wa arimasu ka. ここに水道水はありますか? *Is there running water?* p74

mizugi 水着 *swimsuit* n

mo ～も ～*too (also)* adv

mochi kaeri yō no menyū 持帰り用のメニュー *takeout menu* n

modoru 戻る *return, to return (to a place)* v

mōfu 毛布 *blanket* n p45

moguru もぐる *dive* v

sukyūba daibu スキューバダイブ *scuba dive* p141

moku yō bi 木曜日 *Thursday* n p17

mondai 問題 *problem* n

mosuku モスク *mosque* n

motsu 持つ *have* v

motte imasu. 喘息を持っています。 *I have asthma.* p152

motto sukunai もっと少ない *less* adj

mottomo chiisai, mottomo sukunai 最も小さい、最も少ない *least* adj

mukashi no eiga 昔の映画 *old movies* n p112

murasaki no 紫の *purple* adj

mushi yoke 虫除け *insect repellent* n p148

mushi 虫 *bug* n

mushiba 虫歯 *cavity (tooth cavity)* n

mushiba ga aru yō nandesu. 虫歯があるようなんです。 *I think I have a cavity.*

mushinron sha 無神論者 *atheist* n p109

mushiro むしろ *rather* adv

musuko 息子 / musuko san 息子さん *son* n p102

musume 娘 / ojōsan お嬢さん *daughter* n p102

muttsu no 六つの *six* adj p7

muzukashii 難しい *hard* adj (difficult)

myūjishan ミュージシャン *musician* n p105

N

nagai 長い *long* adj p15

nagaku 長く *long* adv

dore kurai nagaku. どれくらい長く? *For how long?*

nagame 眺め *view* n

bīchi no nagame ビーチの眺め *beach view*

shigai no nagame 市街の眺め *city view*

nagareru, nagasu 流れる、流す *flush, to flush* v

kono toire wa nagare masen. このトイレは流れません。 *This toilet won't flush.*

naibu 内部 / naka 中 *inside* n p77

naifu ナイフ *knife* n p83
naito kurabu ナイトクラブ
 nightclub n
nakusu 失くす *lose, to lose* v
 watashi wa pasupōto o
 nakushi mashita. 私はパスポ
 ートを失くしました。*I lost my
 passport.*
 watashi wa saifu o nakushi
 mashita. 私は財布を失くしまし
 た。*I lost my wallet.*
 watashi wa mayotte shimai
 mashita. 私は迷ってしまいまし
 た。*I'm lost.*
namae 名前 *name* n p1
 watashi wa ____ to
 mōshimasu. 私は___と申しま
 す。*My name is ___.* p1
 anata no namae wa nan desu
 ka. あなたの名前は何ですか？
 What's your name?
nan demo 何でも *anything* n
nan no 何の / 何 nani *what*
 adv p2
 donna shurui no ____. どんな
 種類の____？ *What sort of
 ____?*
 ____ wa nan ji. ____は何時？
 What time is ____? p16
nana ban me no 七番目の
 seventh adj
nana jū no 七十の *seventy*
 adj p8
nanatsu no 七つの *seven* adj p7
nani ka 何か / nani 何
 something n

nanika 何か / nanimo 何も /
 any adj
nanimo nai 何もない / sukoshi
 mo nai 少しもない、全くない
 mattaku nai *none* n p15
nanpa sen 難破船 *shipwreck* n
naosu 直す *correct* v
napukin ナプキン *napkin* n
nashi de 〜なしで *without* 〜
 prep
natsu 夏 *summer* n p19
nebiki 値引き *discount* n
 watashi wa nebiki no taishō
 ni narimasuka. 私は値引きの対
 象になりますか？ *Do I qualify
 for a discount?*
neko ねこ *cat* n
nesshin na 熱心な *enthusiastic*
 adj p104
nettowāku ネットワーク
 network n
nezumi ねずみ *mouse* n
ni gatsu 二月 *February* n p19
ni kakoku go o hanasu 二ヶ国語
 を話す *bilingual* adj
niban me no 二番目の *second*
 adj
 sekyuritī chekku pointo セ
 キュリティ チェックポイント
 security checkpoint
 sekyuritī gādo セキュリティ ガー
 ド / keibi in 警備員 *security
 guard* p36
nichi yō bi 日曜日 *Sunday* n p17
nihon no, nihon jin no 日本の、日
 本人の *Japanese* adj p106
nijū no 二十の *twenty* adj p8

nikaragua no, nikaragua jin no ニカラグアの、ニカラグア人の *Nicaraguan adj*

nikibi にきび *acne n*

niku 肉 *meat n* p84, 90, 95

nimotsu 荷物 / ryokō kaban 旅行カバン *luggage n* p36, 55

ryokō kaban no funshitsu wa doko ni hōkoku shimasu ka. 旅行カバンの紛失はどこに報告しますか？ *Where do I report lost luggage?*

funshitsu shita ryokō kaban o uketoru basho wa doko desu ka. 紛失した旅行カバンを受け取る場所はどこですか？ *Where is the lost luggage claim?*

nimotsu kensa 荷物検査 *security* p35

nin niku にんにく *garlic n* p88

ninki ga aru 人気がある *popular adj* p144

ninshin shita 妊娠した *pregnant adj*

nioi o kagu 匂いをかぐ *smell, to smell v*

no hō o konomu の方を好む *prefer, to prefer v*

no mukō gawa の向こう側 *across prep* p6

kono michi no mukō gawa この道の向こう側 *across the street* p6

no yō ni mieru のように見える *look, to look (to appear) v*

kore wa dō mie masu ka. これはどう見えますか？ *How does this look?*

noboru 登る *climb, to climb v*

yama ni noboru 山に登る *to climb a mountain*

kaidan o noboru 階段を昇る *to climb stairs*

nomi komu 飲み込む *swallow, to swallow v*

nomi mono 飲み物 *drink n* p78, 145

nomi mono o kudasai. 飲み物をください。 *I'd like a drink.*

nomu 飲む *drink, to drink v*

non arukōru no ノンアルコールの *nonalcoholic drink n*

non fikushon ノンフィクション *non-fiction n* p112

nori okureru 乗り遅れる *miss, to miss (a flight) v* p42

notte iku 乗っていく *ride, to ride v*

nozomu 望む、like, desire *v (to please)*

_____ ga suki desu. _____が好きです。 *I would like _____.*

nuno 布 *fabric n*

nuru 塗る *paint, to paint v*

nusumareta 盗まれた *stolen adj* p47

nusumu 盗む *steal, to steal v*

nuu 縫う / saihō o suru 裁縫をする *sew, to sew v* p111

nyūjirando no, nyūjirando jin no ニュージーランドの、ニュージーランド人の *New Zealander adj*

nyūjirando ニュージーランド *New Zealand n*

nyūjōryō 入場料 admission fee
n p127

nyūkō suru 入港する board v

nyūkoku shinsa 入国審査
immigration n p35

O

oba おば / obasan おばさん aunt
n p100

ōbāhīto suru オーバーヒートする
overheat, to overheat v

kuruma ga ōbāhīto shimashita.
車がオーバーヒートしまし
た。The car overheated.

ocha お茶 / cha 茶 tea n p83

ochido 落ち度 fault n p55

watashi ni ochido ga arimasu.
私に落ち度があります。I'm at
fault. p57

sore wa kare ni ochido ga
arimasu. それは彼に落ち度が
あります。It was his fault.

ochikonda kibun no 落ち込んだ
気分の depressed adj p104

ochiru 落ちる fall v

odoru 踊る / dansu o suru ダンス
をする dance v p112

ofuro ni hairu お風呂に入る
bathe, to bathe oneself v

ofuro お風呂 bath n

ōgoe de yobu 大声で呼ぶ
shout v

oi おい / oigo san 甥御さん
nephew n p100

oji おじ / ojisan おじさん uncle
n p100

okane お金 money n

okawari お替わり refill (of
beverage) n

ōkii 大きい big adj p16

ōkii 大きい large adj p129

okkē オッケー okay adv

okotta 怒った angry adj

oku 置く place, to place v

oku 置く put, to put v

okure 遅れ delay n

dono kurai okurete imasu ka. ど
のくらい遅れていますか? How
long is the delay? p42

okuri mono 贈り物 gift n

okuru 送る send, to send v
p121, 122

okyaku お客 guest n

omocha おもちゃ toy n

omocha ya おもちゃ屋 toy
store n

kodomo no omocha wa
arimasu ka. 子供のおもちゃ
はありますか? Do you have
any toys for the children?

omoi 重い weigh v

watashi wa taijū ga _____
arimasu. 私は体重が_____あり
ます。I weigh _____.

kore wa _____ no omosa ga
arimasu. これは_____の重さ
があります。It weighs _____.
See p7 for numbers.

omosa 重さ weights n

omutsu おむつ diaper n

omutsu wa doko de kaerare
masu ka. おむつはどこで替
えられますか? Where can I
change a diaper?

ongaku 音楽 music n p109

nama ensō 生演奏 live music

onna no ko 女の子 girl n

onrain chekku in wa deki masu ka. オンラインチェックインはできますか？ *Is online check-in available?* p39

onsei no 音声の *audio adj* p127

opera オペラ *opera n* p110

operētā オペレーター *operator (phone) n*

orenji iro no オレンジ色の *orange (color) adj*

orenji jūsu オレンジジュース *orange juice n* p45

orību オリーブ *olive n*

osara お皿 *plate n* p84

oshaburi おしゃぶり *pacifier n*

osoi 遅い *late adj* p17

dōka okure naide kudasai. どうか遅れないでください。 *Please don't be late.*

osoi 遅い *slow adj*

osou 襲う *mug, to mug (someone) v*

osowareta 襲われた *mugged adj*

osu 押す *push, to push v* p38

ōsutoraria no, ōsutoraria jin no オーストラリアの、オーストラリア人の *Australian adj*

ōsutoraria オーストラリア *Australia n*

oto ga urusai 音がうるさい *noisy adj*

otoko no ko 男の子 *boy n*

otoko 男 *man n*

otsuri おつり *change (money) n*

otsuri o kudasai. おつりをください。 *I'd like change, please.*

kono otsuri wa tadashiku arimasen. このおつりは正しくありません。 *This isn't the correct change.*

otto 夫 / shujin 主人 / go shujin ご主人 *husband n* p100

oushi 雄牛 *bull n*

oya 親 *parent n*

oyogu 泳ぐ *swim, to swim v* p31

koko dewa oyoge masu ka. ここでは泳げますか？ *Can one swim here?*

P

painto パイント *pint n* p15

pan パン *bread n* p83, 94

panama no, panama jin no パナマの、パナマ人の *Panamanian adj*

paraguai no, paraguai jin no パラグアイの、パラグアイ人の *Paraguayan adj*

parēdo パレード *parade n*

pasu suru パスする *hold, to hold (gambling) v*

pasu suru パスする *pass, to pass v*

pasu shimasu. パスします。 *I'll pass.*

pasupōto パスポート *passport n*

watashi wa pasupōto o nakushi mashita. 私はパスポートを失くしました。 *I've lost my passport.*

pasupôto o onegai shimasu. パスポートをお願いします。 *Your passport, please.* p41

pâtî パーティー *party* n

seitô 政党 *political party*

pâtonâ パートナー *partner* n

perú no, perú jin no ペルーの、ペルー人の *Peruvian* adj

piano ピアノ *piano* n p110

pînattsu ピーナッツ *peanut* n

pinku no ピンクの *pink* adj

pittari au ぴったり合う *fit (clothes)* v

pittari atte iru yô ni miemasu ka. ぴったり合っているように見えますか？ *Does this look like it fits?*

pondo ポンド *pound* n

ponpu ポンプ *pump* n

poppu myûjikku ポップミュージック *pop music* n

poppukôn ポップコーン *popcorn* n p125

posuto kâdo ポストカード *postcard* n

pôtâ ポーター *porter* n p35

pôto wain ポートワイン *port (beverage)* n

pueru토riko no, puerutoriko jin no プエルトリコの、プエルトリコ人の *Puerto Rican* adj

puragu プラグ *plug* n

purasuchikku プラスチック *plastic* n p47

purei suru プレイする *play, to play (a game)* v

purei プレイ *play* n

purofesshionaru na プロフェッショナルな *professional* adj

puroguramu プログラム *program* n

puroguramu o itadake masu ka. プログラムをいただけますか？ *May I have a program?*

purotesutanto プロテスタント *Protestant* n

pûru プール *pool* n p63, 66

R

rabendâ iro no ラベンダー色の *lavender* adj

raigetsu 来月 *next month* n p4

rajio ラジオ *radio* n

ramu shu ラム酒 *rum* n p82

ranpu ランプ *light* n (lamp) p45

rappu toppu ラップトップ *laptop* n p155

raunji ラウンジ *lounge* n

rea no レアの *rare (meat)* adj p79

regê レゲー *reggae* adj p110

reibô 冷房 / eakon エアコン p48, 65, 71 *air conditioning* n

reibô o sagete / agete itadake masen ka. 冷房を下げて / 上げていただけませんか？ *Would you lower / raise the air conditioning?*

reitô shokuhin 冷凍食品 *frozen food* n p94

rekishi teki na 歴史的な *historical* adj

rekishi 歴史 *history n*

remonēdo レモネード *lemonade n*

ren ai shōsetsu 恋愛小説 *romance (novel) n*

rentogen レントゲン *x-ray machine n*

reshīto レシート *receipt n* p116

ressha 列車 / densha 電車 *train n* p56, 57

> tokkyū ressha 特急列車 *express train*

> futsū ressha 普通列車 *local train*

> kono densha wa ____e ikimasu ka. この電車は____へ行きますか？ *Does the train go to ____?*

> densha no jikokuhyō o itadake masu ka. 電車の時刻表をいただけますか？ *May I have a train schedule?*

> eki wa doko ni arimasuka. 駅はどこにありますか？ *Where is the train station?*

ressun レッスン *lesson n*

resutoran レストラン *restaurant n* p36

> yoi resutoran wa doko ni arimasu ka. よいレストランはどこにありますか？ *Where can I find a good restaurant?*

rihatsu ten 理髪店 *barber n*

rikai suru 理解する *understand, to understand v*

> wakari masen. わかりません。 *I don't understand.* p2, 98

wakari masu ka. わかりますか？ *Do you understand?*

rikon shita 離婚した *divorced adj*

rimujin リムジン *limo n* p55

rippa na 立派な *great adj*

rittoru リットル *liter n* p14

riyōken 利用券 *voucher n* p42

roiyaru furasshu ロイヤル フラッシュ *royal flush n*

rōka 廊下 *hallway n*

rokkā ロッカー *locker n* p137

> hokan rokkā 保管ロッカー *storage locker*

> rokkā rūmu ロッカールーム *locker room* p138

rokku ロック *rocks (ice) n* p81

> rokku de onegai shimasu. ロックでお願いします。 *I'd like it on the rocks.*

rokku kuraimingu ロッククライミング *rock climbing n*

rokku ongaku ロック音楽 *rock music n* p109

roku gatsu 六月 *June n* p19

rokujū no 六十の *sixty adj* p8

romanchikku na ロマンチックな *romantic adj*

rōpu ロープ *rope n*

ryō 量 *amount n*

ryōgae 両替 *currency exchange n* p36, 116

> koko kara ichiban chikai ryōgae jo wa doko ni arimasu ka. ここから一番近い両替所はどこにありますか？ *Where is the nearest currency exchange?*

ryōkin puran 料金プラン *rate plan (cell phone)* n

ryōkin 料金 *fare* n

ryōkin 料金 *fee* n

ryōkin 料金 *rate (for car rental, hotel)* n p44, 67

ichi nichi atari no ryōkin wa ikura desu ka. 一日当たりの料金はいくらですか？ *What's the rate per day?*

isshūkan atari no ryōkin wa ikura desu ka. 一週間当たりの料金はいくらですか？ *What's the rate per week?*

ryokō kaban 旅行カバン *(luggage)*, **toranku** トランク *(in car) trunk* n

ryokō suru 旅行する *travel, to travel* v p40, 42, 66

ryokō 旅行 *trip* n p56, 59, 97

ryōri suru 料理する *cook, to cook* v

ryōri suru koto ga dekiru heya o onegai shimasu. 料理することができる部屋をお願いします。 *I'd like a room where I can cook.*

ryōri 料理 *dish* n p80

S

sābisu ryō サービス料 *service charge* n p67, 116

sābisu サービス *service* n

hikadōchū 非稼動中 *out of service*

sāfin suru サーフィンする *surf* v p142

sāfu bōdo サーフボード *surfboard* n

sagasu 探す *look for, to look for (to search)* v

pōtā o sagashite imasu. ポーターを探しています。 *I'm looking for a porter.*

sai aku 最悪 *worst*

saibā kafe サイバーカフェ *cybercafé* n

saibā kafe wa doko ni arimasu ka. サイバーカフェはどこにありますか？ *Where can I find a cybercafé?*

saiban sho 裁判所 *court (legal)* n p54, 153

saifu 財布 *purse* n

saifu 財布 *wallet* n p44

watashi wa saifu o nakushi mashita. 私は財布を失くしました。 *I lost my wallet.*

dareka ni saifu o nusumare mashita. 誰かに財布を盗まれました。 *Someone stole my wallet.* p44

saigo ni 最後に *last* adv

saikō no 最高の *best*

saisho no 最初の *first* adj

saishō 最小 *least* n

saizu サイズ *size (clothing, shoes)* n p129

sake 酒 *liquor* n p43

saki e 先へ / **mae e** 前へ *forward* adj p6

sakka 作家 *writer* n p104

samui 寒い *cold* adj p72, 84

samui desu. 寒いです。 *I'm cold.*

soto wa samui desu. 外は寒いです。 *It's cold out.*

san bai no 3倍の *triple adj*

san banme no 3番目の *third adj*

san gatsu 三月 *March (month)*
n p19

san rūfu サンルーフ *sunroof n*

san 三 *three* p7

sango shō さんご礁 *reef n*

sangurasu サングラス
sunglasses n

sanjū no 三十の *thirty adj* p8

sanka suru 参加する / shusseki
suru 出席する *attend v*

sanso tanku 酸素タンク *oxygen*
tank n

sarada サラダ *salad n*

sarubadoru no, sarubadoru jin
no サルバドルの、サルバドル人
の *Salvadorian adj*

sashi komu 差し込む *plug, to*
plug v

sasu 指す *point, to point v* p2

_____ no hōkō ni sashi
shimeshite itadake masen ka.
_____の方向に指し示していた
だけませんか? *Would you*
point me in the direction
of_____?

sayōnara さようなら *goodbye*
n p98

seibetsu 性別 *sex (gender) n*

seifu 政府 *government n* p107

seigen sokudo 制限速度 *speed*
limit n p54

seigen sokudo wa nan kiro desu
ka. 制限速度は何キロですか?
What's the speed limit?
p54

seihin 製品 *product n*

seikatsu 生活 *living n*

nani o shite seikatsu shite
imasu ka. 何をして生活してい
ますか? *What do you do*
for a living?

seiketsu na 清潔な *clean adj*

seikyū suru 請求する *bill v* p119

seikyū suru 請求する *charge, to*
charge (money) v p120

seikyū 請求 *claim n*

baishō o seikyū shimasu. 賠償
を請求します。*I'd like to file*
a claim.

seki o suru 咳をする *cough v*

seki 咳 *cough n* p147

sekken 石鹸 *soap n*

sekyuritī gādo セキュリティガー
ド / keibi in 警備員 *security*
guard p36

semai 狭い *narrow adj*
p16

sen 千 *thousand* p8

senaka o sasuru 背中をさする
back rub n

senaka 背中 *back n*

senaka ga itami masu. 背中が痛
みます。*My back hurts.*

senchi mētoru センチメートル
centimeter n

sengetsu 先月 *last month n* p4

senkyo 選挙 *election n* p108

senmen dai 洗面台 *sink n*

senmen yōhin 洗面用品
toiletries n p94

sennuki 栓抜き *bottle opener*
n p70

senpūki 扇風機 *fan n*

sensō 戦争 *war* n p108

sentaku / randorī 洗濯 *laundry* n p70

serufu sābisu no セルフサービスの *self-serve* adj

sētā セーター *sweater* n p43, 130

setsudan sareta 切断された *disconnected* adj

operētā san, denwa ga kirete shimai mashita. オペレーターさん、電話が切れてしまいました。 *Operator, I was disconnected.*

setsumei suru 説明する *explain* v

sewa o suru 世話をする *mother, to mother* v

shanpū シャンプー *shampoo* n p70

shanpan シャンパン *champagne* n p82

sharin tsuki 車輪付き *wheeled (luggage)* adj

shatoru basu シャトルバス *shuttle bus* n

shatsu シャツ *shirt* n

shawā o abiru シャワーを浴びる *shower, to shower* v

shawā シャワー *shower* n p65, 74

sore niwa shawā ga tsuite imasu ka? それにはシャワーが付いていますか? *Does it have a shower?*

shi gatsu 四月 *April* n p19

shi 市 / **machi** 街 *city* n p65

shiai 試合 *match (sport)* n

shiawase na 幸せな / **ureshii** 嬉しい *happy* adj p103

shichaku shitsu 試着室 *fitting room* n

shichaku suru 試着する *try, to try on (clothing)* v

shichi gatsu 七月 *July* n p19

shichimenchō 七面鳥 *turkey* n

shīfūdo シーフード / **gyokai rui** 魚介類 *seafood* n p80

shiharau 支払う *pay, to pay* v

shihei 紙幣 *bill (currency)* n p115, 116

shikaku shōgai no 視覚障害の *visually-impaired* adj

shikke no aru 湿気がある *humid* adj p107

shima no 縞の *striped* adj

shimai 姉妹 / **go shimai** ご姉妹 *sister* n p100

shimatta しまった! / **zan nen** 残念! *Damn!* expletive

shinbun uriba 新聞売り場 *newsstand* n p36, 133

shinbun 新聞 *newspaper* n

shindai 寝台 *berth* n

shindai 寝台 *sleeping berth* n

shinkoku suru 申告する *declare* v p41, 43

shinkoku suru mochimono wa arimasu ka 申告する持ち物はありますか? *Do you have anything to declare?* p41
shinkoku suru mono wa arimasen. 申告するものはありません。 *I have nothing to declare.* p43

shinpai na 心配な / shinpai na shiteiru 心配している *anxious adj* p104

shinseki 親戚 *relative (family) n*

shinsen na 新鮮な *fresh adj* p81, 95

shinzō 心臓 *heart n*

shinzō hossa 心臓発作 *heart attack n* p149

shio no nagare 潮の流れ *current (water) n*

shio 塩 *salt n* p87

sore wa gen en desu ka. それは減塩ですか？ *Is that low-salt?*

shiraberu 調べる *check, to check v*

shiroi 白い *white adj*

shiruku シルク *silk n* p129

shiryoku 視力 *vision n*

shishoku suru 試食する *try, to try (food) v*

shita ni 下に *down below adv*

shita no 下の *below adj* p6

shitagi 下着 *underwear n*

shitataru 滴る *drip v*

shitate ya 仕立て屋 *tailor n* p70

yoi shitate ya o susumete itadake masen ka. よい仕立て屋を勧めていただけませんか？ *Can you recommend a good tailor?*

shite yoi してよい *may v aux*

＿＿＿ shitemo yoi desu ka. ＿＿＿してもよいですか？ *May I ＿＿＿?*

shītsu シーツ *sheet (bed linen) n*

shitsumon suru 質問する *ask a question v*

shitsunai gaku 室内楽 *chamber music n*

shitte iru 知っている *know, to know (someone, something) v*

shiyō kanō na 使用可能な *available adj*

shiyōryō 使用料 *toll n*

shizuka na 静かな *quiet adj*

shō ショー *show (performance) n*

shō wa nanji desuka? ショーは何時ですか？ *What time is the show?*

shōgai sha ni taiō shita 障害者に対応した *handicapped-accessible adj*

shōgai 障害 *disability n*

shōgo 正午 *noon n* p16

shohōsen 処方箋 / shohōyaku 処方薬 *prescription n* p44, 147

shōka furyō 消化不良 *indigestion n*

shōkai suru 紹介する *introduce, to introduce v* p99

anata o ＿＿＿ ni shōkai shimasu. あなたを＿＿＿に紹介します。 *I'd like to introduce you to ＿＿＿.*

shoku nin 職人 / kōgeika 工芸家 *craftsperson n* p105

shokuji 食事 *meal n* p40, 45, 85

shokuryō hin 食料品 *groceries n*

shomei 署名 *sign, to sign v*

doko ni shomei sureba ii desu ka? どこに署名すればいいです か? *Where do I sign?*

shōnika i 小児科医 *pediatrician n*

osusume no shōnika i wa imasu ka. お勧めの小児 科医はいますか? *Can you recommend a pediatrician?*

shoppingu sentā ショッピングセン ター *mall n* p128

shori suru 処理する *process, to process v*

shōsetsu 小説 *novel n*

shōyō de 商用で *business adj* p102

bijinesu sentā ビジネス センター *business center* p69

shōzō ga 肖像画 *portrait n*

shū 週 *week n* p4

konshū 今週 *this week* senshū 先週 *last week* raishū 来週 *next week*

shufu 主婦 *homemaker n*

shūmatsu ryōkin 週末料金 *weekend rate* p50, 67

shumi 趣味 *hobby n*

shuppansha 出版社 *publisher n*

shuppatsu suru 出発する *leave, to leave (depart) v* p37

shuppatsu 出発 *departure n*

shurui 種類 *kind (type) n*

sore wa donna shurui desu ka. そ れはどんな種類ですか? *What kind is it?*

sobakasu そばかす *freckle n*

sobo 祖母 / obāsan お祖母さん *grandmother n*

sōda sui ソーダ水 *seltzer n* p82

sōda ソーダ *soda* p45, 82

daietto sōda ダイエット ソーダ *diet soda*

sodatsu 育つ *grow, to grow (get larger) v*

doko de sodachi mashita ka. ど こで育ちましたか? *Where did you grow up?*

soe mono 添え物 *side n*

yoko ni soete 横に添えて *on the side (e.g., salad dressing)* p81

sofu 祖父 / ojīsan お祖父さん *grandfather n*

sofubo 祖父母 *grandparent n*

sofuto uea ソフトウェア *software n*

sōji suru 掃除する *clean, to clean v*

kyō, heya o sōji shite kudasai. 今日、部屋を掃除してくださ い。 *Please clean the room today.*

soko ni そこに *(nearby)* / asoko ni あそこに *(far) there (demonstrative) adv*

arimasu ka. ありますか? *Is / Are there?*

asoko ni あそこに *over there*

sokudo kei 速度計 *speedometer n*

sokudo o otosu 速度を落とす *slow, to slow v* p56

sokudo o otoshite kudasai! 速度を落としてください! *Slow down!* p56

sono その *that (near) adj*

sonshō shita 損傷した *damaged adj* p47

sorerano それらの *those adj*

sōsu ソース *sauce n*

soto 外 *outside n* p77

subete no すべての *all adj* p13

itsumo いつも *all of the time* ijō desu. dōmo arigatō. 以上です。どうもありがとう。 *That's all, thank you.*

subete すべて *all n* p15

sugiru 〜過ぎる 〜 *too (excessively) adv*

sui yō bi 水曜日 *Wednesday n* p17

suiei pantsu 水泳パンツ *swim trunks n*

sūji 数字 / bangō 番号 *number n* p57, 114

heya wa nan ban. 部屋は何番? *Which room number?*

anata no denwa bangō o oshiete itadake masu ka. あなたの電話番号を教えていただけますか? *May I have your phone number?*

sukejūru スケジュール *schedule n*

suki de aru 好きである *like, to like v (to please)*

watashi wa koko ga suki desu. 私はここが好きです。 *I like this place.*

sukoshi 少し *bit (small amount) n*

sukottorando no, sukottorando jin no スコットランドの、スコットランド人の *Scottish adj*

sukūtā スクーター *scooter n* p48

sukyan suru スキャンする *scan, to scan (document) v* p120

sukyūba daibingu o suru スキューバダイブをする *scuba dive, to scuba dive v* p141

sumi masen すみません *excuse (pardon) v* p53, 83, 146

sumi masen すみません *Excuse me.*

sumi masen すみません *sorry adj*

sumi masen. すみません。 *I'm sorry.*

sumi 隅 *corner n*

sumi no 隅の *on the corner*

sumu 住む *live, to live v*

anata wa doko ni sunde imasu ka. あなたはどこに住んでいますか? *Where do you live?*

sunēku ai da! スネークアイだ! *Snake eyes! n*

sunōkeru スノーケル *snorkel n*

sūpā māketto スーパーマーケット *supermarket n*

supa スパ *spa n* p63

supaisu スパイス *spice n*

supea taiya スペア タイヤ *spare tire n*

supein no, supein jin no スペインの、スペイン人の *Spanish adj*

supein スペイン *Spain n*

supesharu スペシャル *special (featured meal) n*

supôtsu スポーツ *sports n* p111

sûpu スープ *soup n*

supûn スプーン *spoon n* p83

suramu gai スラム街 *slum n*

surirā スリラー *thrillers (movies) n* p112

surôpu, kuruma isu スロープ、車椅子 *ramp, wheelchair n* p61

suru する *do, to do v*

susumeru 勧める *recommend, to recommend v*

sutaffu スタッフ *staff (employees) n* p74

sutajiamu スタジアム *stadium n* p138

suteki na すてきな *nice adj*

sutoresu o kanjite iru ストレスを感じている *stressed adj*

sutorêto no ストレートの / chokumô 直毛 *straight (hair) adj* p135

koko o massugu ここをまっすぐ *straight ahead* p5

sutorêto de ストレートで *straight (drink)* p81

massugu ikimasu. まっすぐ行きます。 *Go straight. (giving directions)* p53

sutorêto ストレート *straight (gambling) n*

sûtsu kêsu スーツケース *suitcase n* p47

sûtsu スーツ *suite n*

suwaru 座る *sit, to sit v*

T

tabako o suu タバコを吸う *smoke, to smoke v* p145

tabako タバコ *cigarette n*

tabako hito hako タバコ 1 箱 *a pack of cigarettes*

tabe mono 食べ物 *food n*

taberu 食べる *eat v*

gaishoku suru 外食する *to eat out*

tadashii 正しい *correct adj*

watashi wa tadashii densha ni notte imasu ka. 私は正しい電車に乗っていますか？ *Am I on the correct train?*

taishi kan 大使館 *embassy n*

taiya タイヤ *tire n* p52

taiya ga panku shima shita. タイヤがパンクしました。 *I have a flat tire.*

taiyô 太陽 *sun n*

taizai wa nan nichi kan desu ka. 滞在は何日間ですか？ *How long will you be staying?* p41

takai 高い / se ga takai 背が高い *tall adj*

takai 高い *expensive adj* p37, 76, 132, 144

takai 高い *high adj*

takaku nai 高くない *inexpensive adj* p76

takuji sho 託児所 *nursery n*

takuji sho wa arimasu ka. 託児所はありますか？ *Do you have a nursery?*

takusan no 多い ôi / 沢山の *many adj* p15

takushī タクシー *taxi* n p38, 55

takushī. タクシー! *Taxi!*

takushī o yonde itadake masen ka. タクシーを呼んでいただけませんか? *Would you call me a taxi?*

tamago 卵 *eggs* n p95

tamari ba 溜まり場 *hangout (hot spot)* n

tamesu 試す *try, to try (attempt)* v

tāminaru ターミナル *terminal (airport)* n p38, 39

tamotsu 保つ *keep, to keep* v

tanomu 頼む *ask for (request)* v

tanomu 頼む *order, to order (request)* v

tanoshimu 楽しむ *enjoy, to enjoy* v

taoru タオル *towel* n

motto taoru o itadake masu ka. もっとタオルをいただけますか? *May we have more towels?*

taryō 多量 / takusan no 沢山の *much* n p15

tasukeru 助ける *help, to help* v

tasukete 助けて! *Help!*

tasukete kudasai 助けてください *Can you help me?* p7

tatsu 立つ *stand, to stand* v

tazuneru 訪ねる *visit, to visit* v

te 手 *hand* n

tebukuro 手袋 *glove* n

tēburu テーブル *table* n p77

futari yō no tēburu 2人用のテーブル *table for two*

tegoro na nedan no 手頃な値段の *moderately priced* adj p63

teikyō suru 提供する *offer, to offer* v

teinei na ていねいな / shinsetsuna 親切な *courteous* adj p74

tekuno テクノ *techno* n p109

tenimotsu no 手荷物の *baggage* adj

tenimotsu hikiwatashi jo 手荷物引き渡し所 *baggage claim* p38

tenimotsu 手荷物 *baggage* n p36, 44**38**, **46**tenisu テニス *tennis* n p63

tenisu kōto テニスコート *tennis court* p63

tenji 展示 *exhibit* n

tenji, amerika no 点字、アメリカの *braille, American* n

tenki yohō 天気予報 *weather forecast* n

tento テント *tent* n

terebi テレビ *television* n

tetsudai 手伝い / ashisutansu アシスタンス *assistance* n p41

tetsudau 手伝う *assist* v

to issho ni 〜と一緒に *with 〜* prep

tōchaku suru 到着する *arrive, to arrive* v

tōchaku 到着 *arrival(s)* n

tōgyū shi 闘牛士 *bullfighter* n

tōgyū 闘牛 *bullfight* n

toire トイレ *bathroom (restroom)* n p59, 65, 74

koko kara ichiban chikai kōshū toire wa doko ni arimasu ka. ここから一番近い公衆トイレはどこにありますか? *Where is the nearest public bathroom?*

toire トイレ *restroom n* p36, 40, 61

kōshū toire wa arimasu ka. 公衆トイレはありますか? *Do you have a public restroom?*

toire トイレ *toilet n*

toire no mizu ga afurete irun desu. トイレの水が溢れているんです。 *The toilet is overflowing.* p72

toire ga tsumatte imasu. トイレがつまっています。 *The toilet is backed up.*

toiretto pēpā トイレットペーパー *toilet paper n*

toiretto pēpā ga naku nari mashita. トイレットペーパーがなくなりました。 *You're out of toilet paper.*

tojiru 閉じる *close, to close v*

tojita 閉じた *closed adj*

tōjō ken 搭乗券 *boarding pass n* p44

tōjō 搭乗 *board n*

tōjō shite 搭乗して *on board*

tōkei 闘鶏 *cockfight n*

tokkyū no 特急の *express adj*

tokubetsu yūsen chekku in 特別優先チェックイン *express check-in*

tokudai no 特大の *extra-large adj*

tōkuni 遠くに / **tōi** 遠い *far* p5

made wa doredake tōku hanarete imasu ka. ＿＿＿まではどれだけ遠く離れていますか? ＿＿＿ *How far is it to ＿＿＿?*

tokuten 得点 *score n*

tomaru 停まる *stop, to stop v*

tomatte kudasai. 停まってください。 *Please stop.*

tomare 止まれ *STOP (traffic sign)*

tomare, dorobō. 止まれ、泥棒! *Stop, thief!*

tomaru 泊る / **taizai suru** 滞在する *stay, to stay v* p67, 103

＿＿＿ nichi kan taizai suru yotei desu. ＿＿＿日間滞在する予定です。 *We'll be staying for ＿＿＿ nights.* p67. For full coverage of numbers see p7.

tōmei na 透明な *clear adj* p141

ton トン *ton n*

tōnyōbyō no 糖尿病の *diabetic adj*

tori kesu 取り消す *cancel, to cancel v* p41

watashi no furaito wa kyanseru saremashita. 私のフライトはキャンセルされました。 *My flight was canceled.*

tori 鳥 *bird n*

torihiki 取引き *deal (bargain) n*

nante subarashii torihiki da. なんてすばらしい取引だ! *What a great deal!*

torinozoku 取り除く / **nugu** 脱ぐ *remove, to remove v* p43

toshi 歳 *age n*

nan sai desu ka. 何歳ですか?
What's your age?

totemo とても *very* p73, 74

tozan 登山 *climbing* n p139

tozan dō 登山道 / toreiru トレイ
ル *trail* n p139, 140

tozan dō wa arimasuka.
登山道はありますか?
Are there trails?

tranpetto トランペット
trumpet n

tsuā ツアー *tour* n

gaido tsuki tsuā wa arimasu
ka. ガイド付きツアーはありま
すか? *Are guided tours
available?*

onsei gaido tsuki tsuā wa
arimasu ka. 音声ガイド付きツ
アーはありますか? *Are audio
tours available?*

tsugi 次 *next* prep

no tsugi の次 *next to*
tsugi no eki 次の駅 *the next
station*

tsukareta 疲れた / tsukarete iru
疲れている *tired, exhausted*
adj p104

tsukau 使う *use, to use* v

tsukuru 作る *make, to make* v

tsuma 妻 / okusan 奥さん *wife*
n p99

tsumatte iru つまっている *backed
up (toilet)* adj

toire ga tsumatte imasu. トイレが
つまっています。*The toilet is
backed up.*

tsuno 角 *horn* n

tsureteiku 連れて行く *take, to
take* v

eki made tsurete itte kudasai.
駅まで連れて行ってください。
Take me to the station.

____ made iku niwa ikura
kakari masu ka. ____まで行く
にはいくらかかりますか? *How
much to take me to ____?*

tsuri zao 釣竿 *fishing pole* n

tsūro 通路 *aisle* n

tsūyaku 通訳 *interpreter* n
p153

tsūyaku ga hitsuyō desu. 通
訳が必要です。*I need an
interpreter.*

tsuzukeru 続ける *continue, to
continue* v

tsuzuku 続く *last, to last* v

tsuzuru つづる *spell, to spell*
v p99

tsuzuri o itte kudasai. つづりを
言ってください。/ tsuzuri o itte
morae masu ka. つづりを言っ
てもらえますか。*How do you
spell that?*

U

ubau 奪う *rob, to rob* v

gōtō ni aimashita. 強盗に遭いま
した。*I've been robbed.*

ude 腕 *arm* n

ue ni 上に *up* adv p5

ue no 上の *above* adj p6

ueitā ウエイター *waiter* n

ueku appu kōru ウェークアップ
コール *wake-up call* n

uesutan no ウェスタンの *western* adj

ugoku 動く *move, to move* v

uke ireru 受け入れる *accept, to accept* v

kurejitto kādo wa tsukae masu ka. クレジットカードは使えますか？ *Do you accept credit cards?* p137, 67

uketoru 受け取る *receive, to receive* v

uma 馬 *horse* n

ume awase o suru 埋め合せをする *make up, to make up (apologize)* v

unten shu 運転手 *driver* n p54

unten suru 運転する *drive* v

uokka ウォッカ *vodka* n p82

ureshii 嬉しい *delighted* adj

urikire 売り切れ *sold out* adj

uru 売る *sell, to sell* v

uruguai no, uruguai jin no ウルグアイの、ウルグアイ人の *Uruguayan* adj

urusai うるさい *loud* adj

urusaku うるさく *loudly* adv

usagi うさぎ *rabbit* n

USB pōto USB ポート *USB port* n

ushi 牛 *cow* n

ushiro no 後ろの *behind* adj p5

usu chairo no 薄茶色の *hazel* adj

usui 薄い *thin* adj

uta 歌 *song* n p146

utau 歌う *sing, to sing* v

utsusu 移す *transfer, to transfer* v

okane o idō shitai no desuga. お金を移動したいのですが。 *I need to transfer funds.*

uwagi 上着 *jacket* n p43, 78, 130

W

wai fai ワイファイ *wi-fi* n

wain ワイン *wine* n p45

waipā ワイパー *windshield wiper* n

waipā ワイパー *wiper* n

wakai 若い *young* adj p102

wakareta 別れた / bekkyo shite iru 別居している *separated (marital status)* adj p101

wakeru 分ける *split (gambling)* n

wakkusu ワックス *waxing* n

wāku auto ワークアウト *workout* n

ware yasui 割れやすい / waremono chūi 割れ物注意 *fragile* adj p121

watashi no kodomo ga maigo ni nari mashita. 私の子供が迷子になりました。 *My child is missing.* p7

watashi tachi (ni, o) 私たち(に、を) *us* pron p25

watashi wa 私は / *I* pron

watashi wa me ga mie masen / me ga fujiyū desu. 私は、目が見えません / 目が不自由です。 *I am blind / visually impaired.* p62

webbu dezainā ウェッブデザイナー *web designer* n p105